A Journey into the Unknown and Unexpected

Witchcraft, Whispers, Shadows and Strange Sights

A Journey into the Unknown and Unexpected

By

SIMON KING

CONSCIOUS CARE PUBLISHING PTY LTD

WITCHCRAFT, WHISPERS, SHADOWS AND STRANGE SIGHTS

A Journey into the Unknown and Unexpected

Copyright © 2017 by Simon King. All rights reserved.

First Published 2017 by: Conscious Care Publishing Pty Ltd
33 Crompton Road, Rockingham, WA 6168, Australia
PO Box 776, Rockingham, WA 6968, Australia
Phone: (61+) 1300 814 115   www.consciouscarepublishing.com

First Edition printed June 2017.

Notice of Rights
This book is sold subject to the condition that it shall not, by way of trade or otherwise, be lent, resold, hired out, or otherwise circulated without the publisher's prior consent, in any form of binding or cover, other than that in which it is published, and without a similar condition, including this condition being imposed on the subsequent purchaser. All rights reserved by the publisher. No part of this publication may be reproduced, stored in a retrieval system, or transmitted in any form, or by any means, electronic, digital, mechanical, photocopying, scanning, recorded or otherwise, without the prior written permission of the copyright owner. Requests to the copyright owner should be addressed to Permissions Department, Conscious Care Publishing Pty Ltd, PO Box 776, Rockingham, WA 6968, Australia, Phone: (61+) 1300 814 115 or email: admin@consciouscarepublishing.com

Limits of Liability/Disclaimer of Warranty:
While the publisher and author have used their best efforts in preparing this book, they make no representations or warranties with respect to the accuracy or completeness of the contents of this book and specifically disclaim any implied warranties of merchantability or fitness for a particular purpose. No warranty may be created or extended by sales representatives or written sales materials. The author of this book does not dispense medical advice or prescribe the use of any technique as a form of treatment for physical, emotional, or medical problems without the advice of a physician, either directly or indirectly. The advice and strategies contained herein may not be suitable for your situation. You should consult with a professional where appropriate. The intent of the author is only to offer information for a general nature. Neither the publisher nor author shall be liable for any loss of profit or any other commercial damages, including but not limited to special, incidental, consequential, or other damages. The author and the publisher assume no responsibility for your actions. Where photographic images have been provided by the author and people are depicted, such images are being used for illustrative purposes only. Certain stock imagery© Shutterstock. Product names may be trademarks or registered trademarks, and are used for identification and explanation without intent to infringe. Conscious Care Publishing publishes in a variety of print and electronic format and by print-on-demand. Some material included with standard print versions of this book may not be included in e-books or in print-on-demand. If this book refers to media such as a CD or DVD that is not included in the version you purchased, you may download this material at www.consciouscarepublishing.com

National Library of Australia Cataloguing-in-Publication entry:
Author: King, Simon 1950-
Witchcraft, Whispers, Shadows & Strange Sights / by Simon King
ISBN 9780648085416 (Paperback)
Hudson, Rocky, Editor.

Printed by Lightning Source
Typeset & cover design by Conscious Care Publishing Pty Ltd

133.8

ISBN: 978-0-6480854-1-6

This book is dedicated to all people
who may have personally encountered
supernatural phenomena or in some ways
had their life directly affected by such events,
and who may have reservations about their
experiences. Exploring these encounters
through a diverse range of historical stories,
myths and folklore will hopefully provide
some useful insight into the realms of the
unusual and sometimes inexplicable.

A Graveyard Watcher: The Lone Sentinel of a Graveyard

PREFACE

There is more to the universe than was ever dreamt of by you or me. Perhaps contact with strange 'otherworldly' beings, ethereal entities or mystifying spirits who share our world with us is not fully understood or even tolerated without some dread. However, such encounters have certainly been extensively investigated and reported over considerable time and across numerous cultures. To appreciate the diversity and complexity of these unusual and often frightening encounters, this book explores a vast selection of both historical and contemporary experiences from a somewhat different perspective.

It examines the manifestation and communication processes of an array of fearsome spirits, often in haunted locations, and charts encounters sometimes to quite an unexpected outcome, when people may be faced with almost becoming 'one of those spirits'. Many selective personal experiences gained throughout my own life have been incorporated into various chapters, as well as anecdotal stories shared by others. The role of witchcraft and treatment of many witches' companions, such as cats, crows, ravens, owls, foxes, bears and wolves to name but a few, is scrutinised, reinforced by accounts of reported hauntings by animals or in association with animals.

The book also explores various supernatural tales of myth and legend documented in folklore, bygone chronicles and works of literature to both decipher explanations for these strange events and characters, and most importantly, to spin a really good yarn. To provide the reader with an interesting historical perspective about folklore is probably just as valid as attempting to disprove it actually occurred. A considerable number of oral tales have been passed down over generations and, as a result of this process, sometimes became exaggerated or distorted. However, if kept in the right context, such lore does serve an entertaining purpose in identifying various entities consistently mentioned in certain tales, myths and legends over the centuries.

The power of the human imagination and belief in paranormal encounters and events that almost defy logical explanation is encompassed in several stories relayed in the book. These stories show people are capable of accepting that there are some circumstances that are simply beyond our comprehension. For the reader, it will be a matter of deciding for yourself, because my selection of stories will certainly challenge many of you.

CONTENTS

Listing of Figures	I
Reflections of the other side	1
Spectres and shadows	9
The black dog and others	21
The bear and the wolf	35
Whispers	41
The last moment	51
Ocean wanderers	60
The sea marauders	70
Mysterious lighthouses	81
Genesis of witchcraft	96
Witches	101
The black cat	110
Crows and ravens	117
Enjoy the ghost train	127
Eerie fog	136
The possessed	146
Masque	156
Hobbins and bobbins	166
The scarecrows are watching	170
Momentary respite of silence	182
Encounters of the animal kind	187
The strange ones	195

Paranormal magicians	204
Epilogue	212
References	214
Bibliography	229
About the author	240

LIST OF FIGURES

Figure 1: Celebratory Revellers and Other Beings   11

Figure 2: Visitor to My Home   14

Figure 3: Simon's Black Dog (R.I.P.)   24

Figure 4: The Sun Bear   37

Figure 5: Bizarre and Grotesque Erosion of Siltstone Formations   45

Figure 6: Unfortunates of The Last Moment   53

Figure 7: Pirate Guardian of Buried Treasure   75

Figure 8: Believer, Non-Believer, Sceptic and Watcher*   97

Figure 9: The Wicce Astride   103

Figure 10: Beware a Black Cat   110

Figure 11: The Black Cat with Everything   112

Figure 12: The Mysterious Owl   124

Figure 13: Olde World Charm of Steam Trains   130

Figure 14: The Eerie Fog   145

Figure 15: I Am Waiting For You   148

Figure 16: Be My Friend   151

Figure 17: Strange Happenings   154

Figure 18: Look Behind The Mask   159

Figure 19: Up Close and Personal   168

Figure 20: The Lonely Scarecrow   177

Figure 21: The Night Swimmer   189

Figure 22: Patiently Waiting*   199

Figure 23: Still Watching You   211

*Source Unknown. Publisher wants to give credit with copyright owner.

REFLECTIONS OF THE OTHER SIDE

Why write a book about such ephemeral subjects as whispers and shadows, not to mention the uncertain, almost implausible realm of real-life witches? Perhaps the popularity of the occult, witchcraft and other mysterious traditions associated with the supernatural may be sufficient motivation, or possibly even the fascination with paranormal phenomena which cannot be realistically explained by science or logic.

My motivation is based upon first-hand experience and observation of mystical events which have occurred only for relatively brief periods, yet have persisted across most of my life. One of these significant episodes which affected me greatly occurred when I was a young tertiary student in Victoria, Australia in 1971. I had been visiting a fellow student one evening at his old rented house in a leafy and affluent inner suburb of Melbourne, and was enjoying a quiet drink with him in the lounge. The house had probably been built somewhere near the beginning of the 20th century or earlier. I was seated with my girlfriend on a rather spacious couch on one side of the room, and my friend was sitting directly beneath a massive mirror hanging along the opposite wall. That mirror would have more appropriate in a palace, given its generous dimensions and regal ornate frame.

We had a most convivial and relaxing time until a moment very late into the evening when I stood up to replenish my drink. To my astonishment, staring at me from the mirror was not my own reflection but rather a woman in her thirties and a young girl around 10-13 years of age. Both were dressed in late 19th century costume reminiscent of the Victorian era, with the woman wearing a broad hoop skirt and a bonnet. The girl had long dark hair, was well groomed and wore a demure skirt with frills. If that description was not unsettling enough, their steely gaze was certainly disturbing to me, sending a chill through my bones. The couple appeared forlorn, with sorrowful, almost mournful facial expressions. I turned around momentarily, assuming these visitations were actually standing behind me, and then looked back into the mirror to see only my own reflection instead. The appearance lasted a few seconds but is still as lucid today as the visitation was forty-six years ago. The others in the room had remained seated and so did not see the woman and child.

A search of this house revealed some interesting history of is past occupation. On the wooden door frame of the main entry into the kitchen, someone had carved distinctive horizontal knife marks into the wood in several places. We deduced these marks indicated the various growth stages of the young girl, who would have stood there to have her height marked for measurement. The carvings ceased dramatically at a certain height, possibly when she reached early teenage years. The house had been built at an age when people wore that type of charming clothing I had seen on the woman and girl, and the mirror involved certainly appeared to be from that bygone era. My friend had no similar experiences about the mirror visitors, so we let the matter rest without further investigation until much later in my life.

According to some literary sources, certain types of spirits were thought to reside inside mirrors, which perhaps acted as a type of portal allowing communication with our world. In various ancient cultures, mirrors were used for summoning of spirits, and of course in some folklore traditions, they were paramount for foretelling the future. Interestingly, mirrors have been around for a mighty long time. Before the advent of glass used in modern mirrors, it was common to use highly polished metal or a reflective glass-like volcanic rock known as obsidian for mirrors.[1] The visitation that I had experienced in the mirror was to resurface for me many years later whilst living interstate in Western Australia.

This time the encounter with an apparition was briefer and did not involve a mirror, but was incredibly detailed. I had been visiting a married couple's home one afternoon for a celebratory party and was walking from the lounge into the kitchen. The woman's mother had died many years earlier at a young age and was greatly missed by her. I had never met the mother nor seen her in any photographs, yet was able to describe her following this experience. As I walked into the kitchen, a movement in the lounge to one side of me caught my eye. It was a lady smartly dressed in white casual slacks with a loose fitting, buttoned dark shirt who was running quickly from one room to the next. The episode would have lasted for only a second, but I distinctly recall that she was perhaps in her late forties, had short dark hair, and was wearing make-up. There was an expression of sheer desperation on the woman's face, as if she was hopelessly late for an appointment or had missed the last train home. The running woman, as I recollect, moved sprightly across the room before vanishing from my view. Upon being told of my fleeting encounter, the party host produced an old photograph of her deceased mother. The woman in the photo appeared remarkably similar to the woman of the visitation. To this day, I remain convinced that the running woman was the host's mother still inhabiting her daughter's physical domain.

Coincidentally, my unusual glimpse had a strange similarity to a very famous black and white ghost photograph first published in 1959.[2] In March of that year, a woman and her husband were on a visit to her mother's grave in a cemetery in Ipswich, England. As her mother had only recently been buried, the woman took some photographs of the headstone and then, to complete the roll of film, took the remaining photograph of her husband sitting in the car. When the photograph taken of her husband was developed, it appeared to show the woman's bespectacled mother sitting in the back seat of the vehicle. The ghost in the picture was all the more realistic as this apparition was seated exactly where the woman's mother usually sat for drives.[3] Debate about whether the photograph depicting this spirit was genuine continues on relentlessly today.

Another less dramatic but nonetheless still quite unsettling encounter with the paranormal occurred whilst I was staying overnight in an old hotel (or pub) that had been built well over one hundred years ago, located in the South West timber milling region of Western Australia. Of course the pub had many owners over such a prodigious history but a persistent rumour remained that the building was haunted. Various drinkers recounted to me tales of strange happenings inside the hotel at night, tales sometimes flavoured in colourful language and possibly embellished to an extent by the effects of the demon drink. The most recent rumours during my overnight stay concerned a publican from the 1960s-1970s who was considered a local legend and was highly respected throughout the community. Even today so many years later, some locals still acknowledge the calibre of this publican, who passed away whilst still working in this pub.

The locals warned me against staying overnight due to the presence of this ghostly publican, who was thought to still wander restlessly through the establishment after closing time. Undaunted by these warnings, I elected to stay over one night during an unplanned visit to the region, and I must admit, I had a decidedly uncomfortable night's rest. When a pub is closed at night on a weekday in a small country town, there is usually no traffic noise, no barking dogs or other neighbourhood disturbances in the early hours likely to disrupt your sleep. In this hotel on that night, I was the only resident and there was no night staff on duty. The only accommodation was located on the hotel's first floor and was accessed by a wooden staircase from the ground floor. All the bedrooms and even the adjoining corridor had polished timber floors without any carpeting to muffle the sound of footsteps.

The total silence in the hotel was quite disarming for someone who lived in a capital city and quite accustomed to incessant traffic noise, even late at night. Sometime around midnight, I was awoken by the sound of a door closing and presumed it was probably some staff returning to the hotel, or possibly just a draft shutting the door. On that calm night, there was not even a slight breeze. A few minutes later, I distinctly heard someone very slowly coming up the stairs towards the first floor, then abruptly stopping upon reaching the landing. All older wooden buildings develop creaking noises as the seasoned timbers expand in the heat or contract in the cold weather, or sometimes flex with the building's structure. Such timber movements are spontaneous, and certainly do not sound like repetitive shuffling footsteps. However, timbers can creak on staircases if a person's weight is applied to the steps.

Despite listening intently for at least 15 minutes, I could not detect the sound of any further footsteps and drifted off to sleep. A few hours later I was again awoken by that discernible shuffling noise in the corridor outside my room, as if someone was dragging their feet along the floor. This time the footsteps continued slowly along the corridor to the outside verandah overlooking the street below. Convinced that someone was playing games with me, I turned on the light in my bedroom and then in the corridor outside and went looking for the prankster. There was no-one in the corridor nor on the verandah, so I returned to bed.

At last, a peaceful night's sleep was to be enjoyed. Then just before dawn that morning, further shuffling footsteps were clearly audible, only this time they were returning down the staircase. I know that ghostly footsteps (known as footfalls in bygone days) are a contradiction in terms, as phantoms do not have a physical form or weight, and would walk or shuffle noiselessly. I wondered if ghosts realised it as well? American poet Henry Wadsworth Longfellow certainly understood this point when he produced this verse from his extended poem *Haunted Houses* in 1858: 'All houses wherein men have lived and died Are haunted houses. Through the open doors The harmless phantoms on their errands glide, With feet that make no sound upon the floors …'[4]

I never stayed overnight in that building again and even the hotel's cook just raised his eyebrows the next morning at breakfast in the kitchen and said nothing about my encounter. The poem *Alone* by contemporary American author Sharon Hudson says it all:

> Alone in a house with no one to talk to,
> With the floorboards squeaking,
> And the wall boards creaking,
> Windows rattling like ghost tapping.
>
> Rustling trees, knocking knees,
> Scaredly, I walk down the hall;
> Footsteps following I call,
> No one answers, no one at all.[5]

It would not be unusual for one's imagination to conjure bizarre explanations for ordinary events given the right circumstances, such as sleeping in a supposedly haunted hotel without any residents. The slightest noise to break the deathly silence and creaking floorboards can contribute to creating a ghostly atmosphere in an old hotel. I have heard the saying that 'your mind can play tricks on you', particularly if you are fatigued, stressed or ill. We can all be forgetful sometimes, simply mislaying that essential garden tool or favourite pen just when we needed it to complete a task. However, this was certainly not the case in my early childhood when I would visit my elderly maternal grandmother in Sydney, New South Wales. In the late 1950s to mid-1960s, my mother would take me to spend the Christmas holidays with Grandma in her old weatherboard house in Penshurst, near Hurstville, one of the original suburbs of Sydney. Many houses in these areas were built around the beginning of the 20th century and were probably at least 60-70 years in age.

Although I was probably an impressionable youngster from seven to eleven years of age through those years, one distinctive memory about my grandmother's house always remained with me. Everyday items would inexplicably go missing just when you wanted them, only to reappear the following day, often in a totally different location. Although my grandmother lived alone and was in her late 70s, she was surprisingly alert and very meticulous in her daily household routines.

If she required some firewood cut for heating purposes, for example, she would provide me with a small axe and I would go to the woodshed and cut a sufficient quantity of wood off-cuts and old timbers for a few days use. The axe would always remain in the woodshed lodged firmly in a chopping block over that time, but upon returning to use it later in the week, I would discover it missing. The next day, the axe would reappear in the shed still lodged in the same position in its chopping block. This also happened to other household items, such as paintbrushes, brooms, mops, various gardening tools and on one occasion, Grandma's precious scissors.

Sometimes furniture originally left in one room would be mysteriously moved to another room, be knocked over or turned around, and open doors would close without any assistance. Grandma's theory was that the house had a resident mischievous troll; an 'otherworldly' supernatural being who selectively hid these items or simply moved them elsewhere to cause angst and confusion for the house occupants. In hindsight, I think that she was probably right, as other odd events occurred sporadically, including the front door bell ringing at various times of day or night without anyone evident outside the house, lights in unoccupied rooms coming on and then turning off, and, most disconcertingly, bathroom taps flowing water without being physically turned on by anyone. Trolls have also been known by some as mystical magicians, so their conjuring performance would have been unconvincing unless the missing object was returned to your sight eventually.

The troll in this house was neither malevolent nor pernicious, but certainly had a wry sense of humour. One type of everyday item that unfortunately never magically disappeared was the breakfast, lunch and dinner crockery, which therefore still had to be washed and dried by hand as one of my daily chores. After my grandmother passed on, the incidents decreased in the house but still continued intermittently. Perhaps my grandmother finally sorted out that transient vagabond in the afterlife.

When you look into a mirror to see your own reflection and view your appearance, you may inadvertently have noticed your surroundings in the background. If indoors, this may have included interior furnishings, windows, furniture and other inanimate objects. If outdoors, it may have been other people or vehicles passing by. Typically your focus was directly upon your own features rather than anything in the background. Suppose that you noticed out of the corner of your eye that there appeared to be an odd shape, a blurry dark form, something stationary standing behind you.

You cannot quite discern who or what it was in the background so you turned to see for yourself and there was nobody there. You must have imagined it of course, or perhaps your eyes played tricks on you. You looked into the mirror again and continued looking until ever so subtly, the shape behind you came into view again. This time you turned around immediately only to be disappointed once again.

Finally, you decided to ignore the inexplicable shape if it should reappear, and for a minute or two, you saw only your own image in the mirror. You continued to focus solely on your own reflection, ignoring the likely distraction of anything else in the background. Then as if upon command, you noticed a dark blurry shape forming just behind your shoulder, as if someone or something was directly behind you, peering over your shoulder. It was hard to distinguish the shape other than as a presence. You closed your eyes momentarily and it was no longer there when you reopened your eyes.

To attempt understanding what you may have seen, one needs to appreciate our worst imaginings and fears; the dark side of our nature that lurks in the recesses of our minds. These include the childhood bogeyman, the monster of the dark, the dreadful shape that loomed in the corner; all these are age-old reminders of our murky past and that part of us we would prefer not to face. These are the extraordinary shape-shifters that can change their form into anything they want, anytime. They are the shapes reflected in the mirror of the deepest psyche.[6] Of course, this was still a story without any real substance to confirm such shapes. It may have been something totally different looking at you after all.

SPECTRES AND SHADOWS

Sometimes the things that you see in the shadows are more than just shadows. Throughout the world there are countless theories and speculation concerning what constitutes a ghost, also known as a spectre, apparition, phantom, manifestation or even transient spirit. It is probably best to first understand the commonly accepted meanings of these descriptions before proceeding too much further.

A ghost is the non-physical part of a human being, or sometimes animal, manifested after death to the living. It has no material existence, often appearing in a translucent, shadowy or even misty, ethereal form, able to pass through solid matter. It may also remain invisible, and only be detectable through various signs, such as unexplained movements of physical objects, unexpected noises, distinctive odours and temperature changes. The word ghost originates from the old English term *gast* for spirit, soul, breath or life, with respect to describing something immaterial. Other words used to describe a ghost include spectre, apparition, phantom and spirit which are derived from French and Latin etymological roots and suggest different meanings. Spectre is a visual manifestation of a menacing ghost, whilst the terms apparition and phantom both suggest the viewer is experiencing an illusion.[1]

The following old Scottish prayer gives the best illustration of all: 'From ghoulies and ghosties And long-leggedy beasties And things that go bump in the night. Good Lord, deliver us!' If one thinks back to those ancient times, ghosts are even better described in Lewes Lavatar's 16th century publication *Of Ghosts and Spirits Walking by Night:* '…hallucinations of the insane, superstitions of the ignorant, or corpses under demonic or angelic possession …'.[2] However, I will not attempt to explain the complexities of how and why we perceive these ghosties, as this subject has been extensively investigated, examined and comprehensively interpreted by many accredited people and is not relevant to this book. The debate continues relentlessly.

I am interested in understanding more about apparitions, why such phenomena persist throughout the history of human development, and the surroundings where such appearances are commonly observed. Apparitions are said to represent a person, an animal or even an inanimate object such as a sailing ship, steam train or aeroplane, that was not physically present at the time of the visitation. They may occur both before and after bodily death - that is, they can represent living people and animals as well as deceased ones—without being linked to any particular location.

One common feature of visitations is usually how realistic the apparition appears until something dramatic occurs, such as their vanishing act into thin air or perhaps through a solid physical object, such as a wall. Apparitions appear spontaneously and can be most unpredictable.[3] They also do not cast a shadow like a living person or a physical object. When a ghost frequents the same location, or revisits a specific person, it is haunting the aforementioned. Why does this happen?

Sightings are often associated with particular physical locations, such as cemeteries, churches, hospitals, theatres, schools, hotels and residential dwellings, as well as places where violence and death has resulted, such as crime scenes, traffic accidents or battlefields. The most popular belief about these places is that ghosts are attracted to them as rich sources of composite psychic residues from the past which are imprinted on the surroundings. For theatres, this would result from the passionate emotions of performers as expressed on the stage, whereas for hotels, it would be from the social camaraderie of rowdy gatherings of drinkers.

In the case of houses, former residents who have died may reappear as visitations, as their homes would be natural and comfortable places for them to which to return, particularly where they were subjected to a painful illness. The mourning process of family members would also occur within such dwellings, generating significant memories of the deceased.[4] Scottish novelist and playwright James Mathew Barrie who famously created *Peter Pan*, also wrote the following: 'A house is never still in darkness to those who listen intently; there is a whispering in distant chambers, an unearthly hand presses the snib [fastening] of the window, the latch rises. Ghosts were created when the first man awoke in the night.'[5]

Figure 1: Celebratory Revellers and Other Beings

Houses also offered many suitable spaces for these apparitions to enter our world, such as windows, doorways, staircases and corridors, seen by some as possible entrances from beyond the present. Many visitations around the world have appeared around or above such potential portals.[6] I am reminded of an appropriate warning extracted from an ancient Mesopotamian spell which reiterates this matter:

> …No door can shut them out,
> No bolt can turn them back,
> Through the door like a snake they glide,
> Through the hinge like the wind they blow;
> Estranging the wife from the embrace of a husband,
> Snatching a child from the loins of a man,
> Sending the man forth from his home…[7]

The warning is reinforced by the following dire commentary:

> It is they [the spirits] who rush over a city on the storm clouds, bringing devastation in their train, and from them come all hurricanes and tempests. They unsettle everyone that they meet, bringing unrest, disorder and confusion into the world, and to them is due the restlessness and desire for wandering which comes upon men.[8]

Graveyards are yet another type of physical place thought to attract visitations, due to the obvious concentration of the deceased with supposedly so little to do, although this theory is based upon relative time. This is where the discussion gets tricky and the language complex and difficult to grasp, so I shall maintain a sense of purpose about it. The time when an apparition appears to us in the present world has no significant importance with respect to the deceased. The relevant time is when the deceased had actually passed away rather than when they reappeared.

One of the oldest tales of the sea, probably dating from the late 17th century, is about a phantom sailing ship the *Flying Dutchman*, whose entire crew purportedly perished attempting to round the Cape of Good Hope despite a divine warning to turn back. Recurrent sightings of this spectre, of a sailing ship condemned to an eternal voyage with a single skeleton for a crew, have been recorded by other mariners and various eyewitnesses in the 19th and 20th centuries. The most recent sighting was in 1942 off the coast of Cape Town.[9] Of course, the sea and combined weather conditions have been known to create hazy-looking mirages of ships on the horizon from the refraction of sunlight, particularly during periods of high humidity and prevalent sea mists.[10] It would however be difficult to imagine that an ancient three masted merchant brig under full sail could be easily mistaken for a mirage at sea. Sceptics of such a prolonged legend would clearly disagree.

The sea has been known to play tricks on the human eye, by possibly distortion or inversion to create a mirage. Given the right atmospheric conditions, such as the onset of bad weather around sunrise or sunset, or even on a clear moonlit night, the eye may perceive a ship's image borne more of tiredness and strain than reality.[11] In particularly foggy conditions, shapes appearing briefly in the haze can be readily distorted into outlandish forms. However, sometimes these peculiar apparitions are heard or seen by many on board.

Occasionally a visitation may even occur in unusual earthly spaces like swamps, isolated or derelict buildings or bleak, secluded landscapes. It may involve some spectral manifestation with no obvious connection to that location. Spectres can be intent on mischievous ways, such opening and closing doors, and creating other irritating disturbances. They may also use modern conveniences used for communications, such as telephones, television media or today's Internet to disrupt transmissions by creating their own 'noise'. Where the spectre is perceived as discontented, restless, malicious or even vengeful, get out of its way and vacate the premises, particularly if it is in an obvious state of decomposition. Any such encounter can only spell trouble for the unsuspecting. The following warning by an unknown poet is certainly prudent advice:

> Listen to the night as it whispers your name, It is calling.
> Watch as leaves dance like tongues of flame, It is calling.
> Feel a chill rattle through your frame, It is almost here.

The timing of spectral visitations is perhaps the least understood facet of hauntings. Various authors across the ages have linked the twilight hours and the midnight hour as key times for some of these unexplained otherworldly visitors. Such popular literature has reinforced the assumption that these fleeting spirits are particularly active in the night hours when most of us are asleep and the busy physical world is mostly at rest. These days of course, the world hardly ever slows, let alone stops, and telecommunications are almost instantaneous.

The rise of supernatural movies depicting paranormal events inside houses and typically at night for optimum effect, usually during a wild thunderstorm with prolific lightning shocks, only embellishes the myth. The reality is probably inconclusive, given spectres and perhaps the less daunting apparitions may appear at any time and in various places, often without any reason. It could be that we perceive these appearances better in the quieter hours of the night than amongst the chaos and distractions of the daylight waking hours. Where a haunting is a repetitive experience, the visitation may be more appropriate during the night hours, and excluding the tropical regions of the world, cooler air certainly dominates at night. That sudden chill or unexpected drop in temperature is much more evident in the night hours for most people. It can get your attention very quickly.

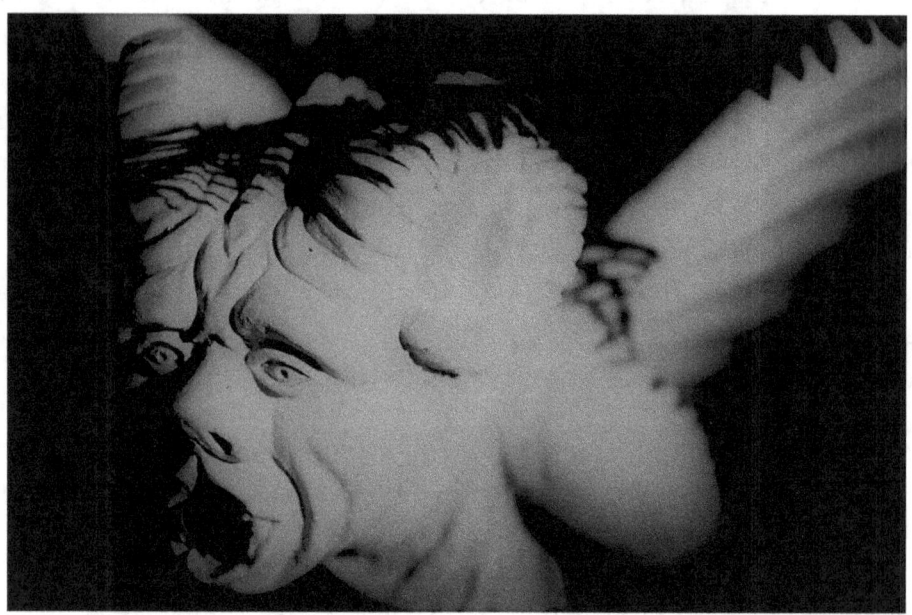

Figure 2: Visitor to My Home

Reasonable explanations for why apparitions occur at all or in some cases, recur at various times, can be difficult and almost confusing to substantiate. There is a belief that when a person is close to dying or has perished recently, particularly involving violent or traumatic circumstances, those closest to the deceased may encounter them again. It does not address why it only involves select family members or only some individuals who are about to die or have passed away. This is further compounded when one considers that some apparitions who return may seem unaware of their surroundings and their relatives.[12]

Acclaimed poet, author and anthologist Myra Cohn Livingston seems to have understood this dilemma in the following way: 'Wailed a ghost in a graveyard in Kew, "Oh, my friends are so fleeting and few", For it's gravely apparent, That if you're transparent, There is no one who knows it is you!'[13] The description of most apparitions as having ghostly characteristics, such as a translucent or vapour-like appearance, a hazy or shadowy almost unrecognisable form, or an ability to float above the ground, seems to be consistent across many centuries and various civilisations. Perhaps the inference here is that the shadows represent a darker side of the apparition and, of course, suggest the unknown, possibly something to be avoided, or at least treated with caution. [14]

The *Shadow March* compiled by the famous Scottish novelist and poet Robert Louis Stevenson recognises the shadows encountered by us all:

> All around the house is the jet-black night;
> It stares through the window-pane;
> It crawls in the corners, hiding from the light,
> And it moves with the moving flame.
>
> Now my little heart goes a beating like a drum,
> With the breath of the Bogies in my hair;
> And all around the candle and the crooked shadows come,
> And go marching along up the stair.
>
> The shadow of the balusters, the shadow of the lamp,
> The shadow of the child that goes to bed -
> All the wicked shadows coming tramp, tramp, tramp,
> With the black night overhead.[15]

A haunting by an apparition is considered to be a persistent and uninvited or unwelcome visitation, usually associated with a specific location or place.[16] These habitual visits are believed in many cultures to represent a portent of misfortune for those being haunted, and have resulted in annual cultural festivals throughout some countries to celebrate these rituals.[17]

To effectively capture these ghostly manifestations on photographic film has always been a technological challenge. In the earliest days of photography, long exposure times could result in unusual shadows or inexplicable transparent images presenting that were not necessarily apparent in the original subject matter. Even in modern times, with sophisticated cameras and fast print technology, the accidental merging of photographic negatives in the laboratory can still create unusual shadows, and photographic effects may be intentionally altered to create mysterious images. Perhaps new digital technology cameras not requiring film will remove any trace of such processing anomalies. If these apparitions are present in the subject matter being photographed, and yet they remain unseen by the naked eye, it may be that their images do appear as shadows in this medium rather than from any trickery resulting from poor lighting or the background in the photo.

Prior to the late 19th century, when electric lighting was introduced, people relied upon gas lamps in the town streets, and oil or perhaps kerosene lamps in their dwellings. Wax candles were also a suitable alternative in some developed societies. The reliance on such weak sources of illumination meant one simply tolerated the shadows at night, particularly in outdoor areas. Unlit country roads and gloomy living rooms readily contributed to the premise of the unknown lurking in the shadows so popular in fictional literature and poetry of the time, as suggested by this anonymous writer of *Shadows of the Night*:

> Dark shadows float through the moonlight.
> Their wings don't make a sound.
> Their claws are long, their eyes burn bright.
> As the witching hour comes round.
>
> They screech and wail. They shriek and cry
> As the wind, it shifts and heaves.
> The creatures land upon your roof
> And crawl beneath the eaves.
>
> You curl up in your bed so small
> And the night wind holds its breath.
> The shadows creep across your wall,
> And all is still, as still as death.

I would be struggling to find a more appropriate poem to aptly describe old houses that were dark, gloomy and peculiar, in which strange things were thought to happen, than some select verse, taken from *Ode on the Anniversary of the Fifth Half Century of the landing of Governor John Endecott*, who was the first Governor of the earliest English colony of Massachusetts Bay. It was compiled by the American poet and sculptor William Wetmore Story, who was born in the New England settlement of Salem, Massachusetts, USA in the early 19th century:

> … How oft, half-fearfully, we prowled
> Around those gabled houses, quaint and old,
> Whose legends, grim and terrible,
> Of witch and ghost that used to in them dwell,
> Around the twilight fire were told;
> While huddled close with anxious ear
> We heard them quivering with fear;
> And, if the daylight half o'ercame the spell,
> 'T was with a lingering dread
> We oped [opened] the door and touched the stinging bell …
> … For with its sound it seemed to rouse the dead,
> And wake some ghost from out the dusky haunts
> Where faint the daylight fell … [18]

Having been born in Salem so renowned for the persecution of witches in the 17th century, Story must have had a reasonable appreciation for the shadows and sounds of unusual things dwelling inside or trying to enter the house. Salem has an enormous diversity of famous landmark sites associated with hauntings and witchcraft, as well as many historically interesting places dating from 1626 during America's early settlement by the English. The following selected verses from his mid-1800s poem entitled *Shadows and Voices at Twilight* capture the moment perfectly:

> … The fire-light flickers – on wall and ceiling
> Wild uncouth shadows dance,
> To the corners dark so swiftly stealing,
> When the flame darts up with a glance.

I know there's a great black shadow mowing
And mocking above me there,
As over the fire my figure bowing
Into its coals I stare …

… What voice is that at the window wailing ?
That wails in the sobbing rain –
That wails and moans with a voice, now failing,
Now rising with screams of pain.

Is it a friend that shakes and rattles
And beats at the panes [glass] so thin ?
Or some lost soul with the Fiend [Devil] that battles,
imploring to enter in …

… No ! 'tis the wind alone that clatters
Against the shuddering pane,
And some tree-branch on the blind that patters
With the gusts of the windy rain.

The world is weird; in these twilight regions
Are shapes of fear and fright –
I shrink from their nightmares that gather in legions [hordes], –
Bring in the light ![19]

For a story that certainly stretches your imagination, try a disused facility built at the start of the 20th century to treat and isolate patients with tuberculosis, a common, highly contagious disease. Those were times when an effective cure for the poor souls was uncertain, resulting in many patients ultimately succumbing to the complaint. However, in its day, the Waverly Hills Hospital in Louisville, Kentucky, still offered the best medical option for many seeking to survive and hopefully recover. It was subsequently occupied for almost twenty more years as a nursing home for the elderly after a suitable cure was eventually discovered for the contagious disease, but finally closed towards the end of the century.[20] Perhaps it was due to the early history of treating patients with severe illness and the uncertainty of survival, but the building certainly appeared to still have a residue of entities remaining well after its eventual closure.

On a particular floor of this multi-storey building, strange occurrences had continued since its closure. To best explain these appearances, one needs to describe them methodically. When someone walks along a long, dark corridor with no lighting other than natural daylight entering through windows, it is usual to cast a shadow. If it is at night and only a ceiling light is illuminated in that corridor, you would still cast a shadow as you walked past. The painted walls may also contribute to this shadow by reflecting the available light somewhat. At night, the only lighting inside a building would be from artificial sources, such as ceiling lights. There would no other artificial light entering from outside of a building several stories high. Now walk slowly along that partially lit corridor alone and how many shadows would you expect around you? On this floor, people had not only experienced shadows all around them but occasionally running past them. Sometimes these shadows had even moved between rooms adjoining the corridor. Time to turn on all the lights and head home.

To attempt to establish some order of logic to the appearance of unusual ephemeral shadowy figures, various explanations have been proposed to explain their recognition only by some people and not others. For instance, it has been claimed such figures are possibly interdimensional beings who are only able to enter our physical world in this form, sometimes for the purpose of hauntings and other times for unknown reasons. These shadows may manifest themselves to receptive people experiencing turbulent emotional upheavals, or simply to those who are just prone to perceive psychically more easily than most others. The figures have even been broadly categorised into various types, such as haunting presences, bedroom watchers, background visitors and moving shadows.

Figures that appear and disappear suddenly and are associated with haunted places may even follow people. They may also be known as 'watchers' for good reason. Conversely, bedroom watchers can remain still for long periods, simply observing sleeping people, before disappearing through walls and ceilings once observed. The nature of human consciousness during sleep may possibly permit these shadows their means to appear as 'thought-forms'.

Background visitors are only visually identified in photographs, whilst moving shadows appear abruptly and move quickly. These moving shadows may appear to have no particular concern for the people present, or alternatively, may watch them intensely.[21] As with the nature of mysterious shadows, their origins and purposes will probably always remain unanswered to mere mortals.

The following anonymous quotation captures the moment: 'Don't rely upon anyone too much. Even your shadow leaves when it's dark.'

THE BLACK DOG AND OTHERS

We still have much to understand about animals. They have served mankind in a diversity of ways throughout recorded history, providing devoted companionship and immeasurable pleasure for their owners. They have also been used for sport, to work the land, and for meat, milk and wool. Their unusual or special qualities have also been recognised and occasionally exploited for further benefit, such as an uncanny ability in some animals to sense imminent danger or impending disasters, to communicate telepathically, and remarkably, to return unaided to their owners over substantial distances. To an extent, the more we learn about these unique traits, the less we understand. This possibly also applies to animals who have passed away.

Many ancient cultures highly valued certain animals for their strange, almost mystical powers. Some popular examples include the common entombment of cats with the deceased pharaohs of Egypt to assist in the passage of these rulers into the afterlife, the supernatural folklore associated with cats and witches prevalent in Europe in the past few hundred years, and the perceptive, perhaps psychic abilities of domesticated pets to anticipate unplanned calamitous or traumatic events. Apparitions of deceased pets, such as dogs and cats, is another most intriguing development, and possibly quite steeped in history.

H.P. Lovecraft, the American horror fiction author, wrote of these animals in his 1920 fictional short story entitled *From Beyond*: '…We shall see that at which dogs howl in the dark, and that at which cats prick up their ears after midnight…'[1] To understand more about why deceased animals and particularly pets revisit the living, it is first essential to fully appreciate the extraordinary abilities of some animals.

Many pet owners would be acutely familiar with the ability of some animals, such as dogs, to accurately predict their unexpected return by their pet's excited behaviour or hospitable greeting well before the owner's actual arrival. This natural ability to perceive future events extends to impending disasters, including earthquakes, tsunamis, volcanic eruptions, cyclones and lightning strikes. In these cases, the animal's sensory apparatus possibly detects minute changes in vibrations, barometric pressures and static electrical charges preceding the events, and increases their erratic behaviour as these indicators increase. It does not explain the bizarre behaviour exhibited by animals when the future calamity is quite subtle.

Some unusual examples of this conduct include the distress suffered by various cats and ducks well in advance of some airborne bombing raids by Allied forces in Europe during World War II, or the howling and agitation of Abraham Lincoln's dog, which raced around the White House shortly before the President was assassinated in Ford's Theatre located elsewhere in Washington.[2] In 1922, the famous archaeologist who was instrumental in the discovery of the tomb of the ancient Egyptian ruler Tutankhamen died in Cairo, whilst his favourite dog reportedly cried out and dropped dead 5,000 kilometres away in England.[3]

How does a beloved animal distinguish almost to the exact moment that their owner is about to face danger or even death, sometimes on the other side of the country or the world? How do animals demonstrate such remarkable homing behaviour, sometimes travelling thousands of kilometres to be eventually reunited with their owners? It has partially to do with the way animals exploit the five senses known in humans, and some animals also have senses humans do not possess.

These latter senses include navigating in the dark; detecting other animals approaching by changes in temperature, and perhaps controversially, by telepathic communication. Is it any wonder that deceased pets, particularly those who were close to their beloved owners in this world, might revisit them as an apparition from the afterlife? These visitations may be for many reasons, such as comforting or reassuring their owners, warning or guarding them, or simply to say goodbye. It does not always have to be a deceased pet which returns to greet you.

Many years ago when I was experiencing severe personal upheaval in my life and the future was looking decidedly devastating, I received a visit from a live dove, purportedly an iconic symbol for peace. The wild bird had managed to fly into my house by slipping past a heavy glass sliding door and entering another room elsewhere in the building. It continued to fly around this room for several minutes despite my feverish attempts to capture it. Inexplicably, the dove then quietly acquiesced and permitted me to catch it by hand and gently stroke it before releasing this messenger back into its natural environment.

No bird had ever flown into my house in the past fifteen years prior to that time, or in the considerable years since that visit. Shortly afterwards, my life's journey improved markedly and never returned to such a low emotional point. When the visitation is less than friendly or far more concerned with haunting, the stories certainly become lively and I shall share some of these more unusual tales.

In terms of overseas hauntings, the 'Black Dog' was probably one of the most commonly reported animal apparitions, particularly throughout the counties of the United Kingdom. The legend of a ghostly black dog can be traced back to the Vikings, who brought tales of their 'Black Hound of Odin' with them on their sea voyages to Britain and the Americas. These canine ghosts of something resembling a dog vary considerably in size, colour, species, and most certainly in their diverse behaviours. A 'Black Dog' is not something that you would want visiting late at night, or during a storm, particularly if it has red glowing eyes the size of saucers.

Black Dog visitations even dated back to the 2nd century. Large black dogs featured strongly in the ancient folk myth, the ghostly 'Wild Hunt' which was led by the spectre huntsman and said to include twenty black horses and twenty black hounds. This folklore of a supernatural wild hunting party of ghastly riders had many variations and names between countries, but in Britain, the hounds were described as jet black, with eyes like saucers, and horrible. The symbolic depiction of such ravenous black dogs certainly would make anyone cautious when it came to any actual hauntings.

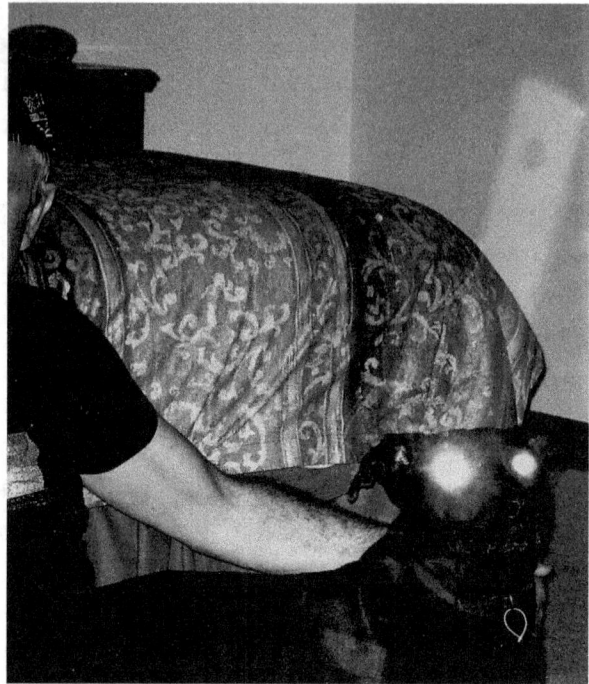

Figure 3: Simon's Black Dog (R.I.P.)

'Black Dog' can be a term used to distinguish apparitions of creatures that resemble canines of various colours and types, precluding pets of course.[4] Indeed, three separate divisions have been nominated, more for our mere convenience, as there were considerable overlaps. Firstly, there is the *Barguest/Shuck/Padfoot* amongst many other locally-known names, and this is a dog which changes its shape, a thing that no true black dog ever does. These are not the names of individuals, but of an impersonal creature which is distributed over certain areas. Secondly, there is the dog that is always black, always a dog and nothing else…It is always associated with a definite place or 'beat' on a road. It is always an individual. Sometimes it is associated with a person or a family, or a witch. Thirdly, there is the rare variety of black dog which appears in a certain locality in conjunction with a calendar cycle.[5]

These apparitions may occur in a diverse range of settings and appearances with varying outcomes, but from a general perspective, are best avoided if at all possible. Many of these hauntings have involved decidedly nasty intentions, so I shall shift my focus onto other animals, and reflect on part of the poem The *Owl and the Pussy-Cat* by British poet Edward Lear, first published in 1871.

> The Owl and the Pussy-Cat went to sea
> In a beautiful pea-green boat;
> They took some honey,
> And plenty of money
> Wrapped up in a five-pound note.
>
> The Owl looked up to the stars above,
> And sang to a small guitar,
> "O lovely Pussy, O Pussy, my love,
> What a beautiful Pussy you are,...
>
> ...and were married next day
> By the Turkey who lives on the hill.
> They dined on mince and slices of quince,
> Which they ate with a runcible spoon;
>
> And hand in hand on the edge of the sand
> They danced by the light of the moon,...[6]

Edward Lear's sequel entitled *The Children of the Owl and the Pussy-Cat* was only partly finished at the time of his death, but its completed opening is particularly fascinating: 'Our mother was the Pussy-Cat, our father was the Owl, And so we're partly little beasts, and partly little fowl, The brothers of our family have feathers and they hoot, While all the sisters dress in fur and have long tails to boot.'[7]

With this in mind, I commence my tales of animal hauntings with the very strange and enigmatic story about a talking mongoose named Gef which commenced in September 1931. This mysterious creature was variously reported to have inhabited a remote farmhouse occupied by a poor farming family near the hamlet of Dalby on the Isle of Man, a small isle in the Irish Sea. The family consisted of a husband, wife and their thirteen year old daughter. The family's first contact resulted from strange audible noises coming from behind the house's wooden wall panelling, resembling the sounds similarly made by rats. As these noise persisted over the following days and baiting was not successful, the farmer's dog was used to flush out the vermin or at least scare it, but with a surprising outcome.

The creature growled back at the dog. Over time, the farmer tried imitating a range of bird and animal noises only to discover they were being mimicked by the intruder behind the panelling. At other times, gurgling sounds would be heard, much like when an infant tried to form their first words. The unseen entity also appeared to have phenomenal hearing powers and gradually learnt the human language by listening to the family talking. The farmer only had to name an animal before the entity mimicked that animal. Then the entity began to talk and identified itself to the family.

The haunting story certainly became involved and somewhat complicated from now on. The mysterious creature said that his name was Gef (pronounced Jeff) who spelled his name phonetically because '…he didn't know how to spell…' Gef described himself as a mongoose who had been born in India in 1852, which was almost eighty years before this haunting. This description varied: '…I am an earthbound spirit…' sometimes and '…a ghost in the form of a mongoose…' at other times.[8] From all accounts by the family, Gef's appearance resembled that of a stoat, a ferret, or a weasel, with yellowish fur and a large bushy tail speckled with black, and a body about nine inches (23 centimetres) long.

Given that a neighbouring farmer had actually imported mongooses to the Isle of Man 20 years earlier hoping to curb the local rabbit population, it would not be unreasonable to find a mongoose in the district. However, Gef simply did not resemble a mongoose and was considerably smaller in size, more like a weasel or squirrel. According to his newly adopted family, Gef had many attributes, particularly his ability to recite anything that he heard, like simple nursery rhymes or songs. He could even spout witty remarks and words of wisdom. Remarkably, at times he acted as a guard dog by alerting the family when they had overslept in the mornings or when guests or unfamiliar dogs approached the farmhouse. When mice were detected in the farmhouse, Gef would scare them away like a family cat.[9]

The darker side to this mysterious creature was not quite as pleasant. He could be frequently irritable, aggressive and foul-mouthed towards the family, provoking them without any warning. At other times, Gef would fly into a rage and create mischief for them. Most disconcertingly, the creature had the ability to hear whispering from 15 feet to 20 feet (5-6 metres) away and to repeat exactly what was spoken.

What was this mysterious creature, which from various descriptions by the family shifted from that of a real, verbally active, live mongoose to something of a telekinetic sprite? Gef was rarely seen by those outside the family, despite many investigative visits to the farmhouse over some years from parapsychologists, ghost hunters, journalists and other interested parties including locals seeking physical evidence of its existence. Strange, unexplained noises and disembodied voices echoing through the walls were the only indication of this entity to these outsiders.

Investigators had a field day with the legendary talking mongoose, explaining much of the paranormal activity away on the farm's long hair sheepdog, and the unusual design of the old stone farmhouse as the origin of the weird sounds.[10] In *Confessions of a Ghost Hunter* compiled by British psychic researcher Harry Price and published in 1936, the author observed that the double walls of wood panelling which lined the interior rooms featured considerable internal air space between stone and wood walls that 'makes the whole house one great speaking-tube, with walls like soundingboards. By speaking into one of the many apertures in the panels, it should be possible to convey the voice to various parts of the house'.[11] There was further doubt cast on the existence of Gef that the strange voices heard may have possibly been a result of some creative ventriloquism by the family.

If the entire haunting was an elaborate hoax by the family who colluded to maintain the illusion for years, what was their motive by living in such a lonely, isolated location? Another possible suggestion was that Gef may have been a poltergeist (a noisy and disruptive spirit that often causes trouble and mischief). They make their presence known by noises, including by knocking, tumbling things, rattling or blustering. These intelligent imps possess certain unpleasant characteristics, and are beings perceived to have evolved from the lower elemental nature of man, or to constitute it. A poltergeist infests an abode rather than haunts it, prefers your company rather than seeking solitude, and may cause trouble and devilment at any time of day or night.

After the death of the family's father, the house changed hands in 1945, but the new owner had no contact with Gef, precluding an incident where he claimed to have killed a strange looking, black and white animal which seemed to be neither ferret, stoat nor weasel. 'It answers to all descriptions', he informed the local press. The animal was much larger than the famous mongoose and the wrong colour. The farmhouse was demolished after the new owner eventually left.

Before the family's surviving daughter died in 2005, she gave an interview late in her life about Gef in which she admitted, 'Yes, there was a little animal that talked and did all those other things ... He said he was a mongoose and we should call him Gef ... But I do wish he had let us alone.' Appropriately, I shall leave the last comment to Gef himself who was quoted as saying 'If you knew what I know, you'd know a hell of a lot!'[12]

Animal hauntings do not appear to be at all common compared with the plethora of reported paranormal sightings of humans. Conversely, their visitations are widely acknowledged throughout the centuries and across many cultures in myths and folklore, often represented as the messengers of omens.

Since ancient times superstitious people have placed much credence in omens, particularly where these signs were delivered through birds or animals, such as the raven or perhaps the black cat so popular in published supernatural literature. The message did not seem to attract quite the same attention when it was delivered by a fox. These carnivorous mammals are recognised more for being cunning and wily, with an innate ability to baffle and to avoid capture, rather than as a creature of foreboding. In John Masefield's narrative poem *Reynard the Fox* or *The Ghost Heath Run*, published shortly after World War I, the fox survived a protracted hunt by horsemen and hounds to live another day:

… And the hunt came home and the hounds were fed,
They climbed to their bench and went to bed ;
The horses in their stable loved their straw.
"Good-night, my beauties," said Robert Dawe.

Then the moon came quiet and flooded full
Light and beauty on clouds like wool,
On a feasted fox at rest from hunting,
In the beech-wood grey where the brocks were grunting.

The beech-wood grey rose dim in the night
With moonlight fallen in pools of light,
The long dead leaves on the ground were rimed ;
A clock struck twelve and the church-bells chimed.[13]

For one of the strangest stories concerning the behaviour of foxes, try medieval Ireland in 1478, when the Prestons of Gormanstown were made the first viscounts in the country. A viscount is usually conveyed as a rank above a baron but below that of an earl. The crest of such a noble family was that of a running fox, with another standing erect supporting the coat-of-arms. Legend has it that foxes would gather at the Gormanstown castle shortly before the death of the head of this family. This castle was built in the early 19th century on the site previously occupied by a manor house in which the Prestons had always lived since 1363.

When the 12th Viscount was dying in 1860, witnesses saw foxes gathering around the ancestral home for some days, before congregating in pairs under the Viscount's bedroom window, and barking and howling the entire night. The following morning, they were observed crouching around and in front of the home, and disappeared after the funeral. Remarkably, the foxes even walked through the poultry kept on site without harming them during this time. Brings to mind a French proverb that states 'A wise fox will never rob his neighbour's hen-roost'.

The foxes were there again for the 13th Viscount's death in 1876. He actually seemed to be improving in health until the foxes appeared, barking under his bedroom window, and, contrary to expectation, the Viscount died that night. The 14th Viscount died in 1907, this time in Dublin, but yet again, several foxes were observed around his dwelling and the nearby chapel, with some appearing to be distressed.

Two days later, with the Viscount's body lying in the chapel, the strangest episode of all occurred. About 3 a.m. that morning, the Viscount's son was inside the chapel and '…heard outside a consistent and insistent snuffling or sniffing noise, accompanied by whimperings and scratchings at the door'. He subsequently observed foxes outside various entrances to the chapel, and '… one so close that he could have touched it with his foot'. The noise from these foxes continued until 5 a.m. when it suddenly ceased.[14]

The humble horse, or steed as it is known when ridden, is another animal distinctively associated with omens and particularly folklore involving the supernatural. It has remained sacred to mankind, both as a reliable and sturdy servant for farmers and other workers alike, and has carried men into countless battles. Its value could best be gauged by the following old proverb beginning as early as the 13th century:

> For the want of a nail, the shoe was lost,
> For the want of a shoe, the horse was lost,
> For want of a horse, the rider was lost,
> For want of a rider, the battle was lost,
> For the want of a battle, the kingdom was lost,
> And all for the want of a horseshoe nail.[15]

Interestingly, the horseshoe and the nails supporting it also served another useful purpose with respect to witchcraft, as indicated in folklore superstitions from Suffolk, England that '… a witch cannot pass over the threshold on which a horseshoe is nailed with the open part upwards or at least, that she cannot perform her diabolical feats within the door to which it belongs…'[16] There was some rather stringent conditions allocated to this superstition, including that the nails should not be driven through the shoe but only positioned to hold the shoe by its sides, and ever be removed or disturbed.

For those only able to afford a donkey instead of a horse, nailing the donkey shoe under the threshold of any witch with a reputation of being suspected of sorcery would also suffice. It would presumably '…avert the exercise of her craft by confining her all night within doors, as witches cannot cross iron.'[17]

Of the considerable number of horse mythologies from the Irish, Scottish and Welsh, I think the 'pooka' or 'puca' seems a fitting example of a demonic creature able to transform into various animals. Such a mischievous sprite has been depicted as a water-horse in various supernatural occurrences involving lakes and other bodies of water. If the horse arose from the water and was captured, it would make a splendid steed but could also rip apart those who approached. In Scotland, a folktale recounts a foolish young girl who decided to try the Halloween fortune-telling custom of dipping her sleeve in water, and vanished forever. She left behind only her screams in the night and shreds of clothing found next morning near a hoof-print. Halloween night, May eve and Midsummer's eve are known to the Welsh as the 'Three Spirit Nights' of the year. On these nights, the spirits of those who had drowned might surface once again, riding white horses atop the waves.[18]

Encounters with ghostly horses can have dire outcomes if you are the unfortunate one to cross their paths; alternatively, they may represent an early warning from the supernatural of something yet to happen. It is worth recounting some real-life experiences to appreciate the differences. These examples occurred in the 1800s, when the coach and horse were the common form of road transport throughout the developed world. The coach of passengers would be driven by coachman who sat atop the front of the carriage and controlled its horses with a set of reins. The coachman would encourage them to maintain a suitable speed, sometimes even by using a small whip on occasion. The phantom coach and its horses, or the ghost-carriage as it came to be known, was always heard but only seen intermittently. In those bygone days, many roads were paved in cobble stones which contributed to considerable noise as the horse's hooves and then the coach wheels passed over them.

My example occurred on a moonlit night when a coachman was transporting his passenger along such a road and heard another coach approaching from the rear. The other coach made such noise from the roll of its wheels, the clatter of hooves and the jangling of its bits, that the coachman felt obliged to let it pass and pulled over to one side of the road, but nothing passed. When he looked back down the road, it was empty, so he continued on for a further 15 minutes, still with the noise of another coach behind him. Upon reaching a crossroad, the coachman turned down the side road only to clearly hear the phantom coach dash past him along the straight road.[19] It appeared that this spectral phenomenon represented no distinctive warning, unlike the sinister apparition of the headless coachman which is part of folklore in north-western Europe and which foretold approaching death, usually of a family member.[20]

From eyewitness accounts through the 19th century, the death coach always involved a loud rumbling of noise as it travelled and appeared as a shadowy dark shape which could pass directly through locked gates. The family member who passed away shortly after the visit may have had ailing health already or would die without any apparent health problems. On one decidedly scary occasion in 1821, it was reported that a family member who had been travelling in vain for his health was returning home that evening. When a coach arrived that night, a servant at the house reached out to open the coach door, and instead of the ailing family member, saw a skeleton looking out and promptly fainted. When the servant recovered shortly afterwards, the coach was nowhere to be seen. A little later, the sick family member arrived but died the following morning.[21] If one travelled further back in history to the medieval mansion Wolfeton House in Dorset built in the late 15th century, or to a Jacobean mansion on the northern outskirts of London, England, built in 1611, the spectral coach was reported to have actually passed through the main doors and up the grand staircase before de-materialising. The omen of impending death remained the same.

These events seemed to have ceased with the demise of horse-driven coaches. However, one account from a car driver on a quiet country road in Cornwall on a rainy afternoon might surprise. The sole occupant of the vehicle reported a phantom coach drawn by four ghostly horses at full speed suddenly appearing and coming directly towards him down the road. He provided an incredibly detailed description of the coach, its coachman and guard, and the calamitous event. Fortunately, the spectral coach vanished before colliding with his car, but not before the roaring cacophony of noise from the coach's wooden wheels, the horses' hooves and the warning horn of the coach terrified him.[22] His description of the coach as viewed at such close range was meticulous and I would suggest difficult to fault. Such a coach would have probably transported mail between local villages in the area two hundred years previously.

Supernatural horses are an integral part of another truly frightening apparition—the Ankou, also known as the Harbinger of Death, the Graveyard watcher and, less commonly, the Grim Reaper. Ankou folklore is Celtic in origin, but has persisted mainly in French Brittany, a region which blends the oral traditions of Paganism with Catholicism. The Ankou came in many guises, but most commonly appeared as a tall, skinny, almost skeletal and ageless man or man-shaped living shadow, with long flowing white hair and supposedly had a gaunt, haggard face (although apparently no one living has ever seen his face). He wore a large, wide-brimmed, old felt hat that concealed or shaded his face, and a long, black robed-costume, cloak or cape.[23]

The Ankou was said to drive a ghostly black cart, small coach or even a hearse drawn by either two black horses of which one was youthful, strong and healthy, and the other was old, thin and ill-looking, or by four black horses of unspecified age. He was assisted by two ghostly skeletal figures whose features were always hidden from view and who walked beside the cart/hearse leading the horses, and helping the Ankou gather the dead.[24]

For this was the mission of the Ankou, to deliver an inevitable warning of death to living people who were about to die and to fetch the unfortunates in his cart. Just the ominous roar of the creaking solid wooden wheels of his cart as it approached your house was enough warning of this impending doom, usually preceded by a cold gust of wind. It is said no-one can ever stop the Ankou or be immune to his visit, as Death comes to us all and cannot be escaped, no matter how hard we try. As an old Irish proverb says 'When Ankou comes, he will not go away empty'.[25] Fortunately, however, many tales report that some people, having seen the Ankou, were given enough time to organise their affairs before he returned to collect them.

How did this frightening phantom come to be known as the Graveyard Watcher? For this explanation, one needs to resort to an ancient custom concerning the creation of a new graveyard. In tales found throughout Europe, it would be customary to bury some unfortunate victim alive in the first grave in order to create a ghostly guardian (the Ankou) to frighten away anyone who might disturb the peace of the departed buried therein. Interestingly, this Graveyard Watcher is believed by some to be the cause of the involuntary shiver one gets from time to time that can cause a person to remark, 'someone just walked over my grave'.[26]

So why do spectral horses figure prominently in various sightings of animal apparitions throughout the world? For some guidance, one should look to the acknowledged qualities of horses as detailed in folklore and myths across so many cultures. By virtue of their size, both domesticated and wild horses have traditionally commanded respect from people. Coupled with their strength and tenacity, horses exhibited fearsome qualities, particularly when ridden into battle. They could also be unpredictable, and it would not be uncommon for horses to bite people in certain circumstances. Permit an unbridled horse to run freely and it would truly be a sight to behold. With this is mind, it seems only right that a horse would be the creature pulling a spectral coach or being ridden by a ghostly phantom.

The following excerpt from an old book about mythical horses captured the sentiment:

> And the breed of horses they reared could not be surpassed in the world – fleet as the wind, with the arched neck and the broad chest and the quivering nostril, and the large eye that showed they were made of fire and flame, and not of dull, heavy earth.[27]

A final intriguing thought in folklore about a horse is that it '… is believed to have the power of seeing ghosts…'[28] and given the many admirable qualities of the horse, why does that not surprise me?

THE BEAR AND THE WOLF

Of all the wild animals that have been reported to appear as apparitions and are inextricably linked to cultural folklore, the bear and the wolf are possibly the most recognisably predatory and fearsome species. Both share voracious appetites, threatening appearances when agitated or otherwise aggressive, and an ability to grow to enormous sizes; both command considerable respect and apprehension from humans when confronted. They are also highly protective of their young until their offspring are experienced enough to survive on their own, or for wolves, at an age where they may usurp their status in the group.

A wild bear without cubs is a loner, a fighter with extreme strength, powerful claws and the ability to attack anything that gets in the way. It is a brave man who must have iron nails that would scratch a bear. In different cultures these beasts have gained a well-deserved reputation for nobility, on account of their survival skills in the face of adversity, such as being able to survive the entire winter without eating.[1] Their enormous strength and strange habits, including a tendency when so required to rear themselves on the hind legs, to kill by hugging an adversary, and leaving footprints similar to adult people, meant the bear became highly respected as a courageous opponent and not a malevolent species.[2,3]

Interestingly, the collective name for a group of bears is a 'sloth' which somewhat understates their actual ferocity and tenacity. In witchcraft, it was believed bears were often selected to become witches' companions (known as 'familiars') because of their extreme strength and tenacity to fight to the death. These skills were considered essential for the protection of a witch and her magic.

Wolves by contrast hunt and fight in packs, and use the skills of cunning and patience to exploit any weakness in their prey.[4] A wolf will always isolate the weakest and most vulnerable of the hunted to satisfy its appetite, in preference to blindly attacking a sizeable herd. It can be a ruthless and mean adversary, even attacking other wolves in its group if necessary to affirm its status.

These qualities and characteristics of wolves and bears were valued by human cultures from the earliest of times, and recognised in various myths, tales and even poems. The wearing of bear skins, wolf skins or perhaps even the head of such an animal to symbolise these attributes has been known across ancient cultures.[5]

The ferocity of these animals has also been translated into popular myths with respect to shape-changing; the ability to transform between people and animals. Everyone has probably heard of the mythological were-wolves, also known as man-wolves—from the Old English term 'wer' for 'man'—but wolves were not the only animals into which man could change. Bears were certainly another such animal. Shape-shifters, as they are known in folklore and legends, could be animals, ghosts, spiritual entities or other various things which could change into others at will or under special conditions, such as when under a curse or possibly when bitten by another shape-shifter for example. What is not commonly known is that shape-shifters were not necessarily evil or sinister. For this book however, I shall confine myself largely to apparitions and other ghostly shape-changers, rather than delve far into the realms of magic and superstition.

To understand more about a wild bear and why it may return as an apparition, I quote in part from *Turi's Book of Lapland*, as translated from the Danish by E.G.Nash (1931): ' The bear is a wonderful animal who lives through winter without eating. And he is not angry with a person who comes up to him and does not do anything to him …' It was also felt that the bear had no natural antagonism towards human beings.[6]

Figure 4: The Sun Bear

Interestingly, I particularly like the supposed supernatural abilities deemed in Newfoundland that distinguished a bear from most other animals and qualified as follows:

> The threats involving bears are used to discourage children from going into the woods (berrypicking, etc.), to get them indoors before dark and discourage them from going out after dark, to discourage them from going to other dangerous or forbidden places, to encourage obedience and good behaviour in general and to dissuade them from making fun of bald-headed men![7]

For the purposes of describing a ghostly bear, it is important to turn to folklore for some relevant guidance. *Barguest* is a name used widely to describe a shape-shifting creature, which can also appear in the shape of a bear, possibly derived from German for 'bear-ghost'. The derivation of the word *Bar-geist* is disputed, with some explaining it as 'bear-demon' in German, in allusion to its alleged appearance at times as a bear. Elsewhere, in the northern counties of England for example, the name *Barguest* applies to a large nocturnal spectre-hound whose appearance is a portent of death; a mythical monstrous goblin-dog with huge teeth and claws that can also be described in folklore under various other names.[8]

Reported sightings of ghostly bears are relatively uncommon throughout the world, yet documented folklore had many historical accounts of the appearances of *Barguests/Bahrgeists*, and I shall look to such commentary pertaining to their existence. Whatever the entity supposedly described in such folklore, it certainly had common attributes observed between various counties and locales. These seemed to include haunting a specific location in a neighbourhood, usually in a lonely rural setting, with quite half the places associated with movement from one locality to another; they include roads, laneways, footpaths, corridors, staircases, bridges, fields, hedges, hollow trees, graves or even stretches of waste land, that could all be considered as possible gateways/passages between our physical world and elsewhere.[9]

Ghostly bears are also considered to utter a roar totally unlike the voice of any known animal, to be able to readily change shape and form. They are best avoided if encountered. If anyone came in its way, the entity could inflict a terrible wound by its paw and that wound may never heal properly, if ever. Its presence would represent an ominous warning or prophesy of imminent death.[10] Beware the roar of the *Barguest* and leave the beast alone.

The following excerpts from verses compiled in 1644 by William Paulden in the North Riding of the county of Yorkshire in England probably best illustrate the nature of the *Barguest*:

> … About midnight, when they saye
> Greislye [Grizzly] ghosts have leave to playe,
> And dead menn's [men's] soules [souls], with courage brave,
> Skipp [Skip] from out each severall [several] grave,
> And walke the roundes [rounds]; when the bar-guest [ghost of York]
> Comes tumbling out of's [his] smoakye [smokey] nest,
> Sometymes [Sometimes] having suche [such] a face
> As promiseth an human race;
> Sometymes he bee [be] a beare [bear], a dogg [dog],

> Sometymes the lykeness [likeness] of a hogg [hog]…[11]

Why are wolves so feared and detested for their behaviours? There may be several reasons but two possibilities warrant discussion. Wolves have an enduring history recorded over the centuries of ferociously attacking and eating people and livestock. The wolf has been perceived as the great destroyer and despoiler of flocks and herds, and in Europe and northern Asia, was considered to be man's most dangerous enemy. There was no compassion for such activity, particularly when it involved hunting in large wolf-packs. The ability of a wolf to be sly and cunning in tracking its prey, and the physical deception that such a wild dog closely resembles a domesticated dog, could also be why wolves are hated and feared.

The outcome for an unsuspecting person confusing man's best friend with his worst enemy could have fatal consequences. As the Spanish proverb goes: 'The wolf loses his teeth but not his inclinations.' I particularly like this brief description of a likely encounter between man and wolf as prepared circa 1554, summarised as follows: 'The property of a wolf is that if a man sees the wolf after the wolf sees the man, then the man shall not be dumb. But if the wolf sees the man before the man sees the wolf, then is the man dumb and cannot speak.'[12]

Additionally, ancient myths and legendary tales have recognised that wolves have the shape-shifting ability to become werewolves. In the northern European country of Estonia between Latvia and Finland for example, belief in werewolves was widespread in the 17th century, with numerous trials convened of people who confessed to transmuting into such creatures by the wearing of wolf skins and attacking animals. This eventually ceased by the end of the century when belief in such superstitions waned amongst the population, although the sinister development had still fuelled apprehension about the wolf.[13]

In modern times, wolves have become extinct in many regions of the world and remain only as an unpleasant memory in some areas. Their reputation as ruthless killers persists in other areas, with savage attacks of various livestock still being reported up until the middle of the 20th century. As the old warning goes: 'Beware of false prophets, which come to you in sheep's clothing, but inwardly they are ravening wolves'. These animals have also been associated with witchcraft and, according to Germanic lore, were actually ridden by witches. Similarly, ancient Nordic female spirits known as Valkyries were thought to be transported by wolves. A European gypsy folk tradition nominates that a wolf howling may signal a witch approaching.[14]

Because of their remarkable similarity to some breeds of domesticated dogs, wolves may be mistaken for a large black dog in the dark or mist, and consequently apparitions of wolves over time may have been inadvertently reported as those of the 'Black Dog'. This is based more upon some unusual characteristics of large wolves, such as their prominent pointed ears, ferocious long teeth, piercing eyes and shrill howling at night, than upon reported sightings. Then again, if confronted by a rather large, fearsome and aggressive hound in the dark on a lonely path, one could be excused entirely for mistaking such an entity for any number of creatures just from sheer panic.

'In the calm, deep waters of the mind, the wolf waits.'[15]

WHISPERS

Have you ever listened intently to the wind at night as it howled and wailed around your house, cabin, apartment or flat? When the wind becomes a raging tempest, it can sound like the discordant clanging of metal chains or the shrill clinking of a multitude of empty glass bottles as it mercilessly buffets your dwelling. The wind almost seems to have a voice at those times. Sometimes, just occasionally, if you listen intently, it is possible to imagine that the wind is whispering, particularly as it whistles through the cracks in windows and doors.

I am reminded of my early childhood life at a country primary school where a huge evergreen conifer tree dominated the school's playground. Its dense foliage of wispy, fine needle-like leaves perfectly filtered even the strongest winds, often resulting in a distinctive 'whispering effect' as the tree's prolific branches swayed and twisted. If you played directly beneath this unusual tree's canopy on particularly windy days, it always seemed as if there were several voices whispering to you simultaneously. These childhood memories should evaporate in adulthood but oddly, have been reinforced by recent events. Whilst parked in a suburban supermarket car park in daylight hours, and on the opposite side of Australia to the primary school of my childhood days, I realised that there was several identical evergreen conifer trees growing adjacent to my parking bay.

There was a slight breeze blowing through these trees on that day but not enough to cause much rustling of their needle-like leaves. When I returned to my car, I heard that distinctive whispering so prevalent in my childhood days, but thought no more about it. Unfortunately all the trees were removed from the car park before my subsequent visit a few weeks later, , possibly due to safety concerns from falling branches, so I shall probably never know whether it was all in my imagination. Eugene Field, the American writer known as 'the poet of childhood', captures these sentiments succinctly in the first verse of his 19th century poem *The Night Wind* as follows:

> Have you ever heard the wind go "Yooooo"?
> 'T is a pitiful sound to hear!
> It seems to chill you through and through
> With a strange and speechless fear.
> 'T is the voice of the night that broods outside
> When folk should be asleep,
> And many and many's the time I've cried
> To the darkness brooding far and wide
> Over the land and the deep:
> "Whom do you want, O lonely night,
> That you wail the long hours through?"
> And the night would say in its ghostly way:
> > "Yoooooooo!
> > Yoooooooo!
> > Yoooooooo!"... [1]

Night whispers are probably founded in one's imagination and perceptions rather than reality. The wind can readily conjure tricks with one's mind in the darkness, and in some ancient cultures, may be indicative of communication from deceased spirits. Whilst early British explorer Lieutenant John Lort Stokes was visiting the remote North West coastline of Australia in 1838, he reflected briefly on the local Aboriginal people's trepidation about inclement weather at night; '... in wild stormy weather, when the creaking trees, and moaning wind, give them a dread of a visit from the Evil Spirit'.[2]

In my direct experience, such whispers have usually been associated with my long departed parents and have occurred late in the evening whilst sleeping alone on calm nights without the slightest breeze. Regardless of the quality of your sleep, someone clearly pronouncing your first name on a quiet night with no evident external sounds can certainly get your attention. Did I just imagine that someone called out to me in the night or was

I dreaming it?

You tentatively try to resume your sleep only to hear your name loudly whispered again, like somebody urgently trying to hail a taxi. This time you sense the shadowy shape of a person standing over you beside the bed and facing directly towards you. Lying in the darkness, you cannot distinguish any features of the shape other than it is a person. You make the mistake of sitting up to get a closer look and the apparition is gone. These whispers occur infrequently and often years apart in my life, but have always involved someone calling out as if trying to get my attention. I am still listening. In recent years, there have been variations on a theme, including something touching me on the shoulder but when I turn around, no-one is there. Once when indoors on my own, I copped a puff of air in the face as if someone had exhaled directly in front of me.

A rather scary example of the presence of supernatural wind was provided by an account from the late 19th century concerning an old weathered house in a suburb north of London that was inhabited by two elderly maiden sisters. A visitor to the house who arrived in the early evening along with other guests to dine with the sisters encountered something daunting. Once left alone upstairs, the visitor became aware of a rather peculiar sound in the room, best described as 'a sort of shuddering'. Assuming it to be probably from the wind in a chimney or even a local draft around a door, he initially ignored the sound, until it seemed to follow him to wherever he moved in the room. Feeling distinctly uneasy now, the visitor quickly left the room and descended the stairs to another room, only to hear the faintly audible shuddering sound as he was still on the stairs.

Even at the dining table, the sound was remarkably close as if something was seated beside him, yet no-one else at the dinner party appeared to notice anything. This dreadful disturbing sound was unmistakable several times and continued to cause quite some distress to the visitor until he eventually left the house. When he met the sisters again away from the house, it was tactfully explained to him that they were aware of it but it had ceased to be a concern, as it was considered harmless in nature. Sometimes it would be quiet for weeks, before resuming following them about the house from room to room, and floor to floor. No further explanation was provided.[3]

Perhaps I should heed the prophetic advice of the contemporary English writer of children's poems Daphne Lister, as provided in her poem *Under the Stairs*:

> I don't like the cupboard
> Under the stairs,
> It reminds me of caves
> And dragons' lairs.
>
> So I never look in
> Once it is night,
> In case I should get
> A nasty fright.
>
> I'm silly I know
> 'Cos it's only small,
> There wouldn't be room
> For a dragon, at all.
>
> But even in daytime
> It gives me the scares
> To go past the cupboard
> Under the stairs. [4]

Strickland Bay, located at the southern end of the Buccaneer Archipelago on the remote and rugged West Kimberley coast of Western Australia, is a forlorn and desolate place and thankfully I only ever visited it once, in the late 1990s. In the centre of this extensive bay is a group of isolated islands located nearby to a smaller elongated bay known locally by the daunting name of 'The Graveyard'. It is commonly acknowledged that this name originated from the deaths of divers who perished in the late 19th century either by drowning or suffering 'the bends' (decompression sickness) whilst pearling in The Graveyard, which is a relatively deep bay. The name also indicates the presence of up to fifteen graves of these divers buried in mainly unmarked graves through the surrounding islands.

Some of these graves were marked by headstones gathered from the local rocks, and at least one gravestone was also inscribed with a date. Pearling luggers were known to frequent this region of the Kimberley coast in the 1880s, concentrated in Strickland Bay and nearby Cone and Cascade Bays. During my visit to this area by charter boat, the skipper suggested the area may even be the site of graves of early Portuguese whalers who were tracking the whales migrating down the coast from Camden Sound further north of Strickland Bay. He also suspected there may be a submerged vessel or two lying in The Graveyard.

What was particularly unsettling about islands near The Graveyard was the local siltstone rock formations which appear to dominate only this region. Extensive weathering and erosion of the relatively soft siltstone by

Figure 5: Bizarre and Grotesque Erosion of Siltstone Formations

the elements as well as passing cyclones and massive tidal movements, has resulted in a diversity of honeycombed and pitted features of the outcrops, as well as dramatic, seemingly sculptured edifices.

Interspersed between the prevailing, softer siltstone outcrops are more durable and narrow sandstone layers which have resisted prolonged weathering, often standing alone like stark sentinels guarding the graves or as pronounced vertical monuments to the dead. These isolated sandstone columns were also sometimes simply perched precariously on a beach as if dumped there by some 'otherworldly' being. The island with the most graves had a small beach comprising harsh shell grit and weathered stones rather than soft sand. It was certainly not a comfortable beach where you could enjoy yourself.

On the day of my visit to these islands, it was particularly humid and calm without even the hint of a breeze. It was the start of the wet (rainy) season in the tropics and the atmosphere was oppressive. After spending time wandering through the various rocky outcrops and visiting some of the gravestones, I was overcome by the pervasive eerie silence. Even in the middle of the day, there was no a sound of any birdlife, insects or even a waft of air rustling the vegetation. Stone dead silence. After staying for a couple of hours in the stifling humidity, the skipper decided it was time to continue our travels and he returned to the charter vessel to make preparations. As I sat on the beach alone waiting for his dinghy to return for me, I experienced two very strange events. In the heat of that calm day, I suddenly felt a distinctive chill in the air, as if the temperature around me had dropped dramatically. It is difficult to explain how one felt chilly without any breeze or change in weather, but I had the shivers. I felt like I needed to put on a jacket or even a woollen cardigan, but it would be ridiculous in this humidity. A short time later, a slight breeze commenced gently wafting across the beach.

When a strong wind is blowing through and around honeycombed rocks, it tends to generate whistling noises as the air passes over the cavities. When a gentle breeze arises, it does not generate much sound. What I detected in those few minutes before the skipper returned in his dinghy was a distinctive whispering coming from the nearby hillside. It sounded like collective voices whispering together but what they said was indecipherable. As the dinghy approached the beach, the sound of the small outboard motor drowned out all other noise so I was unable to investigate any further. The whispers might have been a case of my imagination running wild or perhaps an odd meteorological effect, but I was very glad to leave that beach and those islands. It was not a place for an overnight stay for me under any circumstances. I would definitely heed the warning of an old Cornish superstition that stipulates fishermen should '…never dare pass the night on a shore near a place where ships have been wrecked. The souls of the dead sailors are said to be haunting these places…'[5]

The belief in the power of certain human agents of strange spirits controlling the elements of winds and waves has existed early in the history of man. The phrase 'a capful of wind' was reputedly coined by Eric VI, of Norway who lived in 907 AD. He was believed to be able to control the winds by turning his cap in the direction sought. Eric was in his time held second to none in the magical art, and was so familiar with the evil spirits whom he worshipped, that what way so ever he turned his cap, the wind would presently blow that way.[6]

Such beliefs are founded in superstition, sorcery and by the incantations of witches, and became almost universal in the Middle Ages. Every ancient culture had their belief in weather-makers who controlled the elements, and there were probably none better known for having the supreme power over the winds than witches. Legends of spirits who wailed or howled through storms have been noted in coastal parts of Cornwall in the west of England, whilst elsewhere, many believed that the spirits could raise or bestow winds or tempests.

Tregeagle, the troublesome ghost of Gwenvor Cove, was known as the Cornish storm-fiend and was just such a spirit. It was believed he wailed at the failure of his efforts to accomplish certain difficult tasks. This howling or roaring in such frustration was commonly believed in the Cornish district to represent not only a forewarning of the onset of stormy or blustery weather, but also such howls could be heard mingled with the winds of the storm before it scattered the spirit away.[7] The basis as to why Tregeagle behaved in this manner is lengthy and would not add much more to the actual legend of wind-raising.

There are innumerable folktales from throughout the world and over the centuries concerning the mystical powers of witches to control the elements, but I particularly like the tale of an old woman who was said to have raised a storm off the coast of England by blowing a tin whistle. Although her son's vessel was wrecked in that particular storm but without loss of life, seamen affirmed they often heard the old lady's whistle in a gale. Another less fortunate witch on the Isle of Man, who was believed to have caused a storm resulting in the loss of an entire fleet of herring fishing vessels, met with a most tragic demise, by being rolled down a hill inside a spiked barrel.[8]

Whistling on board is probably one of the most enduring of nautical superstitions. There is a common belief that whistling for a wind at sea is tantamount to inviting a gale, unless there is no wind and only a favourable breeze is sought. To whistle softly in a calm may bring fair winds by appealing to the patron saint of breezes and winds. To whistle during fair winds or during inclement weather is thought to only increase the winds, possibly to gale force or stronger and subsequent potential calamity. Sailors believed that you were mocking the god of the wind who in turn could become furious and deliver destructive winds instead.[9]

The presence of deceased sailors on maritime sailing vessels of the past has led to many explanations for the occurrence of curious wind phenomena. In one belief described in 1639, where a vessel is only able to progress slowly or becomes becalmed (deprived of the wind necessary to move it), it could be caused '... by a kind of mournful sympathy' for the dead.

Perhaps one of the scariest and unpredictable phenomenon to encounter at sea is the sudden appearance of a thick fog-bank. These misty, dense shrouds of fog can envelop a vessel quietly and completely, even on a calm day in still waters. There can be an unusual resonance encountered within such fog-banks, and a chilling dampness that you feel in your bones. Every noise seems exaggerated and a strange feeling of 'being locked in from the outside world' can be experienced. This is when your imagination takes over and ghostly shapes or shadowy outlines appear in the mist. When sailing ships in bygone days were becalmed in such meteorological conditions, sailors might hear and occasionally see something not quite right. These mirages could be explained by the reflections of distant landforms or other ships, or by unusual conditions of sunlight, but at other times, this was not possible. Even the sound of waves on hollow coastal rocks or reefs can generate unearthly noises in a fog, except there are usually no waves on a calm day.

The paranoia can best be described by the following verse in the 8th Canto from *The Revolt of Islam*, by English poet Percy Bysshe Shelley, composed in 1817: '…The Captain stood Aloof, and, whispering to the Pilot, said, "Alas! alas! I fear we are pursued By wicked ghosts; A Phantom of the Dead, The night before we sailed, came to my bed In dream, like that!"…'[10]

Sailors, usually the boldest men alive, are yet frequently the very abject [submissive] slaves of superstitious fear. Innumerable are the reports of accidents unto such as frequent the seas (such as fishermen and sailors), who discourse [speak] of noises, flashes, shadows, echoes, and other visible appearances, nightly heard and seen upon the surface of the sea.[11]

THE LAST MOMENT

Oliver Cromwell, the famous English military and political leader of the 17th century whom, among other things, was a key figure in the first civil war involving all of Britain, was quoted as having said: 'In the meadows of the mind, no one travels so far as he who knows not where he is going.' For most people living on this planet, their last moment in this physical world may be exactly that sentiment. A near-death experience or a near-miss with death has probably happened to each and every one of us in our lifetime. For many, we have possibly experienced this unfortunate circumstance more than once and survived. Where this experience has involved the most extreme example of clinical death or massive trauma, out-of-body cosmic travel also known as astral projection is one common outcome reported.

However, I am more interested in the persistent repercussions and consequences for those people who did not succumb to their final moment. From my actual encounters, a distinctly greater sense of purpose of life and vastly less materialistic outlook has dawned for me. The various encounters have also heightened my intuitive abilities whilst greatly reducing my apprehension of death. In effect, the near-miss has become a clear indicator of what could happen again with terminal consequences. Of the four significant near-death experiences in my life, two were from almost drowning in early childhood, and the remainder from preventable unfortunate incidents.

When I was probably around seven or eight years of age, I scampered across a pond of water lilies on a neighbour's property, assuming that it was an unkempt lawn due to the intricate and tight intermeshing of the vegetation. The thick layer of water lilies entirely camouflaged the underlying pond water and appeared to be part of the surrounding natural terrain. I was fully clothed at the time, including an overcoat and knee-high rubber gumboots, and promptly sank like a stone half way across the pond. Fortunately, my older brother was nearby and immediately responded to prevent me drowning. To this day, I am unsure how he retrieved me from that pond with both my gumboots full of water, which must have added considerably more weight to my body. I recall the extreme cold of the water, how my gumboots quickly pulled me under, and not much more.

The second near-drowning was in the shallows of a popular beach when I was around ten or eleven years of age. The persistent wave action at this beach had over time eroded a deep channel a few metres from the shoreline which was not apparent to any unsuspecting swimmer. As I walked slowly towards the surf, I fell into this tidal gutter and sank underwater without making any noise. Panic is the worst enemy of a poor swimmer. Twice I tried to reach the surface and was going underwater for the third and probably final time when my older sister rescued me. She had seen my flailing arms and heard my shouts, but initially thought that I had been simply skylarking. I had swallowed considerable seawater and was struggling to breathe when she arrived. The rest is largely a fuzzy blur, although I do clearly recollect visions of my short life flashing past in rapid succession. When I eventually asked her why she decided that I was in real trouble, she replied because she had always looked after me and sensed something was not quite right.

My next near-death experience involved a far more dramatic traffic accident when I was around 20 years of age. It was an era when vehicle seat belts were not compulsory in Australia, which as it eventuated, saved my life. I had borrowed my mother's Mini Minor which as everybody knows, is a compact midget of a car. A substantially larger tow truck failed to give way to me at a road intersection, resulting in the Mini crashing into the side of this truck, and everything then appearing to me to occur in ultra-slow motion as perhaps it does in a personal crisis. The force of this sudden impact flung me out of the vehicle through the driver's door and onto the bitumen road, whilst my front seat passenger was likewise propelled out of his door onto the road. The engine of the Mini-Minor was pushed backwards into the front seats which we had both previously occupied one second earlier.

These seats were crushed entirely and so would have anybody who had remained secured in them. When you are lying on the road looking back into your empty vehicle, it is explicitly clear that your final moment had not yet quite arrived. The tow truck involved had a massive protective steel girder affixed to its front to minimise any damage to the vehicle in the event of a front-on collision. Had this vehicle collided with the side of the Mini-Minor, neither my passenger nor I would have survived. It would be another sixteen years before I experienced my last near-death experience, and it was a particularly harrowing episode as well.

In the metalliferous surface mining industry, open pits are excavated to depth usually in a series of uniform benches of fixed height, somewhere between five to twenty metres. As the pit deepens, a narrow safety 'berm' of three to eight metres width is traditionally retained around the excavation final perimeter at each bench level. This is to maintain the stability and integrity of the overall final pit wall slope by leaving a series of small steps (or berms), rather than having one continuous uninterrupted slope which could become very unstable with time and collapse. The instability of this exposed ground along such berms may in some instances ultimately result in localised sections progressively failing and rock material falling into the pit below. To minimise this safety risk, it was usual practice to routinely monitor any physical signs of impending failure of such berms, such as extensive ground cracks and sporadic rock falls. These visual inspections occurred at least daily and often more frequently if ground conditions deteriorated.

In my case, a particular berm had been slowly developing ground cracking along a small section over several months and required such regular but routine physical safety inspections. There had been no indication of any dramatic escalation of the ground cracking for weeks, and nothing likely to trigger any unexpected failure of the berm. On this particular day, I walked cautiously to the monitoring location on the berm at the edge of the ground cracks to record my visual observations. Call it intuition or possibly a premonition, but something made me feel most uncomfortable as I stood there.

As I kneeled to take a closer look at the small rock cracks near my feet, as I had done so many times before, I noticed that they were increasing in width and new cracks were appearing in the solid rock nearby. Instinctively, I retreated a few metres away and the entire section berm in front of me slowly started to subside. In the short time that it took me to reach about ten metres from my original position, the berm section behind me had fallen completely into the pit below with a thunderous roar. There had been no evident noise to indicate this failure was underway and some 10,000 tonnes of rock were about to collapse.

It certainly was not my last moment, but I am sure that my unusual and acute sense of imminent danger had something to do with my eventual fate that day.

The witty and humorous American Sam Levenson certainly appreciated one's final moment when he astutely quoted that 'if you die in an elevator [lift], be sure to push the up button'. What actually is a near-death experience? It probably needs some clarity to avoid confusing it with actual departure from the world of the living. There are also a diverse range of spiritual and religious viewpoints on the matter to be considered, but I shall keep the process relatively simple.

Figure 6: Unfortunates of The Last Moment (*Courtesy of Shutterstock*)

When a person is about to die in circumstances which do not involve unexpected death or perhaps great suffering, they are usually able to adjust and accept what is about to happen to them. Their subjective state of being is comfortable to pass from the living world without undue concern. If however, their demise is likely to be emotionally or physically shocking, a person cannot or will not accept what is about to happen to them. In effect, their state of being becomes trapped in circumstances where it is awkward to make the transition beyond the present. How do some people survive these near-death experiences, and yet so many others succumb?

Humans are a very resilient species and many are gifted with natural physic powers to a varying degree; however they usually either neglect or suppress these until it is warranted. The extrasensory perception one develops in a near-death situation may be an extension of one's five ordinary senses being used beyond their normal limitations. However, it is far more likely to actually be a super sense that operates through the other senses to deliver its messages. The "sixth sense" as it is commonly described is a very effective warning mechanism for individuals in the event of impending danger; it also allows them to perceive apparitions. Without delving into the mystical world of superstitions, omens and other portents of future events, perhaps some individuals survive these experiences because their time is not due. For whatever reason, their unfortunate but significant near-misses are more likely to be hiccups on the journey, and possibly even subtle and timely warnings intended to catch their attention.

Perhaps this brief verse from 1845 will fulfill the moment, albeit the last moment that we all face eventually:

> I never lik'd the world so well,
> It, never seem'd so dear :
> For I beheld it, as I fell,
> And bless'd the little sphere.
>
> And now I breath'd the air again,
> And felt 't was native breath ;
> And I long'd once more to speak to men,

And tell them what is death :

But I was high in the sky-vault yet,
And slow I sunk, and slower :
Oh, how I long'd my foot to set
On the dark green Earth again ! [1]

It appears a most appropriate time to discuss the custom convened in so many countries to mark the passing of the deceased known ubiquitously as a 'wake'. This is a particularly lengthy topic with its origins firmly based in ancient cultures, and hence the variation in definitions attributable to the term *wake*. These include 'to wake up, to be awake, keep watch' in the context of the deceased is attributable to keeping a vigil or watch over the body. In earliest times, this vigil would have been spent over a night in commemorating the passing of the deceased's soul.

It was considered unacceptable to leave the deceased alone for a single moment, with each set of watchers replacing another '…from the moment of the breath leaving the body, till the lifting of the coffin previous to interment.'[2] This custom would eventually change to a solemn social interaction usually held before one's funeral to conduct the necessary lamentations and to quietly celebrate the person's past life. In more recent times, the wake is customarily held directly after the funeral when appropriate refreshments are served to the bereaved participants.

Even in those earliest of times, the relatives, good natured friends and neighbours who volunteered to watch over the body on such a melancholy occasion were liberally served refreshments as a tribute of respect and sympathy for the departed. Where the deceased was a single person with only a modest income and no immediate relatives, sometimes in those bygone days the wake was more akin to revelry which extended for days on end. The watchers may have even consumed everything in the house of the departed before finishing at the nearest public house.[3] A scary lesson is to be learned from this practice and the recently departed.

Take the tale about a sea captain around the middle of the 19th century who perished during a ferocious storm off the Donegal coast in Ireland whilst returning to his ship in a relatively small, frail boat. His body was washed ashore shortly thereafter and suitable arrangements made for the disposal of his body. The island where he was subsequently buried only had a few inhabitants who briefly visited a few times each year from the mainland. Several days after the funeral, these people received a visitor one night who approached their dwelling walking on fine and soft sand, yet still with clearly audible footsteps, as if coming on hard ground. When the door finally opened, the sea captain was standing in the entrance, dressed in the same clothing worn when he perished. Although the inhabitants were visibly shocked and dumbfounded at the sight of the deceased, they still invited him to enter, and then the figure '... without the least word or sign, moved back and disappeared from their view.' Although they rushed outside, they could discover no sign of a living person on the confines of the island.[4] Thankfully, they had not held an extended wake for him over days, because this particular departed had actually returned.

The watching of the corpse prior to interment has also been known in some regions of the United Kingdom by the old Saxon term as a *lyke wake*, from *lic* (a body), and *waecce*, (watch).[5] While the sun was above the horizon, such a vigil was named 'a sitting', and after dark, it became 'a lykewake'. This night watching has also been known as 'lich-waking' or 'a lichwake'.[6] In those ancient times whilst the assembled kindred and neighbours maintained their vigil, it would not be uncommon for a diverse range of games or group activities to occur, to pass the evening, ease the suffering of the deceased's relatives and provide some solace. These may have included reading the Scriptures, singing Psalms, reciting stories or playing games such as cards (incredibly using the coffin as the card table), or hide-and-seek.[7] The latter game may seem a relatively innocent pastime for a gathering, but from one account of the time, it turned somewhat out differently.

On this occasion of playing hide-and-seek at a lykewake, it was reported that some young men decided to remove the deceased from the coffin, and laid one of their number in its place to hide. A search for the youth discovered him in the coffin and quite dead, and the corpse originally removed was nowhere to be found.[8] A sobering thought indeed for those intending to play such a game of mischief at a wake.

The custom of 'watching' a corpse all night usually meant the mourners had considerable time on their hands, and for those of a superstitious nature, it could provide them with some unnerving experiences. The mind can play tricks on you at times, so visions of the dead unexpectedly reviving or the possible appearance of a wraith may not be uncommon for some. There are a variety of ancient customs for wakes. In Ireland for example, upon the death of one in humble circumstances, the body was "waked" by friends and neighbours.

After vociferous and often poetical lamentations, endless food and liquid refreshments provided at great effort was consumed, commonly leading to noisy and sometimes boisterous songs, laughter and crying. However, far from being disrespectful of the dead, the merriment and rigor were taken in good humour. The purpose of the merriment was both to celebrate the past life of the deceased through shared and embellished tales of praise, and to assist the bereaved to stay awake during a mourning process that could last for days.

The wake was the only opportunity to pay their respects for the final time in an appropriate yet emotional manner, with the tone dependent upon the circumstances of the death. In some rural counties of England, such as Norfolk and Suffolk, at least as far back as the 16th century, the drinking customs of mourners involved quite considerable consumption. From one account of the day, wine and beer would be served to each and every mourner, and '…the bearers of the corpse were liberally regaled with cake, and either rum, gin, or brandy'. In one recorded example, the cost of the wine for the gathering was five times more than the cost of the coffin.[9] In more modern times, however, the excesses of bygone days appear to have been replaced by rather sombre wakes of solemn dignity in many districts.

In past times it was hard to get through a funeral without drinking, and as English poet Thomas Shipman recanted in his 1667 poem entitled *The Old Mourner*: 'Grief is thirsty, and must drink'.[10] Even after the ritual interment, the wake represented to the bereaved merely a regrouping to discharge the solemn tension of the funeral and reassert the vitality of the survivors. Sometimes this mirth, feasting and revelry went far beyond simply mourning.[11] Perhaps part of this behaviour can be traced to around the 16th and 17th centuries, when certain celebratory religious festivals of dedication and commemoration in Britain known as annual wakes and vigils included festivals of feasting, music and dancing. These 'wake days', originally held for solemn religious and spiritual purposes, could become far more about excesses of revelry, consumption, dancing, sporting and gaming and other irreverent pastimes amongst the local population.[12]

The 17th century English lyric, poet and cleric Robert Herrick depicted these festivities so well in the following part of his poem *The Wake*, published in his book of poetry *Hesperides* in 1648:

> ...Drencht in Ale, or drown'd in Beere.
> Happy Rustiks [country bumpkins], best content
> With the cheapest Merriment:
> And possesse no other feare,
> Then to want the Wake next Yeare.[13]

The next tale, concerns a lykewake in Scotland. Two young girls who had been close since their childhood days once attended a lykewake for a female acquaintance and were shocked when they observed the dressing of the body treated with a relative indifference and even light-heartedness. They mutually promised that whoever of the two outlived the other would be solely responsible for laying out [preparing] the other one's body for burial. Of course, after parting and leading somewhat separate lives for several years, the girls' mutual promise was forgotten.

Upon learning that her female friend had passed away on the previous night, the remaining girl, now a woman married with an infant and living in a solitary farmhouse, found that she could not possibly fulfill her original solemn promise of attending the lykewake and laying out her friend's body. Her farming husband, his ploughman [farmhand] and their housemaid were away for the day and unlikely to return home at least until the evening, leaving no-one who could mind her infant. In her anxiety, she waited for them on a small hillock near the farmhouse with the best view. However, as the evening descended, the only figure she observed in the far distance was that of a female in white. Assuming this person to be her maid returning home, the woman went back into the house only to hear shortly afterwards the nearby farm livestock snorting and stamping their hooves, as if disturbed by someone passing. Then without further warning, '… a tall figure wrapped up from head to feet in a winding-sheet [burial garment/shroud]…' appeared at the door, before entering and sitting in a chair beside the fire.

The seated figure raised its thin, chalky arms to uncover its face, and exposed the features of the recently deceased woman. She was best described as having '… an expression of anger… dead and glassy eyes glaring at her … livid, unbreathing lips drawn apart, as if no friendly hand had closed them after the last agony…' The terrified woman continued to keep the fire burning with straw, for fear of being left in complete darkness with this apparition, until almost all the straw was expended. Then the sound of voices outside signaled the return of her husband, resulting in the apparition gliding towards the door to depart. However, as this spectre passed by the farm livestock, one of the startled cattle '… struck at it with its feet in the passing…', causing the figure to shriek faintly before vanishing.

To finally fulfill at least part of her original promise to respectfully share the last moment of the deceased woman, the terrified lady attended the lykewake the following morning. To her utter astonishment, upon examining the body, she discovered the mark of a cow's hoof distinctly impressed on the left side of the corpse.[14]

Perhaps the following quotation of the American author, playwright and actor/filmmaker Woody Allen from his 1975 play *Death: A Comedy in One Act* best explains the last moment: 'It's not that I'm afraid to die, I just don't want to be there when it happens.'

OCEAN WANDERERS

What is it about the ocean and those old wooden sailing ships that plied their trade between continents over hundreds of years, enduring treacherous climatic conditions and mountainous seas to reach a port of safety? What could tempt a sailor to risk life and limb voyage after voyage across the unforgiving seven seas for a meagre pittance of pay? The poem *Sea Fever* by British poet and novelist John Masefield first published in 1902 may provide a hint:

> I must go down to the seas again, to the lonely sea and the sky,
> And all I ask is a tall ship and a star to steer her by,
> And the wheel's kick and the wind's song and the white sail's shaking,
> And a grey mist on the sea's face, and a grey dawn breaking.
>
> I must go down to the seas again, for the call of the running tide
> Is a wild call and a clear call that may not be denied;
> And all I ask is a windy day with the white clouds flying,
> And the flung spray and the blown spume, and the sea-gulls crying.
>
> I must go down to the seas again, to the vagrant gypsy life,
> To the gull's way and the whale's way, where the wind's like a whetted knife;
> And all I ask is a merry yarn from a laughing fellow-rover,
> And quiet sleep and a sweet dream when the long trick's [period of duty] over.[1]

The simple answer is that these sailors loved being at sea and probably the unconventional lifestyle away from those landlubbers. Even when voyages lasted several months away from loved ones, sometimes in hostile environments where vessels may only have modest rations, poor living standards and perhaps a ruthless captain, the crews were not subjected to the same dreary and oppressive drudgery usually experienced by those living on shore. Their daily shipboard routines would provide a sense of discipline and order for them, and their variety of life would come from the innumerable changes in weather/sea conditions and ports visited.

With the exception of perhaps buccaneers/pirates, explorers and Royal Navy marines through the 16th to 19th centuries, typical seaboard life was probably not excessively dangerous. In earlier times, however, when sailing vessels were considerably smaller and far less reliable, sea travel could be particularly hazardous and voyages by explorers into the vast, unknown parts of the world fraught with countless dangers.

Sailors in those times could readily feel a very close affinity with their ship and it would be common practice for them to ascribe a distinctive personality to each vessel, thinking of it not as an inanimate object but rather as a living character. Names were selected to either protect the ship from harm and to further her business, or to avoid offending the various spirits that could bring harm or danger to the vessel.[2] Seamen did not usually consign a gender neutral name to a sea-going sailing vessel, but would either call it a 'she' (perhaps in deference to Athene, the ancient Greek goddess of the sea) or, if a fierce fighting vessel, call it a 'man-of-war'. For some ancient reason, the sea was also always spoken of as woman, possibly because the female will go her own way, no matter what the consequence, and so does the sea.

As one old captain once said about his ship, 'She can do anything but talk.' He was wrong about that because those sailing ships could even do that. When ships become unseaworthy and about to break-up as a result of the stresses and strains on the hull by sea conditions or by misadventure, such ships '… have been known to give forth moaning sounds like wailing'. It is not always possible to recognise how this sound originates or from which location on the vessel, but like any human being who is ailing, a sinking ship also makes her lamentations.[3] This incredible companionship formed between the ship and the mariners who spent much of their lives on board could translate into the subsequent folklore, legends and myths, whereby such vessels returned to active service as spectral manifestations or phantom ships, of which there have been many sighted worldwide.[4]

The strange and fascinating tale of the 170 ton brig *Neptune* of London, which was destroyed in a gale with large seas in the Bay of St.Ives on the coast of Cornwall, England, in April 1838, fits this description. A day prior to the disaster, another unknown ship was said to have appeared in some difficulty in the same bay at night. In the description of the day, she had the appearance of a foreign trader, a schooner-rigged vessel with a light over her bows and her hull clearly visible. Several small rescue boats were despatched to assist and in due course, one boat reached the vessel. The crew were close enough to board, so a bow-oarsman attempted a grasp at her bulwarks (an extension of a ship's side above the weather deck).

His hand found nothing solid and he fell, with one of his mates just preventing him from falling overboard. The phantom ship and its lights then vanished into thin air. It was believed that this unknown ship was a warning of the forthcoming disaster.[5] Many nautical tales about the appearance of phantom ships and spectral vessels mention that they were often followed by a storm or squall, and the *Neptune* was wrecked in such a gale the night after the sighting of the ghost ship.

The *Neptune* was found the morning after the gale driven onto rocks commonly known as Godreavy Lodge in the parish of Gwithian, located along the Bay of St. Ives, and all aboard had perished. This was some two and one half kilometres from the original sighting of the phantom ship. The *Neptune* was '… a complete wreck—her masts carried away and her half in pieces'.[6] Local tradition says that there have been sightings of the ghost ship of *Neptune* far out in the same bay, whilst on stormy nights, a ghostly woman in white silks holding a lamp has been seen on the beach at St.Ives. The woman appears to be terrified and was possibly a relative of the crew that perished. Another interpretation of the lady and the lantern is that she and her child initially survived, but that her child was then swept away and drowned. Consequently, when her spectre appears, she is purportedly still searching for the child's body.[7] The Cornish coast has numerous coves and dangerous offshore rock outcrops where various ships have succumbed and sailors have been lost trying to safely reach the shore, particularly throughout the 19th century. It also had a notorious reputation for some considerable time as the Wrecker's Coast and many ships paid the price as a result.

This historical custom of enticing unwary vessels onto the rocks to scavenge their cargoes and anything else of value was perpetrated by unconscionable characters known as 'wreckers'. They would hobble a horse at night with a short strap or rope tied between two legs, hang a lantern from its neck or tail, and leave it to graze along the cliff tops until a ship appeared. Then it would be led hobbling along the high coastal cliffs, usually late at night, as a decoy to create a canny illusion for any vessel out to sea.

At such a distance and in the dark, the lantern bobbing up and down appeared to be the light in the rigging of another vessel safely riding at anchor, prompting the unfortunate passing ship to approach these waters for safe haven.[8] Once the ship was on the rocks, the wreckers would pounce and start the scavenging, although this was still a very dangerous activity given the treacherous conditions. It has been said that from time to time in coves along this coast and usually on a stormy night, a phantom wrecker might be seen for a fleeting moment thrashing around in the waves and clinging to flotsam, having paid the ultimate price for his sinister occupation.[9]

These nautical manifestations and their often dramatic meteorological effects may be more to do with one's imagination than reality, but many stories and superstitions persist containing such elements. On the subject of such apparitions, the Cornish coast has some vivid accounts involving uncanny storms or squalls out of which appears a phantom ship with full sails set and yet not a breath of wind evident. As the spectral vessel passes by borne on the clouds, considerable thunder and lightning accompanies the visitation, and presumably the ultimate demise of the wrecker. [10]

Given the sheer volume of shipwrecks along this coast during the 19th century, there would be a natural propensity for accounts of phantom ships, such as this one: '... Full spread and crowded every sail, The Demon Frigate braves the gale; And well the doom'd spectators know The harbinger of wreck and woe.'[11] The spectral vessels always share a common element: they typically foretell a tragedy or catastrophic event and are usually associated with dramatic stormy or ominous foggy weather. These phantom vessels range from ships which soar over land or sea, are luminescent and pass in total silence, to those having unusual characteristics or peculiar appearances, such as skeleton crews, no sails under full speed or perhaps the ability to vanish without trace. These vessels represent ships lost at sea or destroyed in other tragic circumstances.[12]

Many other seaward locations throughout the United Kingdom, Europe and Scandinavia have similar tales to Cornwall, and I shall share a select few, commencing with an unusual beach in Wales. Rhossili Beach is located at the western extremity of the Gower Peninsula, not too far from Swansea in West Glamorgan, and is the site of over 30 documented shipwrecks. The beach sits at the base of an exposed, wind-swept headland, and is seemingly forever lashed by severe storms rolling in from the Atlantic Ocean. Understandably, given its relative coastal isolation at the tip of the peninsula and the abundance of shipwrecks throughout the area, tales of ghostly apparitions and legendary smugglers abound.

One legendary tale purportedly concerns a 17th century Spanish treasure ship aptly named *The Dollar Ship* that became engulfed in a storm and came to grief here, or was it lured ashore by wreckers? As much of the precious cargo (described as gold in this version of events, but only as silver doubloon coins in all earlier accounts on this beach) as they could carry was scavenged by the crew before they hurriedly deserted the stricken vessel without raising any suspicions of the unwitting locals. The rights to salvage the vessel were also quickly sold to one such local for cash before the crew departed, and it would seem more than enough treasure was left behind.

Unfortunately, before any more of the ship could be retrieved and broken up for salvage, she sank deep into the sands and presumably disappeared without trace. Eventually, it became common knowledge that the submerged wreck had been a treasure ship, culminating in the local Lord of the Manor claiming it for himself. However, nothing more was to happen for an extended period of years as the missing ship lay engulfed in the sands, until one of the family supposedly conducted a secretive investigation to locate the wreck and retrieve more of the treasure. It was subsequently learnt that this person 'died miserably', after absconding overseas, despite the windfall. Enter the black phantom coach pulled by four ghostly grey horses at full gallop at night attempting to drive off any of the villagers from recovering the treasure. This spectral apparition was supposedly the deceased returning to claim the remaining treasure, and was last seen in the early 19th century when the shipwreck re-emerged out of the sands of Rhossili beach on a very low tide.[13]

Extensive and thorough investigation of the legend over many years now has cast doubt on whether the shipwreck found near the treasure was *The Dollar Ship*, and what was found may possibly have been the remains of two shipwrecks which occurred considerable years apart in same the location.[14] The legend of the treasure remains extremely complex with many intriguing twists and conflicting accounts that have modified the story over time. As well, various tales of more retrieved treasure have continued to surface over the years as the wreck reappeared from its resting place only to be engulfed by the sands of this beach once more. However, what remained of the booty is definitely still relevant to this great tale about a spectral coach. On the subject of the Vale [county borough] of Glamorgan, a town named Penarth certainly has an intriguing history.

This tale takes place in a town named Penarth, slightly south-west of Cardiff, in the Vale [county borough] of Glamorgan. What is so unusual about this town, other than being located between the mouth of the famous River Severn (the longest river in Britain) and the Bristol Channel? Its location on the Glamorgan coast is facing westerly into the Atlantic and it is exposed to the ferocious gales that rush in from the ocean and, as you would expect, the area is littered with shipwrecks. Up until almost 100 hundred years ago, deliberate shipwrecking was believed to be very common along this coast. Penarth harbour was formed by the conjunction of the estuaries of three considerable rivers (Ely, Rhymney and Taff) where they enter the Severn Sea, and represented a relatively safe haven for shipping compared to the prevailing marshy and waterlogged areas nearby. The shingle foreshores of the harbour provided the only suitable location for landing, unloading and loading cargo up until the early 19th century, with secure anchorage and sheltered protection from the ocean's treacherous westerly winds.[15]

From at least the 16th century, Penarth was therefore an attractive location for pirates seeking a sheltered retreat from the unforgiving Atlantic Ocean and for a number of infamous pirates who plied their trade along the River Ely before seeking riches elsewhere in the Caribbean or off the coast of Africa. Between the 17th and 18th centuries (the *Golden Age* of smuggling) smugglers using the Bristol Channel made use of the harbour, which was close enough to Cardiff to allow them to efficiently transport their contraband.[16] This section of the coast certainly had a prevalence of pirates, smugglers and other brigands intent on ill-gotten gains.

Kymin House was built in Penarth between 1790 and 1810, and its name appears to be derived from the old Celtic term 'Ki' meaning stream, and the old Norse word 'minni' for stream mouth. The common land surrounding this house was known locally as Kymin due to the confluence of three streams.[17] So what is so important about the house? It appears to have been the place where an 18th century pirate named Captain Ramón Hill was thought by some to have appeared as a manifestation and to have enjoyed scaring people with unworldly experiences. Little appears to be known about this pirate and, given the proliferation of these brigands along the coast of Wales, it would not be unexpected. Perhaps like the pirates and smugglers themselves, it was probably best to keep his identity a secret.

From the Americas comes a tale from the 19th century of a ghostly crew intent on assisting a vessel in distress. Georges Bank (Shoals) is a massive elevated area of seafloor which effectively separates the Gulf of Maine from the North Atlantic Ocean. This impressive but treacherous submerged bank is part of the continental shelf and is located about 100 kilometres offshore between Cape Cod in Massachusetts and southern Nova Scotia in Canada. The shoals are famous for their access to the extensive supplies of Atlantic cod and halibut which have been fished for over 400 hundred years. However, ships have come to grief on such shoals. The *Northern Light* was just such a schooner which found itself in quite some difficulty off Georges Bank, despite being manned by a large crew.[18] It had completed fishing on the Bank and had departed for the shore only to encounter extremely nasty weather, including gales, ice and even snow. The closer the vessel got to safe anchorage, the worse became the weather, making it difficult to maintain course.

Almost on dark and before her crew knew it, the vessel was in considerable trouble in the shallow shoals, buffeted by enormous waves and the raging gale. Even the vessel's small rowing boats (known as dories) which could have been used by the crew to abandon ship were unable to be released safely in such arduous conditions. With the vessel about to founder with little hope of avoiding the obvious calamity, there appeared no obvious way to save the ship. Suddenly, as the tale goes, an entire crew of twenty-four dripping sailors came swarming aboard over the ship's rails. The Master and his crew were then herded to the forecastle by the silent ghost crew and would remain below deck for the entire night. Remarkably, this ghost crew, with their lustreless eyes and livid faces, then assumed control. The only sounds evident thereafter were the wailing wind in the rigging, the noise of the raging sea and of course the groaning and creaking of the ship.[19]

The ghost crew sailed the vessel without uttering any commands or making any other sounds. When the original crew emerged from below deck the next morning, they discovered the strange ghost sailors were gone and the schooner was safely progressing under full sail in calm conditions towards the twin lighthouses on Thatcher's Island just off the Massachusetts coast, with no one else on deck.[20] It is unclear why such spectres elected to assist other sailors in distress, other than the vessel may be have passing the fatal site where the ghostly sailors themselves originally perished. Perhaps part of the following sea shanty (chantey) or shipboard work song entitled *The Ghostly Fishermen* may provide an insight:

> ... But one dark night I speak of, we were off lee shores a way,
> I never will forget it in all my mortal days,
> When in my dim dark watch, I felt a chilling dread,
> That bore me down as if I heard one calling from the dead.

> When on deck that September came sailors one by one,
> A dozen dripping sailors, just wait till I am done.
> On the decks they 'sembled, but not a voice was heard
> They moved about together but neither spoke a word.
>
> Their faces pale and sea-wet, shone ghostly through the night,
> Each took his place freely as if he had a right,
> And eastward steered the vessel until land was just in sight,
> Or rather I should say, saw the lighthouse towers alight.
>
> And then those ghostly sailors, moved through the rail again
> And vanished through the mist, where sun can shine on them.
> I know not any reason in truth why these should come,
> To navigate our vessel till land was just in sight.
>
> They are the simple sailors, I hope God rest their souls,
> When their ship went under that time on Georges Shoal ...[21]

Sailors can be a superstitious group, and so it would seem most likely in bygone days that even the suspicion that a witch was aboard would contribute to a belief of seriously bad luck and misfortune ahead for the ship. I shall write about witchcraft at more length later in this book, but would add that in nautical jargon, the presence of a witch only conjured extreme dislike from mariners. Witches represented malevolent sorcerers and shape-shifters, often mistaken for cats or certain sea birds, and were quite capable, through their perceived supernatural powers, of sending a ship to a watery grave.[22] It was believed that some witches were capable of transforming themselves into any shape whatsoever, though usually a dog, cat, hare lion, bear, wolf, monkey, horse, bull or calf.[23]

Hysteria about witchcraft was prevalent in colonial America in the Middle Ages, particularly around the states of Massachusetts and neighbouring Maine. It was at this time sea hags, as they came to be known, plagued certain seafaring men. It did not matter that they simply were old and wrinkled, often malnourished women who behaved strangely or were just downright different, they were still believed to be witches. According to superstition, the ugliness of a witch was a sign of supernatural strength, and it followed that somebody fitting the popular description of witch—old and ugly with warts and a beard—would be shunned by society.[24] Tales about such women would usually involve a visitation or a foretelling of misfortune on the mariner, who would attack the spectre, only to learn later that the sea hag who had cast the spell had perished or at least been seriously wounded at around the same time at another location entirely. Parts of the poem *The Hag* published in 1648 by 17th century English poet Robert Herrick seem to capture this superstition very well:

> The Hag is astride,
> This night for to ride;
> The Devill & shee together:
> Through thick, and through thin,
> Now out, and then in,
> Though ne'er so foule be the weather …
>
> …While mischiefs, by these,
> On Land and on Seas,
> At noone of Night are a-working.
>
> The storme will arise,
> And trouble the skies;
> This night, and more for the wonder,
> The ghost from the Tomb
> Affrighted shall come,
> Cal'd out by the clap of the Thunder.[25]

For probably the most subtle quote concerning superstitions about witchcraft, it would be difficult to improve on the following nautical gem from the remote Shetland Islands north of mainland Scotland: 'The sea is the greatest witch in all the world.'[26] This phrase was reported in 1882 and was purportedly spoken by an old woman who was regarded as a good authority in local occult lore.

THE SEA MARAUDERS

This chapter is devoted to the scoundrels, buccaneers and miscreants who roamed the oceans at will with the sole purpose of plundering and looting anything of value, particularly through the 1500s, 1600s and into the early 1700s. These 'Brethren of the Coast' were akin to groups of maritime renegades who were relentlessly hunted by various navies of the world intent on punishing them for their ruthless attacks on merchant ships, or in some cases, the navies of other countries. Privateers were commissioned by seafaring nations at war to attack and plunder enemy shipping, including defenceless foreign merchant vessels, thus assisting the war effort. These well-armed vessels were privately owned and could actually be manned by pirates who recognised an ideal opportunity to become very wealthy by sailing and looting under licence to a suitable government.[1]

Unlike traditional pirates who preyed on vessels of all flags, or buccaneers who did likewise but excluded any vessel of their own nation, privateers only attacked vessels of a country at war with their own. They did this by purchasing a licence known as a 'letter of marque and reprisal' from the government, commissioning the privateer to seek, capture or destroy enemy shipping.[2] Privateers were also known as buccaneers in the earliest times of this plundering, predominantly due to their widespread trade in illicit valuable commodities. They were not quite pirates and more like proficient smugglers of essential consumable goods, such as rum for example, and of course they bootlegged the commodity. They apparently first appeared as early as the 13th century in England, and began flourishing around the close of the 16th century when the French and the Dutch engaged in these activities. Intriguingly, one of the English privateers was a woman known as *The Terrible*, with a commander fearsomely called *Captain Death* and a first officer aptly named *Mr. Ghost*.[3]

The romantic and swashbuckling way these men and women were commonly portrayed in literature was very far from the truth. Their lives could be poor, battling prevalent diseases, malnutrition and scurvy arising from an atrocious diet, and dangerous internal conflicts within the crew, if they first survived each sea skirmish without serious injury. Boredom played a major role in their daily lives—with extended periods between fierce encounters with other vessels—as did the risk of treachery from other quarrelsome crew members.[4] Being thrown overboard in the night with a cutlass in the back, or perhaps being marooned on a reef on a rising tide were some likely outcomes. Of course, there were worse things. If a sea marauder was captured and sent to trial, this public humiliation was nothing compared to the hangman's noose which beckoned.

I think the first two verses of *A Ballad of John Silver*, about a villainous but fictional pirate, which was penned by British poet John Masefield at the turn of last century, captures the treasure succinctly:

> We were schooner-rigged and rakish, with a long and lissome hull,
> And we flew the pretty colours of the cross-bones and the skull;
> We'd a big black Jolly Roger flapping grimly at the fore,
> And we sailed the Spanish Water in the happy days of yore.
>
> We'd a long brass gun amidships, like a well-conducted ship,
> We had each a brace of pistols and a cutlass at the hip;
> It's a point which tells against us, and a fact to be deplored,
> But we chased the goodly merchant-men and laid their ships aboard.[5]

The eventual fate of so many of these marauders was a gruesome meeting with the hangman. At the Dolphin Inn in Penzance on the West Cornish coast of England, an apparition of an old sea captain has been seen from time to time dressed in a tricorn hat and coat with laced ruffles as worn in the 1600s. It is believed that he had been a smuggler returning to the inn to claim his booty but came unstuck and was sentenced to the noose by an infamous hanging judge of the day. There must be something in the tale, as casks of illicit spirit which may have been part of his undiscovered treasure were subsequently found behind a false wall in the cellar.[6] Another apparition who was also wearing a 17th century tricorn hat was possibly a coachman reportedly sighted most often lurking in the bar area of the Kirkstone Pass Inn located in Britain's Lake District, Cumbria.

The inn was constructed in the late 15th century, operating as a stopover for horse-drawn coaches, and could be very difficult and treacherous to reach in winter due to its location at the very top of the mountainous Kirkstone Pass. Remarkably, stories about apparitions of other travellers who have perished during these journeys have also abounded and as a result, the inn seems to have a rather unique history of hauntings. However, it is the man in the black tricorn hat who is of special interest, as his manifestation has been known to touch people and even leave a red mark on their skin. The fascinating element to this ghost is that it appeared in the background of a photograph taken in the doorway to the inn in April 1993 by a visiting family.[7] Enough of phantom coach travellers and back to pirates instead.

How many pirates from the 16th-18th centuries actually made a fortune from their escapades and died without meeting some undignified end? Whether from poor judgement, the misfortunes of being a renegade, or perhaps life dealing them the death card once too often, very few succeeded. Even the best known and most feared scoundrels such as Blackbeard and Captain William Kidd floundered throughout their violent careers in making and retaining their fortunes. Buccaneer Henry Morgan duly served his penal sentence when eventually captured and, ironically, turned to suppressing his fellow comrades from their pillaging forays.[8]

Many more pirate captains met particularly grisly deaths at the hands of their own disgruntled crews, and, in some cases, were cut adrift due to their sheer disloyalty to those closest to them. For a band of bloodthirsty cutthroats and brigands to disown their captain because of his/her monstrous cruelty, frightful wickedness and cunning deceitful ways was making quite a statement about evil. Honour among thieves goes a long way, as you would expect. When such prominent pirates finally met their undignified end by the sword or the noose, it would not be surprising that their restless spirits may return in the future on a phantom ship to ceaselessly wander the seas seeking new plunder. Instead of a real crew, however, I would expect no less than such a vessel be manned by skeletons to handle the cobweb sails and gossamer ropes. Such would be the curse for committing murder, mayhem and piracy.

My favourite era for piracy on the high seas was when Spain's naval fleets initially ruled the New World. The Spanish Main, as it came to be known, eventually included the entire Caribbean and the seas of the northern South America region. The almost limitless wealth extracted from these areas during the Spanish conquests was dutifully transported by sea back to Spain and, of course, did not go unnoticed by other nations and pirates. Convoys of Spanish treasure galleons plying this route from the colonies were set upon by various raiders seeking unimaginable quantities of bullion, coins, jewellery and rare artefacts, and such ferocious raids usually resulted in considerable loss of ships and lives.

To describe these treasures as astounding would be truly understating their real worth. Sacks of gold dust, enormous crates of gold and silver bullion ingots, boxes of pearls, assorted gemstones and various jewellery acquired from throughout the Americas certainly would be worth a king's ransom.[9] Recent discoveries of sunken Spanish galleons, such as the 18th century *San José* off Colombia, have uncovered treasure valued in billions of dollars. So, if just one of these Spanish galleons went astray off the Caribbean coast and finished up in the remote region of Newfoundland, a large island in the extreme easterly province of Canada, would it ever be missed? Highly unlikely given the sheer volume of such vessels plundered and sunk by raiders on the Spanish Main. Newfoundland's waters are an extensive graveyard for countless wrecked ships, and it has a distinctive history of pirate activity.

The coasts of this province were frequented at the time by various pirates who preferred such sparsely inhabited regions for their bases, and none more than the most successful privateer-turned pirate Peter Easton. After fleeing his plundering past in England with his ten best ships and crews, he opted to establish his base in Newfoundland and focus on amassing a fortune from captured ships and enforced tributes from fishing vessels.

Initially Easton fortified Harbour Grace on Conception Bay to the north of Chapel Cove. Chapel Cove is near Harbour main, a settlement dating from 1696 and not far from the present local capital of St. John's. Easton later established another base on Kelly's Island on the far shore of this bay and not far from the cove. Before eventually leaving the province in 1614, Easton claimed one of the richest prizes ever captured by a pirate when he looted and then destroyed the Spanish treasure galleon *San Sebastian*[10] (this occurred before there was any recognised effective colonisation of Newfoundland). The pirates purportedly buried the treasure in Chapel Cove. It has been said that once the vessel had been thoroughly looted then burned, the *San Sebastian* was set adrift to ground further up the harbour, where her bones may today still lie buried in the bottom.[11] These areas abound with tales of buried treasure, and given the prolific pirate activity through the 1600s, finding some would not be unexpected.

Although a legend is no more than an ancient myth with some substance, the following tale seems to have merit. In 1895, well over 200 years after the first settlement, some men attempted to find a chest of gold thought to be buried around Chapel Cove. They were thought to have been stopped prematurely when a ghostly galleon appeared in the harbour, with all sails set. Was it possibly the *San Sebastian* returning from its watery grave further up the harbour? The ship crossed the cove, sailing directly towards the men, who fled in terror.

The second attempt to uncover the treasure, in 1909, was when a brave soul managed to find the chest and attempted to pry it open. This attempt faltered because the man was first greeted by an unusual loud noise and then by a spectre which rose up out of the pit, seizing a crow bar and breaking it in half. A later attempt also proved futile, when the man was apparently tormented by ghostly moans and strange figures.[12]

It was customary for some pirates to kill one of their comrades and leave the body in the pit to guard the treasure, and this was probably the case on nearby Kelly's Island.

Figure 7: Pirate Guardian of Buried Treasure

With legends, there are usually different versions. Legends of Captain Kelly describe him either as a lieutenant of the pirate Peter Easton, or as a leader of a group of slaves who successfully commandeered their slave ship off Newfoundland. Eventually, Captain Kelly buried a huge fortune in gold coins on the island named after him, killed one of his crew and left the corpse on top of the gold.[13] It is said that the ghost of that corpse remains to guard the treasure, so I guess the old pirate saying that 'dead men tell no tales' does not apply in this case. I am particularly fascinated with this quotation, which has been attributed to the medieval Persian poet Sa'di around 1250: 'So I finished the rogue, notwithstanding his wails, With stones, for dead men, as you know, tell no tales'. A similar saying attributed to the Greek biographer Plutarch, is 'Dead men don't bite'.

Not far from Newfoundland is Cap d'Espoir (Cape Spear) in Gaspé Bay in the Gulf of St Lawrence. It is the location of another legendary ghost galleon. In 1711, English Queen Anne despatched a powerful fleet comprising seven or eight thousand troops to vanquish French power in Canada forever. The grand plan was destroyed by a violent storm, which not only dispersed her Armada in the Gulf, but cost eight vessels and all those aboard them. Whether it be superstition or supernatural visions or both, sightings by fishermen of the manifestation of a phantom warship off the Cap d'Espoir have persisted.

When the ocean was seemingly smooth like a mirror, mountainous waves would suddenly appear, with a phantom ship bearing on their foaming crest. Lights were seen on the vessel and it was crowded with soldiers wearing uniforms of a bygone age. On the bow stood a superior officer with one foot resting on the spar extending forward from the ship's prow (part of the bow above the waterline), as if he was prepared to jump ashore. The officer appeared to be pointing shoreward with one hand whilst supporting a female clad in white flowing robes on the other arm. Travelling at almost lightning speed, the doomed vessel rushed to its destruction, the lights went out, a mighty crash was heard, and the wild cry of despair of a woman's voice was clearly distinguishable before the phantom ship disappeared beneath the roaring surge. The phantom vessel is said to be the ghost of the flagship of the fleet, with all hands lost.[14]

Ghostly galleons have been sighted throughout the world, and given Newfoundland's maritime history of shipwrecks, it would not be surprising to find them there. Great Yarmouth, a coastal town east of Norwich in Norfolk, England, is yet another place with a rich history of manifestations. This time, the legend involves an entire fleet of galleons sailing on Breydon Water towards Burgh Castle; a third century Roman 'Saxon Shore' fort, which is now a village and civil parish. Breydon is where confluent rivers combine to form a large sheltered inland lake on the western side of Yarmouth, effectively acting as a natural backwater to the Yarmouth Harbour.

This lake or estuary is also known as the *Broad Water* of the Saxons.

Roman galleons would have sailed up to their encampment at Burgh Castle across Breydon Water in ancient times.[15] On the retirement of the Romans, the Saxons, who had established a colony, were promoted to authority and entrusted with confidence in 426 AD.[16] Sightings of the ghostly fleet purportedly identified scores of ships overcrowded with phantom sailors singing and shouting loudly as the vessels progressed. Each ship's sails bore emblems of the sun and were fitted with brightly lit lanterns, resulting in the entire fleet being bathed in an overwhelming glow of luminescence, which when combined with the raucous noise of the rowdy sailors, presented quite a sight to behold at night.

One opinion is that the mysterious ghostly galleons possibly represent ancient Saxon warriors who apparently migrated into the region around the middle of the 5th century.[17] Given the significant turmoil and loss of life in those bygone days, it was little wonder ghostly galleons might eventually appear. Consider the remarkable tale from 495AD of a battle between a Saxon chief, with as many troops as five ships could convey, and the local Britons, which took place where Yarmouth now stands. Despite being vigorously attacked, the Saxons prevailed after a short conflict and the shore was subsequently named to commemorate this victory.[18] Whatever the reason for their appearance on Breydon Water, the ghostly galleons certainly invoke a strong sense of heritage of the Anglo-Saxon settlement of Britain during those historical early years.

Even the Americas have their fair share of ghostly pirate vessels, although surprisingly, sometimes there is no particular reason why they should appear. Take for example the vessel the *Fame* of the French-American pirate and privateer Jean Lafitte who plied his trade in the Gulf of Mexico in the early 19th century. The distinctively black-hulled vessel supposedly carrying a fortune in jewels and bullion sank after his death in the 1820s, taking most of the drunken crew with it. The vessel continued to be frequently sighted in Galveston Bay and in adjoining Gulf waters towards the end of the 19th century and even reportedly off Central America. It was observed by two different ships in 1892, which provided some interesting commentary concerning the vessel's crew: they 'looked like living dead, and 'paid not the slightest attention', despite the *Fame* almost colliding with their respective ships. Perhaps it was the additional comments provided about the *Fame* being luminescent and casting no shadow which are most of interest.[19]

What of the incredible treasures that pirates such as Lafitte, Easton or Kelly purportedly hid away for safe keeping and probably never retrieved? Usually their booty was buried in an obscure secret location known to a select few crew who participated in the exercise but may or may not have survived afterwards. Occasionally a chart or treasure map was prepared to delineate the 'secret location', which, as you would expect, would go missing for centuries, and would be enigmatic, with vague descriptions, cryptic clues, and often misleading information. These maps were never quite the same as those depicted in the popular fictional literature about pirates and buccaneers. Buried treasure could be difficult to locate and even harder to retrieve, especially if it was protected by a spectral guard or perhaps a maritime curse. Many stories from around the world recount the endless searches for pirates' treasure which eventually proved fruitless and frustratingly elusive. In the rare instances where the booty was located, almost akin to the dead pirate's curse, a final dilemma would face those attempting its recovery.[20]

It was never going to be easy. This is where myth, legend and fact collide head-on and it becomes confusing. In the simplest case, where the treasure location was marked by a distinctive object, such as buried beneath a unique coconut palm tree or identified just by a very long iron rod protruding from the ground, it was still possible to find the treasure. Of course this was unless the marker tree eventually fell over in a typhoon or perhaps someone pulled up the iron rod in passing, not realising that it marked the spot. Let us assume for a moment that someone was told where to find the treasure through a dream or possibly by a vision, and attempted to claim the riches. The first hurdle was the ghostly guardians; unfortunates of the original crew who drew the short straw and paid the ultimate price to remain behind permanently.

As one local discovered on a Caribbean island off the coast of Venezuela, this guardian was a persistent apparition, always appearing around the same nearby tree. Investigation eventually uncovered the man's skeleton left buried face first in the ground, but strangely no treasure was found beneath him. The deceased's remains were returned to the grave but this time lying face up, and the apparition no longer returned.[21] Some seeking treasure have not been as fortunate, particularly when diving on sunken shipwrecks. Superstitions aside, it is common to hear tales of unknown forces which prevent any removal of treasure chests.

In 1839 one ship said to be carrying treasure foundered in foul weather before running ashore on a small island off the west Irish coast. Divers sent to retrieve the sunken booty refused to remove it from the vessel, and nor would they return to the wreck. There had been no loss of life during the sinking, so what scared those divers so much that they would not retrieve the treasure? Their only response was that they could not face whatever they found down there.[22] Captain Kidd's legendary 17th century buried treasure location, or one such probable site discovered in 1795 on a small island on the Atlantic coast of Nova Scotia, contains the same fearsome factor for treasure seekers. Phantom guardians are said to appear at the site, such as a spectral stallion with fiery eyes or an apparition of a massive hound roaming through the night.[23] There have been fatalities from trying to discover the hidden booty over the years, which may have more to do with the many attempts at excavating a difficult and intricate burial site, than with the supposed spectral guardians.

The well-travelled Scandinavian sea raiders and ruthless early plunderers of the coastal communities around the North Atlantic Ocean in the British Isles from the late 8th century onwards deserve a brief mention, although given the extreme age of these conquests, this particular tale is probably more folklore than fact. It involves spectral apparitions of Viking longboats which have purportedly been sighted on clear evenings sailing in an inlet on the west coast of Scotland. As with most superstitions about manifestations of supernatural ships, it was always best to avoid them and any potential destruction, mainly because such appearances probably represent something ominous.

It was generally perceived that these Norsemen could be particularly ferocious warriors and as violent as necessary to achieve their conquests. As a consequence, it would not be until the 18th century that some brave local souls decided to confront the visiting apparitions for a closer look in their own small boat. Living or dead, Vikings were always going to be a handful. I am supposing the results of their encounter with the phantom longboats is also now also part of that folklore, because it did not end well for the inquisitive locals. Apparently, the Norse longboats promptly sank and in doing so, pulled the locals' boat underwater with no survivors.[24]

MYSTERIOUS LIGHTHOUSES

The essential navigational aid that all seafaring folk have consistently relied upon since mankind sought to travel the oceans of the world has been a land-based tower or structure housing a suitable beacon to transmit a powerful warning light continuously or intermittently to ships offshore. It has remained the prime source for signalling the navigators of passing ships of the proximity of the shoreline at night, and in particular, hazardous maritime features such as reefs, shoals or submerged rock ledges. As a result, such structures are traditionally constructed at the extremities of the shoreline, sometimes perched on small isolated islands, on rocky headlands or extended sandy spits, or on other suitably elevated promontories such as sea cliffs.

The earliest maritime beacons date back some 3000 years ago to ancient Egypt and were little more than primitive wood-burning fires housed in baskets. The first prominent elevated tower or lighthouse and, as it happens, the largest ever built, is considered to be the Pharos [lighthouse and watchtower] of Alexandria. This 120 metre high stone tower was constructed around 280 BC and was claimed as one of the tallest man-made structures in the world. It lasted about 1600 years until eventually ruined by earthquakes, and was quite an engineering feat by any standard.[1]

The Tower of Hercules built by the Romans on the northwest Atlantic coast of Spain around 20 BC is probably the oldest lighthouse in use today, and stands at a modest height of 55 metres. It served the Roman Empire until the 5th century AD, eventually being reinstated by Spain from the 18th century.[1] The first lighthouse built in England also dates back to Roman days, around 40 BC, but the first purpose-built lighthouse was constructed around 1428 at Spurn Point/Head in Yorkshire.[2] In Australia where European settlement occurred considerably later, the oldest lighthouse still operating is found in Storm Bay, Tasmania and was erected in 1832.[3] Lighthouses have existed throughout the world for many centuries, and due to a number of factors, hauntings of certain lighthouses have persisted as well.

Most lighthouses are erected at inhospitable and usually remote locations, where living conditions can be rugged and lonely. These sites are exposed to the ferocity of the weather and their access subject to tidal or river movements and, in many cases, prevailing sea conditions. To get the construction materials safely to site might involve offloading from ships with limited docking facilities and treacherous tides. Handling and storage of these materials might also involve arduous conditions. Once construction was underway, builders may have to reside on site and rely upon regular deliveries of fresh provisions to survive. Neglect, harsh living conditions and insufficient or unsuitable food supplies—that may have arrived already contaminated—could all contribute to a poor quality of life.

The lighthouse keeper's life could also be quite traumatic, both in maintaining the lights and facing numerous hazards in tending them, particularly given the location of such structures: usually in areas where shipwrecks have occurred and may continue even with the lighthouse functional. It might have been common for lighthouse keepers to actively participate in hazardous sea rescues of shipwrecked survivors along their coast, even into the early 20th century. The daily pressures of perhaps long hours maintaining the warning beacon with inadequate or faulty equipment, the deprivation of fresh meat and vegetables in diets, and the occasional serious accident or unfortunate illness, could certainly take their toll on the human spirit.

Communications for assistance from outside may also have been restricted due to inclement weather and rough seas. This effectively meant a solitary life with a considerable need for self-reliance by resident lighthouse keepers and their families, until such lighthouses eventually became abandoned or automated. But as an old nautical saying states: 'A light without a keeper is but half a light.' The lighthouse keeper fulfilled a vitally important role beyond simply maintaining the lighthouse, and that was to keep watch and report on vessels in distress, and in many cases, go to their assistance.

Many lighthouses were built from the 19th century onwards, perhaps due to a significant increase in shipping throughout the world. As a consequence, many hauntings and other mysterious events relate to this particular era.

The Matinicus Rock lighthouse was fairly remote, located about 30 kilometres off the coast of Maine, in eastern USA. It was perched on a windswept and treeless rock situated in the Gulf of Maine and has operated in various configurations since 1827. As with most lighthouses, it had a keeper's house, which included a storehouse accessed from the living quarters through an adjoining door. At some time in the past, it is believed a keeper committed suicide and that his ghost frequented the storehouse. Whenever anyone opened the door to the storage area, inexplicable episodes occurred, including doors banging or remaining open, items falling off tables for no reason, and most disconcertingly, light bulbs regularly extinguishing. Consequently, any personnel manning the lighthouse knew instinctively to always leave this door shut to avoid these supernatural events. This was until an inspection of the lighthouse was conducted by an officer from offsite who definitely did not believe in such extraordinary phenomena, and categorically ordered the door remain open at all times. Enter from stage left a torrent of unexplained events, including the site's generator stopping and the beacon light being extinguished, as well as all the traditional oddities. Before the officer left site, he commanded that the door remain shut and peace was rapidly restored.[4]

Remarkably, another lighthouse built around almost the same time, in 1825, and located about 30 kilometres away directly on the Maine coast at Owl's Head at the eastern extremity of a peninsula into west Penobscot Bay, also had a famous history of supernatural occurrences. This lighthouse was unusual in various ways which require some elaboration. In the early 1820s, the passage of shipping was increasing through the area, resulting in many shipwrecks caused by storms and fog. By 1823, calls were made for a light station to be constructed at Owl's Head, which was the highest elevation overlooking the bay.

The naming of Owl's Head appears by some to be based upon one's individual perspective about prominent rock features evident in the cliff face: there are two hollow cavities representing the eyes, with an intervening ridge for the bridge of the owl's nose, and rocks jutting out on either side forming the two eyeballs. The selection of this location, at the picturesque entrance to Rockland harbour and close to the nearest 'great landing place' of Lermond's Cove (eventually renamed Rockland), was possibly linked to its original Native American Indian name of Bedabedec Point, which translates in English as 'Cape of the Winds'.[5]

From various historical accounts, the lighthouse at Owl's Head certainly experienced the brunt of high winds, with the wife of the first lighthouse keeper on one occasion blown from the summit by a gust of wind so severe she narrowly avoided falling into the sea, and during extreme weather, the sea spray reached the top of the cliffs.[6] The promontory on which the lighthouse was constructed was already of significant height above sea level for a warning beacon, and so the light tower was unusually short (9.1 metres). Another odd feature about the lighthouse and its dwelling house was that for considerable years after commissioning, they had a deplorable reputation for dilapidation and decay, with many historical accounts recalling that despite repairs, the structures continued to deteriorate and fall to pieces.

It would not be until the mid-1800s, when the light tower was rebuilt and a new separate keeper's dwelling constructed, that this criticism ceased. The new dwelling was a wooden one and one-half storey building, located on the lower ground well below the base of the light tower at the peak of the headland, and quite a distance away, interconnected by an extensive set of wooden walkways and stairs.[7] Although this lighthouse had evidently seen many shipwrecks, loss of life and incredible rescues associated with its past, I am only focused on its more recent history.

This is where the haunting of a lighthouse takes a twist. When reported supernatural occurrences commenced in the 1980s, many incidents occurred in the keeper's house more than in the light tower, possibly involving two different ghosts, and I shall recount reports of them both. In 1980, the spectre apparently appeared to the lighthouse keeper, who awoke to find a sea captain staring at him, and also found unexplained footprints outside in the snow in very peculiar locations. The first documented sighting was in the mid-1980s by another keeper's wife, who reported to a local newspaper she had encountered an invisible presence one night. She identified the supernatural presence by an indentation left in the family bed of the keeper's house, as if a body had been lying there. Only this indentation kept moving, as if some invisible body was still shifting around on the bed. This was supported by the keeper, who had left their bed earlier to go outside and had observed the presence of a mysterious cloud of smoke positioned in one spot over the floor before it passed straight through him and into the same bedroom.[8]

A few years later, in the same house but occupied by a different keeper's family, the three-year-old daughter described an imaginary friend '... as looking like an "old sea captain"...'. Over the next two years she added further detail: he was wearing a blue coat, a seaman's cap and sporting a beard. The girl spoke in very unfamiliar jargon indeed at times, often reminding her parents in the middle of the night that '..."Fog's rolling in! Time to put the foghorn on!"...' prior to any fog appearing. This predictive behaviour continued over a considerable time, apparently always influenced by her imaginary friend.[9] The phantasm of a sea captain was probably responsible for many unexplained occurrences around the lighthouse going back over years, such as footprints in the snow leading to the lighthouse tower yet starting from nowhere, the door to the lighthouse occasionally being left open and even the beacon's fittings freshly being polished.[10]

The last lighthouse keeper at Owl's Head, before it was automated in 1989, later reported that both his wife and their son had seen unexplained presences in the dwelling. A person dressed in white was seen outlined at a window, and the lighthouse keeper's son often insisted that upon waking, he observed a seated woman in his bedroom.[11] This has been suggested by some to be possibly another ghost who frequented the keeper's house, and supposedly has been responsible for slamming doors, rattling silverware, polishing brass fixtures and causing other disturbances.[12] Whatever these spectral occurrences represent, it is certainly clear that they prefer to keep everything ship shape and tidy, as one would expect from lighthouse keepers assigned the imposing responsibility of maintaining a reliable maritime warning system for passing ships.

As well as the critically important beacon light to warn sailors of the proximity of a shoreline or other nautical obstructions, lighthouses could also have an attendant horn, siren, bell or possibly gun as additional safety warning devices. In thick fog or dense sea mist where the beacon may only provide a diffuse beam of light, the use of a noisy horn or bell would certainly raise an alarm about the proximity of the coast.

For the 67 metre long side-wheeler steamer S.S. *Brother Jonathon* steaming north from San Francisco in the Pacific Ocean in 1865, heavily laden with cargo and 244 passengers and crew, no such coastal warning devices were readily available. Prevailing storm conditions and wild seas initially resulted in the vessel seeking refuge in the nearby harbour of Crescent City near the California/Oregon border, before resuming its journey later that day. However, worse conditions were encountered and the vessel endeavoured to return to the harbour, but came to grief on an uncharted rock of the St George Reef instead. These rocks were aptly named the Dragon Rocks, and were acknowledged by mariners for treacherous sea conditions and dangerous currents, particularly in stormy weather. The vessel sank about six kilometres off the shore and within sight of safety, but only nineteen fortunate passengers survived the wreck.[13] From this disaster and numerous other shipwrecks, the outermost rock in the reef, called Northwest Seal Rock, was subsequently selected as the most suitable site for St George to slay the dragon rocks with the erection of a lighthouse.[14]

It was an inhospitable and difficult site for such a project, with extremely rocky terrain and subject to massive seas during gale force winds as well as bitterly cold water temperatures. It would also be the start of a very long and arduous journey for all concerned with the formidable construction and eventual operation of the St George Reef lighthouse. The lighthouse would take 11 expensive years to complete, involving considerable frustrating delays, loss of lives and an unwelcoming reputation for anybody visiting or working there, due to its desolate coastal isolation and exposed hazardous location on a reef. When the beacon was finally illuminated in 1891, it would be about 44 metres above sea level but even this could seem inadequate during extreme storms.[15] To illustrate how vulnerable and isolated the numerous lighthouse keepers who operated the St George Reef Light over the years must have felt at times, one only had to think of waves exceeding 20 metres buffeting the lighthouse. The force of these storms actually cracked the windows of the beacon room.

Perhaps the most daunting feature of the St George Reef lighthouse was that the only way to leave or visit Northwest Seal Rock was by small launch that had to be lowered into the sea using a boom when departing, and likewise retrieved when returning or delivering supplies. Even the sea journey across to the shore could be perilous and in some cases fatal. It has been reported that five lighthouse keepers perished on Northwest Seal Rock and many others whilst travelling between the facility and the nearby coast. The lighthouse was finally decommissioned in 1975 and the current facility is a floating lighthouse buoy.[16] I would think that, given the perils of such a harsh and unforgiving location on the Dragon Rocks, even the legendary St George would have had immense difficulty overcoming these extreme challenges.

Possibly the most mysterious lighthouse in the world is located in the Flannan Islands of the Scottish Outer Hebrides. What a location for a lighthouse! The Flannan Isles off the west coast of Scotland are a very small archipelago largely made up of outcropping volcanic rocks interspersed with seven secluded isles, or in some cases islets, of which Eilean Mòr (Big Isle, or "island-more" when directly translated from Scottish Gaelic) is the largest and one of the two principal islands found to the north-east.

This tiny isle is the site of the Eilean Mòr Lighthouse (also known as the Flannan Isles Lighthouse) as well as the ruins of a chapel established in the 6th century and the remnants of old dwellings dating from ancient times. It had been inhabited, although not by many, probably from very early times. Extensive archaeological evidence indicates it was inhabited into the 7th century, but is then thought to have been abandoned for good. In subsequent years, it seems most likely the island occasionally became the last resting place for shipwrecked sailors who perished from starvation or exposure.

Since the medieval era, visiting shepherds would routinely bring their sheep across to the island for grazing, and would perhaps go collecting the eggs of nesting seabirds.[17] With such a rich history in the medieval era and the extreme remoteness of the area, the location for a lighthouse would appear to already have the ingredients for quite an interesting yarn.

For many years, Eilean Mòr had quite a reputation in local folklore about being a haunt for mysterious supernatural spirits who were to be avoided. It was said that visiting shepherds who grazed their sheep on the plentiful grasses of the isle would never stay overnight, preferring to return to the mainland rather than encounter these magical beings. Fishermen who called into the isle did so only through necessity, as the surrounding waters were considered to be particularly treacherous and had caused various maritime mishaps.[18] Most interesting about this folklore was the persistent superstitions about people disappearing as a result of not avoiding the supposed spirits and instead choosing to stay on the isle at night. Given the medieval history and possibly associated religious traditions of the isle, as well as the presence of ancient ritualistic stone monuments even today, it would not be unusual to consider the place had deep spiritual connections with the past. It has also been suggested that it may have been a final resting place for many in the distant pre-Christian days.

Eilean Mòr was probably selected for a lighthouse because it was the largest isle of the small Outer Hebrides group of about twenty isles, crags and exposed rocks, and the highest above sea level. It is egg-shaped and mostly precipitous, rising almost vertically out of the ocean. It is also treeless and reasonably barren except for grass cover, therefore offered no major obstructions for the proposed beacon light. The Flannan Islands have always been subjected to the full fury of frequent gales from the North Atlantic which virtually strip away the vegetation. Eilean Mòr was a bleak and desolate place. The 23 metre high lighthouse was eventually completed in December 1899, taking twice as long to complete as planned because of delays caused by atrocious weather and rough seas, even though the site had two landing places where building supplies could be safety unloaded, on the east and west sides of the island.

The lighthouse was only in operation for one year before something very strange happened to the three keepers responsible for its care at the time.[19] Fortunately for the fourth lighthouse keeper, he was on his assigned leave at the time of their disappearance. In keeping with the many grim superstitions about the isle, the story definitely demands a prudent approach to seeking what happened to these unfortunate men.

There have been various published accounts prepared about this mystery over the past one hundred years or more and, I might add, considerable controversy as to the accuracy of some of these versions. Consequently, I shall endeavour to recount the tale to the best of my ability based upon available information without delving into the minute detail of events or contrasting versions. The research paper entitled *The Vanishing Lighthousemen of Eilean Mòr*, published in 1998, is the most comprehensive account of the mystery surrounding this lighthouse. Detailed scrutiny of the calamitous events that occurred indicate they were actually more tragedy than mystery, and were unfortunately embellished by subsequent unreliable reporting.

The mystery probably commenced with the arrival of the 2,193 ton cargo ship S.S. *Archtor* on the night of the 15th December 1900. The weather conditions were reported as 'clear but stormy' and the seas were heavy, yet the crew noticed the lighthouse beacon was not operating. Unfortunately, the ship's captain was delayed in reporting this due to a subsequent encounter with submerged rocks less than 48 hours later. Further delay occurred because when the absence of the beacon light was reported, this was not communicated to the relevant statutory authority for lighthouses.

The alarm would not be raised until the fourth lighthouse keeper returned to Eilean Mòr to resume his watch. He came on the steamer S.S. *Hesperus*, which was also delivering stores to the isle, as scheduled, on 26 December 1900. Disconcertingly, when this vessel arrived at Eilean Mòr, no activity whatsoever was observed from the lighthouse. The flag normally hoisted to greet each ship's arrival was not evident on the flagstaff. More importantly, there was no-one to greet the lighthouse keeper at the ship's landing platform, despite the *Hesperus* initially blowing its steam whistle and siren before firing a rocket flare to alert the site. The keeper rowed ashore and headed for the lighthouse to investigate.

What was to greet the relief lighthouse keeper was even more disturbing. No-one was in the living quarters, the door to the lighthouse was unlocked, and the building deserted. In the entrance hall, two of the waterproof oil-skin coats worn by the keepers near the landings in high seas or poor weather conditions were missing, but the third protective coat remained, suggesting the remaining keeper had gone outside in bad weather without a suitable coat. In the kitchen, all pots and pans had been cleaned and stored away, and the kitchen tidied as one would do to complete duty as a cook. The fireplace appeared not to have been used for days, whilst the kitchen clock had wound down and stopped, as had every other clock on the premises. A search of the sleeping quarters revealed empty beds just as they would be left when arising in the early morning.

A thorough search of the entire island found no trace of the missing men. However, some interesting clues about their disappearance were found. At the low west landing, which was closer to the Atlantic Ocean then elsewhere on site and thus more exposed to the effects of severe weather, they detected evidence of recent damage from very heavy weather. The force of the sea rising around this area had dislodged, damaged or twisted some of the permanent fittings at the landing, including a displaced block of stone found on the concrete path of the landing.

A detailed examination of the lighthouse log a few days later cast more light on what possibly happened to these men. The purpose of this log was recording simple factual information including dates and times of weather and sea conditions, and not any irrelevant or unimportant commentary. In some respects, however, the diary entries further compounded the mystery. It should be noted that the written entries in the official log were only up to the 13th December, with particulars on the 14th-15th December compiled in chalk on a slate board, awaiting transference into the log book. The last verified entry on the slate was at 09:00am on the morning of the 15th December, and was a simple record of weather conditions. So what was so important in those entries that may solve the mystery?

The entries described a particularly ferocious gale that raged at least on the 12th-13th December and was finally over by early on the 15th December, as noted by the last recorded entry for the lighthouse. However, some phrases used are both peculiar and mystical in terminology, and also include unusual personal commentary on the moods of the other keepers, possibly suggesting an impending disaster or calamity for the lighthouse from the storm, particularly when all the men prayed together. Much has been written about the veracity of these entries and the controversy of their content, but suffice to say that the tragedy which eventually befell the three men was estimated to have occurred before nightfall on the 15th December, which would have been after the storm had passed and the sea had been reported in the lighthouse log as calm.

Strangely, there had been no reports of exceptionally violent weather from vessels through this area of the Outer Hebrides over the 12th-14th December, and certainly no indication of such a severe maelstrom likely to generate such dangerous conditions for the lighthouse keepers. However, the likelihood of massive rogue waves could not be discounted given the exposed setting of Eilean Mòr in the North Atlantic. Ultimately, it was decided by authorities that just such an abnormal and gigantic freak wave (or possibly successive massive powerful waves) had engulfed parts of the lower west landing of the isle, sweeping the three keepers out to sea. No bodies were ever retrieved and the mystery of their disappearance continues to generate considerable speculation and supernatural commentary.[20] The latter has apparently been fuelled by lighthouse keepers in later years claiming to hear mysterious weird voices whispering on the wind, adding to the reputation of such a desolate area.

According to some superstitious beliefs, when storms came out of the Atlantic, often a piercing, warning shriek was to be heard amongst other storm sounds. It was thought to be the howls of the spirit that are louder than the roaring of the winds. As the storm abated and the sea became calm, the howling became low wailings that crept along the coast and were said to be those of a wandering soul.[21]

The life of most lighthouse keepers could be tedious and even sometimes physically arduous, but conditions were rarely deadly enough to claim a life. The lighthouse on Eilean Mòr had only been in operation for a year and it had been constructed to resist the savage gales common to the Atlantic. The loss of three experienced keepers at the same time was certainly a very rare and bizarre tragedy for any lighthouse in the United Kingdom. The following segments from a verse in 1886 by Thomas Brown, the lighthouse keeper on Deal Island in the wilds of Australia's Bass Strait, are probably a fitting reflection indeed:

> Through the weary hours of darkness in the lighthouse lone and bleak,
> With the tempest around me raging, I my dreary watch do keep,
> Listen to the thunder rolling, watch the lightning's vivid play,
> And in my silent meditation I slowly pass the hours away…
> … But midst the dismal desolation of this wretched spot of land,
> He must do his duty with a heavy, willing hand …[22]

Elsewhere in the world, a lighthouse keeper's life could be particularly hazardous, especially when the structure was built on not much more than a sand bar located in a very treacherous stretch of water. The Sand Island Lighthouse, the first to be located just off the seacoast for the American southern state of Alabama in the Gulf of Mexico was just such a structure. The 17 metre high light tower, associated dwellings and facilities had quite a history of ongoing erosion from tropical storms and sea encroachment, necessitating subsequent rebuilds in various forms, dating from its original establishment in 1838. To appreciate just how precarious was the narrow sand islet selected for this lighthouse, one has to first grasp its exposed nautical location.

The sandy islet is found at the southernmost point of the mouth of Mobile Bay, and located seaward of this entrance, perched between nearby Dauphin Island to the west, and Mobile Point on the peninsula of the Gulf Highlands to the east. As a consequence, it is subjected to the regular tidal movements entering and leaving this bay between Dauphin Island and the peninsula, and is as well as endangered by the direct impacts of sea level surges and storm waves from any passing hurricanes (cyclones) traversing the Gulf of Mexico. Originally around 160 hectares in area, Sand Island has progressively eroded away to a fraction of this size, despite various attempts over time at stabilising the islet by material restoration and protection. Today the current 40 metre high light tower, which was decommissioned in 1933, is virtually surrounded on all sides by the sea, protected only by an artificial barrier of imported broken stone.[23]

In 1906, a very powerful hurricane that roared out of the Caribbean and crossed the coast near the entrance to Mobile Bay wreaked near-total devastation on Sand Island. Only the tiny lighthouse tower survived the onslaught, with the dwellings, other buildings and almost the entire 160 hectares being washed away, with the loss of the lighthouse assistant keeper, his spouse and the wife of the lighthouse keeper.[24] The neighbouring smaller lighthouse further westwards on the substantially larger Horn Island off the coast of Mississippi fared far worse. The result was total destruction of the 14 metre high tower and its dwellings; much of the island was submerged and the resident lighthouse keeper and his family lost their lives.[25]

If ever any island needed permanent and appropriate warning beacons, it would be Sable Island. Located in the Atlantic Ocean 175 kilometres southeast of the nearest mainland at Nova Scotia, Canada, this crescent-shaped sandbar is an incredible 42 kilometres in length yet only 1.5 kilometres across at its widest point. This represents an extremely narrow area of 3,400 hectares. So what is concerning about such an extensive narrow sandbar far out to sea and of such length that it is named an island?

Its reputation in the *Graveyard of the Atlantic* is quite a hint. Around this area of the Continental Shelf, the waters can be relatively shallow and subject to considerably rough sea conditions from the cold arctic currents of the North Atlantic meeting the warmer currents of the southern Gulf Stream originating from the Gulf of Mexico. The result not only generates vast sandy shoals and transient sandbars which are uncharted, but frequent dense fog banks, turbulent winds and unexpected, sometimes severe storms.

Sable Island is always shifting due to these extreme and treacherous currents and weather patterns. Given such formidable navigation hazards for mariners, it should not come as a surprise that literally hundreds of vessels have been wrecked around this area since at least 1583. However, lighthouses were not constructed at each end of the island until 1873. Why did it take almost 300 years for lighthouses to be constructed? The main reason appears to be sea-farers' apprehension about the transient nature of the ever-shifting sandbars and submerged shoals, coupled with unpredictable, irregular currents that could sweep vessels into these shallows.

It was believed as early as 1848 that vessels would be attracted towards the lights on Sable Island and founder. Such concerns and risks of increasing the dangers to mariners subdued any realistic attempt to establish the lights. Instead, the operation of a life-saving rescue station, first established on the island in 1801, was preferred, and even today, a continuous human presence is still maintained on Sable Island.[26] Improved navigation technologies meant dramatic declines in shipwrecks by the mid 20th century. The opening verse from the extensive poem *Sable Island* written by Canadian politician, poet and journalist Joseph Howe in 1831 seems most appropriate for this unusual maritime feature:

> Dark Isle of Mourning! – aptly are thou named,
> For thou hast been the cause of many a tear;
> For deeds of treacherous strife too justly framed,
> The Atlantic's charnel [structure storing remains of dead] – desolate and drear; A thing none love, though wand'ring thousands fear,–
> If for a moment rests the Muse's wing
> Where through the waves thy sandy wastes appear,
> 'Tis that she may one horror of strain sing,
> Wild as the dashing waves that tempest o'er thee fling.[27]

There is another considerably smaller island off the east coast of Canada that has much in common with Sable Island, particularly the atrocious weather patterns and dense fog banks. It also has not only experienced many shipwrecks but was thought to be the final resting place for many of those unfortunate sailors. It had a solitary lighthouse which was built much earlier than those eventually erected on Sable Island. What made this lighthouse somewhat different was reputedly the occasional presence of an unknown spirit or possibly poltergeist. These sporadic episodes occurred throughout the lighthouse keeper's house, and included mysterious thumping noises during the night, and perhaps on a more regular basis, the unassisted opening of closed internal doors even on calm nights with no wind and all outside doors shut.[28]

One could always argue the validity of such events as the natural creaking and groaning noises from settlement of the house, or perhaps the effect of internal drafts around doors during particularly windy weather, or even stretching a point, something else quirky with the house design. On the other hand, poltergeists are thought to be responsible for not only creating unusual and often loud noises, but for mischievous activities such as dragging furniture, moving crockery and of course, turning door knobs. Whatever the mysterious causes of these nocturnal events, it is understood that they have yet to be explained satisfactorily, and given the lighthouse and its dwelling quarters at that time have subsequently been demolished/removed, the mystery will probably never be explained.

GENESIS OF WITCHCRAFT

It is not my intention to dissect and analyse this complex and extensive topic, nor produce a detailed chronology of its history worldwide, as witchcraft has been meticulously examined and thoroughly interpreted by a plethora of competent professional authors over centuries. What is of most interest to me is how witchcraft came to be so intertwined with the practice of sorcery/magic throughout European history, and has probably evolved in modern times to be recognised more as a popular culture for some, rather than viewed as an insidious evil pagan faith from the distant past. To get a proper sense of perspective about what witchcraft actually represents, as it can confusing by definition, one should briefly look to ancient times to understand its fundamental roots.

Let me start with a reasonable definition of a person who practices witchcraft as recognised in modern European times, and in some ways, it is similar to concocting a magical potion. This would be a witch who possesses or has acquired mysterious or supernatural powers to cause either misfortune or beneficent outcomes for others in the future. Now refine this broad explanation by sprinkling in some special ingredients such as the characteristics of such a person, who may be someone isolated by a community; he or she may have a malevolent or mischievous persona, and may possibly be adept at foretelling the future with some certainty. Next stir this brew by adding elements of religious beliefs, such as worshipping demons or possibly mocking other religions, and then add a dash of flavouring to the pot with some idle gossip and malicious innuendo about a witch. Complete the mixture by boiling it furiously to distill the most important ingredient of all – magic.

For when one reviews almost every ancient culture, it appears that sorcery and the effective use of spellbinding incantations, mysterious and ritualistic magic and, to an extent, wizardry, are the common thread throughout. I shall focus mainly on witchcraft from about 1100 AD onwards, to avoid the myriad of legends and superstitious myths so prevalent in those earlier times, and because the 15th -18th centuries appear to have the most extensive records about this topic. I also understand that after 1100 AD, people became far more aware of the activities of witches and sorcerers and their perceived mysterious powers.

It is probably time to now introduce the three types of people who generally would have an opinion about witchcraft, and they can be from almost any era. Of course there were always the believers who were firmly convinced of the relevance of witchcraft and the benefits of such practices. I shall call them the faithful. On the other side, we have the non-believers who were unable to be convinced even when presented with credible physical proof, and they far outweighed the faithful in population. The third group are probably the scariest of all. They were the sceptics or doubters who were unsure about it all but who erred on the side of caution. They hedged their bets in any wager just in case they might be wrong after all. They are also the people who are the last to decide about anything, and that is what makes them frightening.

Figure 8: Believer, Non-Believer, Sceptic and Watcher (*Source Unknown**)

If witchcraft could definitely be attributed to one source of learning (excluding religions and their obvious importance to cultures throughout history), it would have to be sorcery. Black magic or the application of various elements to produce magic definitely prevailed over the early centuries of mankind, and was practised by those who could be termed 'priests to the gods'. These sorcerers had accurate knowledge of their arts and relied upon traditional beliefs and rituals to perform their magic, rather than applying scientific and factual processes.[1] They succeeded in attracting devoted followings across many cultures.

I am reminded of one of my favourite science fiction episodes of the English time-traveller Doctor Who in the BBC's *The Masque of Mandragora* as first screened on television in September 1976. It was based in Italy in the 15th century when superstition, paganism and the secretive cult of the Bretheren of Demnos (Roman god of moonlight) dominated the religious landscape. The use of sorcery dominated the tale, ably assisted by astrology and astronomy in forecasting people's futures and downfalls, and of course, the intervention of an aggressive alien energy force known as the Mandragora Helix. In the final scenes, when Doctor Who thwarts and then successfully eliminates all dangerous threats by using scientific principles over superstitious beliefs, he explains his success as '… a case of "energy squared" sending Mandragora [Helix] back to square one [to whence it came]'.[2]

To someone with scant knowledge of sorcery and its ancient ways, there would appear to be very little difference between it and to witchcraft. The clever citing of incantations, the mixing of strange potions of curious liquids and bizarre powders, and the casting of spells seem remarkably similar. *Maleficium* is a Latin term which could describe harmful magic practised by some ancient sorcerers or some witches, and *malefice* is a type of magic in which an evil spirit intends to harm another individual.[3] Sorcery and witchcraft appear to have shared a very similar history since at least biblical times, but as civilisation has grown, so witchcraft has come to dominate and sorcery has been confined to less civilised, primitive cultures throughout the world.[4]

So let me provide some clearer distinction between sorcery and witchcraft, as they appear almost interchangeable at times. In its simplest form, sorcery is magic by the manipulation of natural forces and powers to achieve a desired objective, and usually this fulfilled a range of useful needs in society. These included protection of people and livestock from disasters, outsiders and enemies for example. Sorcery is mechanistic and intuitive rather than being a set of beliefs. During the 14th -17th centuries, professional sorcerers could also be men of high learning, such as alchemists and physicians, Whereas some were believed to have derived their knowledge from supernormal forces, such as demons, it was not the same as European witchcraft that grew out of sorcery and conjured demons for the purposes of *maleficia* and devil-worship, or *the practyse* of *the blacke scyence*. Anthropologists have attempted to make a further subtle distinction that in some societies, sorcery was performed by professionals often as harmful magic, whilst witches were born with the power to cast spells and perform divination (foretelling the future and deciphering omens, dreams, visions for example), and were inherently evil.[5]

As my book is mostly concerned with witchcraft in the 15th - 18th centuries, I shall simply add that both practices involved the application of ritualistic magic and apparent use of supernatural forces. So why did the power of witches become such a concern across various countries that the foundations for witch-hunting emerged during the Middle Ages, and public trials and ruthless inquisitions eventually flourished to eradicate immense numbers of people suspected of witchcraft? A decidedly complex question indeed, but one which could be answered in several ways, depending upon your personal outlook on life and religious beliefs.

One viewpoint considers that witchcraft delved into the dark supernatural powers of demons and other equally unsavoury beings to effectively create curses, yield strange effects on the weather or produce misfortunes. To do so required a pact with the Devil to possess such powers, effectively idolising the forces of evil, which was considered decidedly wicked and unconscionable.[6] Another viewpoint considered that witchcraft was responsible for virtually every illness or malady known to man and animal alike, and that witches were using unnatural forces to cause these afflictions.[7] This viewpoint is aptly identified with the following words from Canto 5: *Poetas épicos* of *La Mosquea* by the comico-epic poet José de Villaviciosa (1589-1658):

> … Art thou perchance a vile phantasm,
> Or some *lying* witch and sorceress,
> That by force of nature or cataplasm [body poultice to relieve soreness and inflammation]
> Drainest the living substance? …[8]

Yet another viewpoint stretched the former perspective by assuming witches were actually devils in disguise, sent to wreak havoc on civilisation, and should be exterminated.[9] During daylight hours, they might even appear as ordinary people, but come the night when most people were asleep, such witches went to work.[10] They supposedly did this quite successfully by being cloaked in darkness, and travelling either by becoming invisible or shape-shifting into one of their familiars, such as a cat, dog, toad, bat or other suitable creature. Add public hysteria and some physical examples of such witchcraft and you have the basis for a perfect legal system to remove all witches.

I will not delve into the extensive persecutions and subsequent trials, confessions and punishments of witches throughout Europe in the 15th - 18th centuries as it would involve enormous commentary. Suffice to say that there were investigative practices involving dubious claims and convictions, supported by often inhumane execution processes. Enough said on this topic. So how has witchcraft survived into modern times, and how does it probably still remain influential for at least some of the population?

Part of this reason lies in beneficial witchcraft for healing and not harming. Where witchcraft is able to be used to celebrate a fruitful harvest, to appreciate the true value of the seasons, or simply to provide some comfort for the afflicted, it would certainly be of benefit. However, choosing to use arcane powers to delve into black magic and seek the darker side of this practice could produce unfortunate or even tragic circumstances, both for the witches and their victims.

WITCHES

I once read a most interesting inquiry for a special spirit which read as follows:

Witch wanted: Spellbinding pay and must like cats and be able to cackle (whatever happened to cackling?).

Perhaps the following supplementary information could have also been provided to secure the right candidate. It is from the incisive and magical Gothic poem *The Witch* (in the 1976 publication *Nightmares: Poems to Trouble Your Sleep*) by the American writer of children's poetry Jack Prelutsky:

> She comes by night, in fearsome flight,
> in garments black as pitch,
> the queen of doom upon her broom,
> the wild and wicked witch,
>
> a cackling crone with brittle bones
> and desiccated limbs,
> two evil eyes with warts and sties
> and bags about the rims,
>
> a dangling nose, ten twisted toes
> and folds of shriveled skin,
> cracked and chipped and crackled lips
> that frame a toothless grin.
>
> She hurtles by, she sweeps the sky
> and hurls a piercing screech.

As she swoops past, a spell is cast
on all her curses reach.

Take care to hide when the wild witch rides
to shriek her evil spell.
What she may do with a word or two
is much too grim to tell.[1]

Of course this version of a witch could only be based upon myths and misconceptions. In ancient times, it was believed by many that a witch could fly through the night on a broomstick, with her pointed hat and black cape silhouetted against the full moon. Witches, or night-fiends as they were known by some, were also thought to ride on other various implements and items, including pitchforks (ouch!), cart-shafts, on straw and even astride animals, such as goats, horses, roosters and, naturally, on cats.[2] But how could people believe such wild imaginative ideas when physical proof was rarely witnessed, asserted or admitted? Surprisingly, despite numerous concerns expressed about witches riding broomsticks, the first known illustration depicting a woman astride a broomstick did not appear until the mid-15th century, in a French manuscript of Martin Le Franc's poem *Les Champion des dames*.[3]

Perhaps the truth lies in the descriptions obtained from suspected witches in confessions to their interrogators in the witch-hunting days through Europe between the mid-1500s and the 1600s. These include flying on hawthorn and elder trees, as well as on straw bundles and even different but rather impractical types of straw. Less common seemed to be the practice of riding some kind of beast such as a cat, rooster or even a swallow. There is also considerable commentary well into the 1700s about riding other witches or innocent people transformed into horses or similar, and this appears to be far more widespread than riding animals or plants.[4]

These magical modes of transport seem to be less than credible. Yet remarkably, there appear to be very structured reasons in why they were utilised, and they were, certainly in principle, part of a witch's supposed skills of transformation and shape-shifting. It is understood that witches could also travel without the aid of a vehicle when being transported on the wind, and particularly a whirlwind. The duration of a witch's flight and the ultimate destination are extremely difficult to ascertain,[5] as now we are definitely in murky waters indeed. Perhaps it would more sensible to leave them simply as 'unspecified'. In the 1600s, witches' confessions yielded many tales of travel over sea and inland waters for maritime encounters which may involve sinking or saving a ship amongst many other things. Even when flying over land, these flights would not be at any great altitude but rather floating not far above the surface.[6]

Figure 9: The Wicce Astride

The modern English name 'witch' in itself reflects the historical hysteria experienced by ancient civilisations, deriving its origins from people's unusual supernatural behaviours.[7] For those practising sorcery, the Old English word is 'wicce', whilst in Germanic and European origins, 'weid' applies to foretelling and knowing, and 'weik' is to bend or fold, in which witches were certainly considered capable. Were all witches treated the same, considering their perceived diverse supernatural abilities to cast spells, predict the future, influence the elements, to fly and accomplish numerous other extraordinary feats? Apparently not, for from the late 16th century and early 17th century in some English religious quarters, a subtle distinction was made between performing harmful magic and that of using witchcraft specifically to aid and assist the Devil.[8]

The former was considered to be any magical act or malevolent sorcery intended to cause harm or death to people or property, whereas the latter was a consensual willingness to be helped by the Devil for the doing of only harm or only good.[9] So-called bad or binding witches were thus labelled for using the Devil's help to do harm and even bring death to people and animals, as well as causing destruction on sea and land by raising tempests and other supernatural forces. Conversely, so-called good or white witches were deemed only capable of practising healing and curing the harm inflicted by bad witches, and through their beneficial magic, were not able to curse, torment or otherwise harm anything.[10] In modern times, there would probably be many witches who consider themselves white witches, living in harmony with nature and the elements. Such people would be at one with the planet and would direct their abilities for the benefit of others, whilst still celebrating the plentiful bounties provided by the seasons.

The distinction between witches who were a special kind of magician anyway, and those people who were believed to be able to summon demons to achieve their ends was important.[11] Ritual magicians were not considered as horrifying in various European cultures because their work involved the use of magic incantations and recitations, rather than demonic practices. Such magicians could be learned people who chose this path for benevolent or not so benevolent reasons. By contrast, witches freely choosing to practice the paganistic ways of the Devil were considered tainted and capable of inflicting severe harm and hurt on others.[12]

If you really embrace the broad definitions detailed of witches in the 16th-17th centuries, there would be many of us considered to be a witch. I provide a refined selection of some of these descriptions concerning English witches as follows: The English Puritan cleric John Gaule, who was known for his partially sceptical views on witchcraft, produced the following description in 1646: 'Every old woman with a wrinkled face, a furr'd brow, a hairy lip, a gobber [projecting] tooth, a squint eye, a squeaking voice, or a scolding tongue, having a ragged coate on her back, a skull-cap on her head, a spindle in her hand, and dog or cat by her side, is not only suspected but pronounced for a witch.'[13] This was embellished by others to include women with a myriad of disabilities, infirmities or unusual features, such that any woman who was lean, lame or deformed, wrinkly, pale, bleary-eyed, melancholic, sullen, doting, superstitious, without religion, mischievous, devilish or simply mad could be considered a witch.

Of course, the skills of such witches were perceived as endless and omnipotent, including the ability to kill with simply a look or disable with a curse, take on whatever shapes that they wanted, transport themselves anywhere at any time, call up storms or sunshine, and to ruin people at the mention of a few choice words. Some wise and sane men of the day reflected about those times of universal madness, and '... gave their minds to the task of stemming the raging torrent of cruelty and superstition. For the whole world was overrun with witches ...'.

Some witches had particular talents which could be sought by superstitious people intent on having good fortune. Such was the case involving many seafaring men, who preferred to know in advance if their journey would be hindered by the onset of bad weather. Scottish witch Bessie Skebister was roundly acknowledged by all honest men in the Orkney Islands off the rugged North Eastern coast as a person with such adept skill. It was common for these mariners to seek her foretelling regarding the fall of storms prior to sailing their vessels into possible danger. If the seafarers were late returning to shore or had encountered trouble, their relatives would seek her out concerning the condition of the sailors. Unfortunately, her ultimate demise in 1633 arose because she was a 'dreamer of dreams' and a witch who was accused of tormenting sick men and causing livestock to become ill.[14]

Far more prominent as a sea witch was Sarah Moore, also known as Old

Mother Moore by some. She lived well over two hundred years later in Leigh-on-Sea, Essex, England. Much has already been written about this infamous witch, so I shall keep my commentary brief. If there is such a thing as an archetypal witch and I seriously doubt it, then Sarah's appearance and personal characteristics were certainly in keeping, for she apparently had a stooped back, a hooked nose, a harsh tongue, and a propensity for foretelling the future and forecasting storms. And, importantly, she had a habit of cursing those who crossed her. Sarah had a reputation for extracting a coin or two from the many superstitious sailors dockside for foretelling favourable weather, or, as the saying goes, producing it ('Buy a fair wind, buy a fair wind') for those boarding their ships. For those who refused to provide her with this meagre income or who taunted her predictions or otherwise upset her, it was believed that she could raise storms at sea in revenge.[15]

An extraordinary and lengthy description of the powers of English sea witches to most effectively command the weather was compiled by Reginald Scot in 1584 in his publication *The Discoverie of Witchcraft*, when he comprehensively detailed that '...the elements are obedient to witches, and that at their commandment or that they may, at their pleasure, send rain, hail, tempests, thunder and lightning, ... all which things are confessed by witches and affirmed by writers'.[16]

It appears the demise of Old Mother Moore in 1867 resulted from a new sea captain, who was unaware of her skills, putting to sea without buying a fair wind from her. In another version of this tale, the captain was believed to have refused to pay and laughed at the witch. Either way, as the fishing sailboat left the harbour, the sky ominously began to grow dark with storm clouds and the wind dropped away. Worse was to come as the severe inclement weather engulfed the vessel, causing it to roll on its side, tangling the sails' rigging. With his superstitious crew, including very experienced sailors convinced Old Mother Moore was responsible for their misfortune, the captain threatened to kill the sea witch as he attempted to clear this rigging to prevent it pulling the vessel completely underwater.

On the third blow with an axe, remarkably the storm abated and the sun appeared. The vessel returned to harbour and to a truly terrifying sight indeed. Lying on the Strand Wharf at Leigh as they approached was Sarah Moore, who had died with three gashes to her head reputedly not long after the vessel's calamity.[17] This sea witch may have been many things but an ability to cause someone to burst into flames by spontaneous combustion was probably not one of them.

How did this tale originate? In 1852, a small group of young and inquisitive neighbourhood children crept into the witch's house on Victoria Wharf whilst she was out in order to explore this mysterious abode and hopefully find a potion to cure the teenager in their group who suffered greatly from painful itchy skin. The rest were younger than twelve years old. Unfortunately, the interior lighting was so poor the children used a candle left on a table to inspect the premises, at about the same time as the witch returned. As the witch stood in the doorway muttering curses, the children panicked, resulting in a bottle of flammable 'paraffin' falling over and knocking over the candle, as well as splashing over two of the group. It had been a particularly windy day, so as the witch came through the front door, '… the wind had made the flames blaze', effectively fanning them by the sudden in-rush of wind. Realising the danger to the children, Sarah Moore rushed towards them with a sack reputedly to smother the flames. The accounts from the surviving children blamed the witch, suggesting that '… sparks flashed from her eyes and they [the children] burst into flames'.[18] A very sad ending to a witch's story.

Another Englishwoman whose appearance by all accounts resembled that of a witch was the famous and legendary prophet Old Mother Shipton from Yorkshire. Born in a cave in 1488 to a poor, single mother, Ursula Southeil (or possibly Sontheil) was fostered out at two years of age to a local woman, and even in her childhood, was rumoured to use supernatural forces against those who taunted or were particularly unkind towards her. Ursula even seemed able to foretell such punishments. She was eventually married briefly to local carpenter Toby Shipton in 1512, and lived until 1561, gaining considerable notoriety throughout England by using her uncanny predictive abilities to foretell remarkably accurate and sometimes bizarre prophecies recited verbally in verse.

As her reputation for foretelling the future spread, all kinds of people sought her advice, from influential clerics and dignitaries, to petty criminals anxious to repent their crimes. She was also widely believed to possess strange intuitive powers to heal and to suitably punish the wicked, such as people seeking her services to dispense misfortune to other.[19] Why would she wish to punish someone? It may have something to do with her physical appearance, as she had been born with a crooked spine (hunchback). This unfortunate affliction and her amazing prophecies are said to have earned her the unenviable title of a child of the Devil from some people, and no doubt, contributed to her being thought of as a witch in some quarters.

An incredibly detailed description of her unusual facial features and body at birth were compiled in the writings from the late 15th century belonging to an old Monastery in Yorkshire and published in the book entitled *THE LIFE, PROPHECIES AND DEATH OF THE FAMOUS Mother Shipton*. For the sake of brevity, I shall summarise the description of her birth due to its extraordinary extent:

> She was mishapen …the right side of her body stood lower than her left … again, her left side was … as if her body had been screwed together piece by piece, and not rightly placed, … her legs very crooked … her neck so strangely distorted … her head was very long, with very large googling, but sharp and fiery eyes, … a nose of incredible and unproportionable length, having in it many crooks and turnings … her cheeks were wrinkled, shrivelled, and very hollow … her teeth … excepting only two them, which stood quite of her mouth in imitation of the tusks of a wild boar, or tooth of an elephant, a thing so strange in an infant…her chin … turning up towards to her mouth; …[20]

Given the poor woman's afflictions and deprived upbringing, is it any wonder that she would have given short shrift to any such personal criticisms. Mother Shipton lived until the ripe old age of 73, which was miraculous for a so-called witch, though she was actually remembered more as a seer/prophetess who foretold the future. Probably more importantly, the woman was also respected for her ability to help others. The words inscribed on her headstone, believed to be once erected almost 2 kilometres from York but now long since gone, are certainly accurate:

> Here ly's [lies] she who never ly'd [lied]
> Whose skill often has been try'd [tried]
> Her Prophecies shall still survive,
> And she keep her name alive.[21]

THE BLACK CAT

There are many domesticated cat species spread across the world and they provide welcome comfort and companionship as pets, albeit usually with some distinctive traits of solitude and independence when the mood takes them. Ask their owners and the consensus will be that this is what makes them special. Cats are mysterious creatures, persuasive and fawning one moment, then decidedly irritating or aggressive the next moment, like their wild feline cousins.

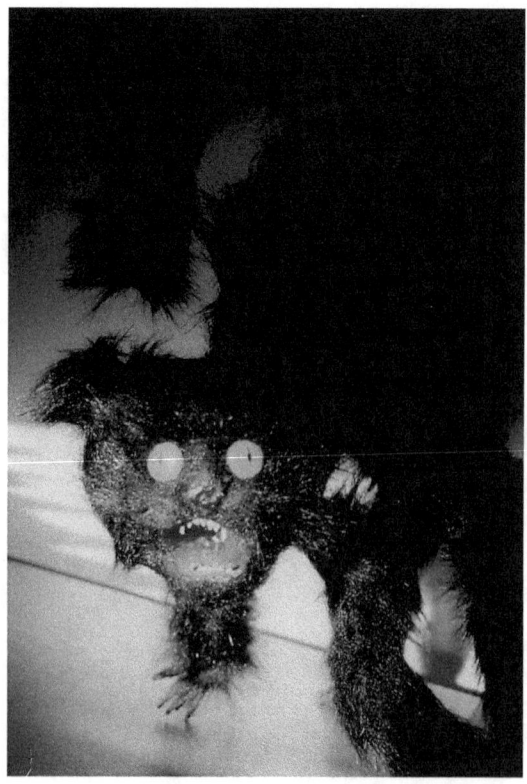

Figure 10: Beware a Black Cat

I owned cats at various times and found them to be considerably fickle, aloof and prone to misbehaviour, but also loyal and therapeutic most of the time. Feed me and pamper me and I will always be your pet. So why has the humble black cat been lumbered for so long with such unsavoury titles as 'the witches' agent', 'demonic worshipper', 'shape-changing magician' or 'purveyor of bad omens'? Is it something to do with the unsettling way a black cat can stare at you so intently with those piercing changeable eyes, or is it perhaps the intuitive way they seem to know what is just about to happen?

Folklore suggests that the most effective way of dealing with werewolves is by using a silver bullet. Fortunately, this not apply to black cats who may be behaving in a supernatural manner or perhaps acting as an agent of sorcery. For those superstitious readers amongst us, it would be heartening to know that a ship's cat would almost always be considered good luck on board a vessel. They provided affection for the seamen whose routine life could be dreary and far removed from shore life, and they were adept at eliminating rodents so prevalent on seaborne vessels. Unfamiliar cats, however, could be treated as unlucky. Sailors in bygone days certainly believed cats possessed some unusual abilities, and the one belief that I find fascinating is their perceived ability to conjure storms. How was this possible?

The simple answer was to stroke the cat's fur on a day with no moisture in the air, thereby discharging static electricity. These miniscule electrical sparks were believed to be mini-lightning bolts which the cat stored in its tail. If the cat was permitted to become too playful around the ship, it could release 'its lightning' and eventually raise a storm, or was it probably just wishful thinking? As a consequence, cats were labelled as storm-bringers.[1] Unfortunately, because of this supposed mythical ability and other natural characteristics, they appear to have been rather unfairly associated with witches by superstitious seafaring folk, and called a witch's familiar. This was particularly as witches were thought to raise storms and tempests as well as sometimes foretell the future.[2]

Cats were believed to be naturally sensitive to meteorological changes in the weather, could see well in the dark and thus detect fearful demons which might approach ships, and appeared to possess an uncanny ability to avoid harm (thus inviting the popular belief that they have nine lives). Many legends also associated cats and witches with the moon and all that it evoked, and consequently, the black cat was viewed as representative of a cloudy, moonless night which did not auger well for sailing.[3]

Figure 11: The Black Cat with Everything

The Chinese and ancient Greeks even believed that the waxing and waning of the moon was reflected in the widening and narrowing of a cat's pupils. As part of the quote from Polish-born English writer Joseph Conrad states: 'There is something haunting in the light of the moon; …' However, cats are believed in some folklore to bring either good or evil luck to a ship, depending upon their behaviour, and this is where it becomes messy.

In January 1885, Frenchman L.F.Sauvé published in this edition of his folklore work *Mélusine* the following account of how a cat on board is believed to foreshadow imminent events:

> 'Fishermen at Santec, in Brittany, have a song, in which presages [signs or warnings] are drawn from actions of the cat. If it wipes the face with its paw, the omen is bad, and if rubs the ear, the helmsmen

cannot steer. If it turns the back to the fire, the boat will upset, and if burns its claws, the crew are lost. If it commences to purr, the omen is good.'[4]

By these accounts, it would seem most difficult to determine what may eventually transpire. Given such a formidable background of superstitions, it should not surprise anyone that apparitions involving black cats could be taken rather seriously. Unfortunately, for black cats in particular, they were singled out for harsh retribution in Europe in the 1600s at the time when witches were being relentlessly persecuted for their sorcery. Even the keeping of a cat through those precarious times was enough to inflame suspicions in some quarters, but without doubt, the tale where it was claimed that a witch assumed the shape of a black cat to harass a servant was a precedent.

It led to a commonly held belief that a black cat was almost certainly a witch in disguise, and ultimately by association, contributed to cats meeting the same fates as those dispensed to witches, innocent or otherwise. A sad tale indeed for our feline friends and companions. I think part of this prophetic verse *On Halloween* by American poet and author Nina Willis Walter says it all: 'The witches fly Across the sky, The owls go, "Who? Who? Who?" The black cats yowl And green ghosts howl, …'[5]

The close association of black cats with witches comes to mind in relation to the case of the Witch of Wapping, a district in East London, England. In 1652, a woman who lived in this area was well known for healing ill people with rather unorthodox suggestive methods rather than by using traditional medicines and processes. A child from the neighbourhood became unwell, described at the time as being 'strangely distempered', and was placed in a rocking cradle to recuperate. She was being watched by a neighbour woman when one evening, a black cat suddenly jumped into the cradle. This woman and another watching the child did not recognise the cat or from where it had appeared, but promptly scared it away by throwing a fire-fork (prong) at it. An hour later, the black cat returned on the opposite side of the child's cradle, only this time the neighbour woman raised her foot and kicked the cat. Suddenly her foot and leg swelled and became very sore and painful. Terrified by this experience, both women left the house but not before complaining to the master of the house that they could not remain in such a place plagued with evil spirits. Now the tale becomes fascinating. On their way home, the women met a baker who remarked that he had just met a big black cat that was so frightening it made his hair stand on end. He also remarked to having seen the suspected witch shortly before his scary encounter. The man had never been afraid of a cat in his life, but he had never seen such a cat before and hoped that he should never see the like again. The mysterious black cat was not sighted again and remained an unsolved matter.[6]

Another witch who reportedly used cats for her own purposes was Ursula Kemp (or possibly Ursley Kempe). Note that she had the same first name as Old Mother Shipton and was also born in Yorkshire. Unfortunately for this Ursula, who was born in 1525, she was ultimately tried and convicted of being a witch, perishing on the gallows in 1582 at Chelmsford in Essex. Her crime was intentionally causing illness and death whilst treating the various ailments of her neighbours through her abilities as a healer and midwife. Part of her confession, provided privately to the presiding justice, involved the sending of four witch familiars (spirits) to the victims to bring them illness and death. So what were these animals and why were they used? If one is to go by the reliability of 'the confession' as reproduced, it appears that Ursula had previously healed herself of lameness because she had been bewitched and was able to remove the spell and recover.

She performed the same ritual on two local women suffering lameness and they also recovered. Accordingly, she believed that she could now bewitch others by using spirits through selected animals. For these malevolent messengers, she chose two female spirits that brought sickness to people and two male spirits that brought death. Her messengers were a male black cat called Jacke (Jack), a male grey cat called Tyttey (Titty), a white female lamb named Tyffin (Tiffin), and a black female toad named Pygine (Piggin). Why these familiars were used at all stemmed from nasty disagreements between Ursula and her patients, with the ultimate result intended to be ongoing punishment for one patient through bodily harm and illness, and death to others.[7]

The witch's most consistent companion or 'familiar' was arguably the domesticated cat, predominantly by association with its most unusual traits. It has been said that some witches have even confessed (under torture) to originally being cats in former lives and so could easily transform into the feline shape to undertake their work. Cats were certainly not the only familiars, and some of the others were selected because they were supposedly repulsive to ordinary folk. These others included dogs, various birds (including crows, ravens, owls, sparrows, even domesticated fowl), moles, hares, mice, rats, toads, frogs, spiders, flies, and hornets.

The perceived mysterious aura of cats probably also contributed to domesticated felines being named as likely agents for sorcerers and witches to practise their magic, healing or harming powers. Consequently, cats in particular may be singled out by superstitious people, like seafarers for example, as being a catalyst for spells, curses and incantations despatched by their owners, such as witches.[8] No wonder the domesticated cat seems to have borne the brunt of such criticism and persecution.

For a broader appreciation of the cat's nature, I turn to a very powerful description provided in a book published in 1887 about ancient Irish legends, myths and superstitions as follows:

> … the mysterious and almost human qualities of cat nature; the profound cunning, the impertinent indifference, the intense selfishness, yet capable of the hypocritical flatteries when some point is to be gained. These traits are not merely the product of brute instinct with unvarying action and results, but the manifestation of a calculating intellect, akin to the human.[9]

'Their intellect is also very remarkable, they easily acquire the meaning of certain words, and have a singular and exact knowledge of hours.'[10] To qualify these findings, the author provides the following commentary:

> The observation of cats is very remarkable, and also their intense curiosity. They examine everything in a house, and in a short time know all about it as well as the owner. They are never deceived by stuffed birds, or any such weak human delusions. They fathom it all

at one glance, and then turn away with apathetic indifference, as if saying, in cat language – "We know all about it."[11]

Unfortunately, the cat's ability to understand everything that is said, as popularly believed particularly by superstitious people, has also has contributed to their reputation for being selfish, revengeful, treacherous, cunning as well as generally dangerous. It seems the poor black cat has certainly been dealt quite an unfavourable hand when it comes to the superstition and myth of arousing the evil spirit in them.

CROWS AND RAVENS

The crow is a member of the genus *Corvus* which belongs to the Corvidae family, also known as corvids. It has always been a feared bird, regarded by some as a bird of ill omen, as indicated by the following common English proverbs: 'Black as night the devil's kite' or 'A crow on the thatch, Soon death lifts the latch'. The collective name for a group of crows is a 'murder', and I have no doubt that the name may have originated from encounters with some people who were less than impressed with their behaviours. In reality, I understand the name originated because, for reasons unknown to scientists, crows have been known to occasionally murder other crows.

They have always been associated with wars, death, and the afterlife, notably in ancient Irish mythology and Cornish folklore, and their calls are said to have been heard before death in battles, acting as messengers from beyond. Conversely, crows are known to frequent battlefields following the carnage and death of the combatants, probably much like vultures seeking to scavenge the bodies of the slain. In effect, they have been revered particularly throughout Celtic Britain as presiding over death and slaughter.[1] So what attributes do these birds possess which suggests these mystical powers?

They are quite large black birds, particularly noisy, smart and gregarious. Crows prefer being in populated areas and easily keep pace with human activities by learning, because these birds are universally regarded as being both highly intelligent and inquisitive. It has been said that they have the largest brain to body size ratio of any birds, and are even thought by some to have the mental capacity equivalent to that of the seven-year-old child. As a result, crows are also known as great imitators, and can generate a diverse range of bird sounds learnt from other sources in their environment.

They also possess a reputation for being sneaky petty pilferers who can winkle a snack from almost any situation. Their glossy black plumage and clever antics have resulted in a close association with various elements of witchcraft. However, unlike witches, who were thought to frequent the dark night skies, crows are actually not nocturnal, and are renowned for starting each day with discordant and loud cries to announce their arrival.

The common raven (*Corvus corax*) is also a member of the Corvidae family of birds, and is remarkably similar both in superficial appearance and intelligence to a crow. However, the raven is substantially larger in all of its physical features, lives considerably longer and tends to be particularly cautious, reclusive and less sociable with mankind. According to folklore, 'The longevity of the Raven is believed to be much greater than that of any other beast or bird, and it has been known to live in captivity fully a hundred years'.[2] Its distinctive croaking call is hoarse, deeper and decidedly less piercing to that of the crow, which in contrast seems high pitched, raucous and rasping.

Ravens were revered in various cultures and are depicted across Celtic, Irish and American mythologies as being far more daring and dignified than crows, which were considered to be more like shuffling, sneaking, common thieves. Ravens are also highly intelligent, clever and crafty, as well as being bold and almost theatrical in nature: they devise innovative and often humorous ways to satisfy their needs or to impress other ravens.[3] They have proliferated because they will reside in almost any structure and consume just about anything. The collective name for a group of ravens is 'an unkindness' which is far more subtle than 'a murder' of crows. Perhaps at some stage, someone took pity on ravens and named them accordingly.

Raven and crow familiars have always been recognised as companions of witches. They enhance the performance of witchcraft magic through their superior intelligence, and provide a means for astral travel between destinations. They were thought to have acted as messengers by collecting information for witches and by spreading the magic across great distances at night, when their black gloomy plumage was virtually undetectable in the sky.[4] This was the perfect partnership with great upside for the witch.

Famous American poet Henry Wadsworth Longfellow certainly captured the moment about these birds in the following segments from *Blessing the Cornfields* in his extended poem *The Song of Hiawatha* published in 1855:

> ... the King of Ravens,
> Gathered all his black marauders,
> Crows and blackbirds, jays and ravens,
> Clamorous on the dusky tree-tops,
> And descended, fast and fearless, ...
> ... Soon they came with caw and clamor,
> Rush of wings and cry of voices,
> To their work of devastation,
> Settling down upon the cornfields,
> Delving deep with beak and talon, ...[5]

In Norse mythology, it was also believed that ravens were incredible messengers, able to traverse the world as servants of the omniscient All-Father god Odin and return to elaborate on faraway places. It was said that although Odin could see all over the world from his heavenly palace, it was too far to know everything that was going on, so he despatched two ravens each day at dawn. When his two ravens Hugin (thought) and Munin (memory) returned each evening, they whispered in his ears about everything they had heard and seen during their flight through the worlds.[6] This folklore is not that unrealistic, given that in certain circumstances, ravens appear to be mimicking human speech, if you listen intently enough, as well as many other familiar sounds detected in their environment.

It was also understood that the raven was the first bird to be sent out by Noah from the ark and '...went forth to and fro until the waters were dried up from off the earth.' However, it did not return with a message, and apparently, it was condemned to be black and eat carrion.[7]

Like ravens, crows were also thought capable of finding land whilst on board ships at sea, even when such landfall was well out of sight.[8] However, probably in part due to the ferocious Vikings embracing the sacred raven symbol as the Bird of Omen, this bird was eventually considered by much of western Europe to be a bird of evil omen. Little wonder if the bird had become associated with death and despair.[9] The raven also acquired quite a reputation for its clever ways, and a diverse range of unusual abilities uncommon to most avian life. Along with a select group of other birds including crows, owls, canaries, magpies and some parrots, it was believed that the raven had a reputation for predicting the onset of one's death. This was achieved by many means, including making exotic noises and/or exhibiting weird behaviours.[10]

In one particular case many years ago, a raven took a considerable interest in a specific household and just would not leave the family alone. Perhaps it was simply chasing a free feed or was overly curious. The raven's cries became downright irritating but eventually it left. Fortunately, the family recorded the date when this incessant visitor started all this bizarre behaviour, because several months later, they were notified of the passing of a direct relative who lived overseas. The date that their relative passed away was precisely the same as the day of the raven's ranting activities.

It all seems to be somewhat creepy to me. No doubt there would be those willing to say it was just a coincidence or even a rarity. Witches on the other hand would certainly think otherwise. Why does a bird for no obvious reason keep flying into a closed window or even persisting to get inside your house? To some birds, it could be seeing their own reflection in the glass window and assuming it to be another bird. To others, it could something more complex. There have been tales of birds feigning death and lying prostrate with legs upwards, then getting up and repeating the whole charade. Another ploy to confuse their aerial adversaries perhaps, or something far more symbolic?

I should say at this point that the incredibly chilling and thought-provoking 1963 avian horror movie *The Birds*, directed by the famous and gifted master of suspense and intrigue Alfred Hitchcock and distributed by Universal Pictures, certainly got it right. Who knows what is really going on with these airborne messengers, and why in that fictional movie, did thousands of various birds descend on a small coastal town and wreak havoc on the entire population with dire consequences for many? Perhaps this is a little too severe as *The Birds* was really just an imaginative movie after all.

Similarly to ravens, crows have also taken the brunt of blame from an association with witchcraft, and as an example, I will refer to a tale emanating more from folklore than fact concerning the humble crow. This tale is based during times of upheaval and turmoil for the British colonies in America, and involves an unfortunate woman known as Peg Wesson who was reputed to be a witch. She resided in Gloucester, on Cape Anne on the southern coast of Massachusetts. Gloucester's first encounter with women supposedly suffering from the delusion of witchcraft was as early as 1692, but it would many years later before this took a more dramatic turn for the community. In 1745, a colonial force including a contingent recruited from this area and supported by a naval fleet, laid siege to a strongly fortified coastal town established by the French at the north-eastern tip of what is now Nova Scotia in Canada.

Prior to the local expeditionary forces departing Gloucester for their siege, some of the soldiers visited Peg and so upset her by their conduct that as they departed, she threatened to inflict vengeance on them. During the siege, the colonial soldiers were armed with long barrel, muzzle-loaded firearms known as muskets, which in the mid-1700s could be inaccurate unless in reasonable proximity to the target. This tale involves two such soldiers who became particularly annoyed by a crow who persistently hovered over them for no apparent reason. Despite throwing stones at this crow, they could not stop its incessant antics nor scare it away, so next they tried shooting the bird but again without any success. The crow appeared almost impervious to musket shot, and certainly was not frightened, keeping up the assault.

Then, unfortunately for Mr Crow, one of the soldiers thought that this bird was actually the suspected witch from Gloucester wreaking her promised revenge on them, and so it would be necessary to fight fire with fire. Now I suspect that we move into the realms of folklore. The solution contrived by the soldier was based on a medieval superstition that only the precious metal silver could effectively injure a witch. So the clever soldier cut-off the silver sleeve-buttons from his uniform to use as rudimentary projectiles from his musket.

With the first shot, the crow was wounded in the leg, fell to the ground, and was soon killed. Now we move into extreme folklore which stretches one's beliefs. Eight hundred kilometres away from this incident, in Gloucester, Massachusetts, the dreaded witch had fallen down with a broken leg at precisely the same time as the crow's demise. She was to die from her injury not long afterwards. As with much folklore, there is always a twist at the end of the story, and this one apparently had quite a twist in credibility. When the witch's fractured limb was later examined closely, the identical silver sleeve-buttons were discovered in the flesh and extracted from the wound.[11] I feel for the crow in this tale because, if the first part of the tale was factual, the bird received a painful death for no apparent reason other than annoying the soldiers.

The poor raven's reputation did not fare much better in this folklore emanating from the Shetland Islands north of mainland Scotland. It concerns a superstitious belief founded on the following tale of witch metamorphosis. For authenticity, I shall recount the superstition as provided from two separate versions, as can happen when folklore is reproduced over time. A witch had taught her daughter some 'tricks of the trade' in her profession, and the girl, proud of her knowledge, changed herself into a raven [known as a *corbie* in Shetland], according to the maternal directions.

But in learning how to become a bird, the girl had forgotten to receive the magic instructions necessary for returning to human shape (or eagerly changed before being told), and would have remained a raven had her mother not guessed somehow the state of the case. It is suggested here in one version that a real raven presented as a comely lass and intimated the situation to the witch that it wished to recover its true form.[12] With great difficulty the witch contrived to restore her daughter's personal appearance and the proper transformation was almost successful, but all her art could not recover the girl's natural voice. Croak she would, and croak she did, and all her descendants after her; and that is how the peculiar sound of a burr in speech called *corbieng* in Shetland originated.[13] Any such person who has this particular kind of hoarse articulation is still believed by superstition to possess witch-blood.

It is probably now the best time to introduce the opening verses of a very old English folklore ballad about the raven, entitled *Bill Jones, a Tale of Wonder*. It was written by novelist Matthew Gregory Lewis in 1808 to appreciate why ravens were so feared as a bird of omen.

> "Now, well-a-day!" the sailor said,
> "Some danger doth impend:
> Three ravens sit in yonder glade,
> And harm will happen, I'm sore afraid,
> Ere we reach our journey's end."
>
> "And what have the ravens with us to do?
> Does their sight then bode us evil?"
> "Why, to find one raven is lucky, 'tis true;
> But 'tis certain misfortune to light upon two,
> And meeting with three is the devil …"[14]

Enough about the crow and the raven. One of my favourite birds probably deserves a minor mention here, given that this bird is also well known in various cultures as a witch's familiar and of course, the ominous messenger of some impending dire calamity. This bird is instantly recognisable not only by its somewhat unique physical features but also by its distinctive nocturnal sounds. No matter which way you look at this bird, it has the hallmark of a truly gothic spirit, a mystical avenger that relentlessly and silently hunts its prey almost exclusively at night. Their intimate association with witchcraft is virtually timeless and in so many ways, linked to those clandestine mysterious habits usually only performed at night. Over two hundred species of this bird typically exhibit the same characteristics of supreme patience, fearsome hunting skills and of course, that intangible quality of somewhat eerie behaviour.

If you guessed an owl, then you guessed correctly. For want of a better descriptive term, *Strega* or the screech owl says it all, and is synonymous with 'witch'. This avian survivor has developed all the essential tools for its lifestyle over millions of years. These include razor-sharp talons, a downward-facing hooked beak for optimum grip and laceration of prey, a flat solemn face for optimum peripheral vision and unforgettable eyes that have night vision second to none. In addition, they have highly developed hearing, supremely balanced and silent aerodynamic flight capability, naturally camouflaged plumage that makes them almost invisible, and who could overlook that haunting war-cry 'hoot, hoot, hoot' of the assassin messenger?

The owl's ominous dismal hooting was considered a disquieting and even mournful cry among superstitious folk, and when combined with its nocturnal hunting habits, gave rise to an owl's cry being taken as a portent of impending death. Indeed, in the Middle Ages, owls were thought to be bad spirits that came to eat the souls of the dying.[15] Just to gaze directly into an owl's large captivating eyes can be an almost spellbinding experience for most. Adult snowy owls in particular have a near-ghostly appearance dominated by their distinctive all-white plumage. It's no wonder witches embraced these curious and mysterious wonders of nature as their own familiars.

> *Now, when the owl makes wild ado*
> *With his sad tu-whit tu-who,*
> *'Tis the night for erie* [sic] *things,*
> *When shadows from unearthly wings*
> *Born in umbrageous* [shady] *solitude*
> *Gloom the meadow and the wood...*[16]

Figure 12: The Mysterious Owl

An interesting selection of excerpts from the poem initially published in 1851 entitled *The Owl* by English poet Bryan Waller Procter (penned under his pseudonym of Barry Cornwall) describes the nocturnal habits of this particular bird.

> In the hollow tree, in the old grey tower,
> The spectral Owl doth dwell;
> Dull, hated, despised, in the sunshine hour,
> But at dusk, – he's abroad and well!...
>
> *... O – when the moon shines and the dogs do howl,*
> *Then, then, is the joy of the Hornèd Owl!*
>
> Mourn not for the Owl, nor his gloomy plight!
> The Owl hath his share of good:
> If a prisoner he be in the broad day-light,
> He is Lord in the dark green wood! ...
>
> *So, when the night falls, and dogs do howl,*
> *Sing, Ho! For the reign of the Hornèd Owl!*
> *We know not alway*
> *Who are kings by day,*
> *But the King of the night is the bold brown Owl!* [17]

Despite the innumerable superstitions that abound about this bird of night and darkness, and its unfortunate label as 'the bird of witches', the owl has many redeeming features, including an unmatched natural ability to cull and devour vermin. It can live in almost all types of habitats and tends to live in harmony with humans. On top of these attributes, I think their very unusual physical appearance and incredible avian skills indicate owls are indeed unique messengers.

Probably one of the most commendable qualities of this enigmatic bird can be found in the following version of an old, traditional and English language nursery rhyme entitled *A Wise Old Owl*, as published during the mid-1930s:

> A wise old owl sat in an oak;
> The more he saw, the less he spoke;
> The less he spoke, the more he heard;
> Now, wasn't he a wise old bird?[18]

For all the wisdom indicated by this exceptional night hunter, its haunting cry has been somewhat harshly treated throughout ancient superstitious times, as illustrated by this 1633 quotation:

> Tis yet dead night, yet all the earth is cloucht [clutched]
> In the dull leaden hand of snoring sleepe [sleep] :
> No breathe disturbs the quiet of the aire [air],
> No spirit moves upon the breast of earth,
> Save howling dogs, night crowes, and screeching owles [owls],
> Save meagre ghosts, Piero [sic], and blacke [black] thoughts.[19]

ENJOY THE GHOST TRAIN

From spectral trains operating late at night along disused tracks, haunted railway stations, signal boxes or tunnels, to ghostly manifestations of deceased train drivers, signalmen or even passengers, the stories abound across the centuries. My first encounter with a ghost train was in the 1950s when as a young boy, I experienced the shivers and frights of riding one in an amusement park. They were very popular attractions for youngsters and even teenagers in those days who wanted to be shocked and thrilled by the unexpected. Television was yet to arrive in Australia, so you made your own fun, and amusement parks and fairs were the obvious choice.

This particular ghost train operated on a seaside pier, which meant one minute I could be inside a dark haunted house with various scary apparitions and luminescent faces appearing directly in front of me, and the next minute, the train would be outside, precariously perched directly above the sea just below the jetty. To travel on this train with a close friend was mandatory, in order to have someone to grab as the intensity of frights increased. To travel on my own was simply too scary and ridiculously courageous. I duly paid my fare, not knowing what to expect, and sat in the little open two-seater carriages of the train waiting to shuffle off into the haunted house and total darkness. Anticipation of the unknown is probably more terrifying than the ride itself. The train followed very convoluted short tracks which deviated sharply, jolting and shaking me intently. At every twist and turn of the ghost train, something or someone suddenly appeared out of the dark to frighten, scream, cackle or shriek at me.

At some stage, a person dressed as a ghostly shape leapt towards me or touched me on the shoulder before disappearing into the darkness. Half way through the journey and my thoughts turned to panic, as I wondered how much more I could tolerate. The total darkness could be daunting even without the unexpected scares. Then just as quickly, the ride was over as the little train emerged from the pitch darkness into bright glary daylight and a sea of eager expectant faces waiting for their turn on the spooky train. As I clambered out of the seat, I asked myself what all the fuss was about. It was not really that scary after all, but I still purchased another ticket to ride the ghost train once more, just to be sure.

For a chilling story about a real ghost train, I revert to the old railway system known as the Highland Railway, which provided transport services to towns and villages north of the city of Perth in central Scotland. Before being amalgamated into the broader British rail system in 1923, with eventual closure of some shorter branch lines, the Highland Railway operated an extensive network of branches for steam-powered trains.

This story involves the railway stations of Dunphail and Dava located on the Inverness and Perth junction line, inland from the nearest major town of Nairn on the North East coast of Scotland. Dunphail had been operating since 1863 and was located in sparsely populated farmland, whilst the Dava station opened in 1864 was located in wild moorland. This rural region was quiet with only the occasional train passing along the lines. Late at night, the regular service would cease and the train lines would remain out of use until daylight.

In 1921, a person walking along these tracks not long after midnight reported seeing a spectral steam train complete with four brightly lit but empty passenger carriages rapidly approaching at full throttle down the line. The phantom train seemed to be floating just above the rails and eventually it disappeared in the mist. The same sightings occurred twice to other members of the person's family at different times, but always with exactly the same descriptions. In one instance, the person was thrown to the ground, possibly by the force of the passing train.[1] The train track is long gone and the station, stationmaster's house and platforms at Dunphail and Dava are all that remains, so it would now be unlikely that any further sightings would occur, but then again, you can never really tell.

Hauntings involving railway stations, tunnels and even signal boxes, particularly in Britain, appear to involve the previous demise of a railroad employee, usually through some calamitous event or traumatic accident. These visitations may also be accompanied by a suitably eerie mist or strange thick fog which envelops the manifestation, adding to the mystery of the haunting. As was so appropriately stated by the creepy stationmaster in a distinctive Cornish accent in the 1941 definitive cinematic British version from Gainsborough Pictures entitled *The Ghost Train*: 'If this be a natural thing, where do it come from, where do it go?' Of course, it may not always be the train that is the dreaded apparition, as this next story indicates. It occurred on a train line which formed part of the south-west network for the Greater London railway system in the early 1930s, and involved a rather unusual journey for one particular passenger.

As the tale goes, this passenger was undertaking a fairly mundane rail trip one morning, travelling for probably far less than an hour up to a station near London, about 24 kilometres away. At that time of day, it was most fortunate to find an empty carriage on the train so the passenger settled in for a comfortable ride. This was not to last, as at the very next station, a nondescript man carrying a neat bundle of books entered the carriage and sat at the opposite end. There was something not quite right about this person, although it was more what you sensed about him rather than any physical characteristics. I presume some people do have a sixth sense or wise intuition about these matters. This feeling of unease became so great that the passenger wanted to get off at the very next station, but was upstaged by the new arrival, who quietly stood up and calmly alighted instead. What a relief that he was gone and now the passenger could return to enjoying the journey.

At the same station where the stranger had left the train, some other people entered the carriage and the train resumed its trip towards London. Feeling far more relaxed sharing the carriage with other travellers, the passenger then got some sleep until the train had almost reached the intended final destination near London, whereupon he awoke to confirm the name of the next station. To the passenger's total astonishment, who should be sitting directly opposite but the same nondescript man who had left the train many stations ago. He was sitting motionless and calmly gazing at the passenger, still with his little bundle of books on his knee. Total panic was now the order of the day because this chap had definitely left the train once already. Without a second thought, the passenger stood up and then hurriedly ran through the carriages until finding an empty compartment in case the man should reappear again before the train reached his final destination. It did not occur and the passenger never saw the mystery apparition again on that eventful journey, and for that little blessing, was most grateful.[2]

With the advent of modern electric and diesel engine trains, and the passing of the age of steam trains still using coal/coke or wood for their boilers by the middle of the 20th century, it seems to me that the mystery and aura of ghostly apparitions on the rail system may have also been consigned to the history books. The mystique of a steam locomotive powering through mountain tunnels with its smoke billowing in through the carriage windows seems to be most appropriate for a supernatural setting, compared to the almost clinical appeal of efficiently clean electric trains with their sealed windows and quiet operation. For anyone who has experienced the olde world charm of travelling on a steam train under full power, and the choking smoke flooding into your carriage compartment through an open window, it hardly compares after all. What a delight arriving at your destination covered in soot from the locomotive's smoke. I should have closed my window after the first tunnel.

Figure 13: Olde World Charm of Steam Trains

Passenger compartments on those old steam trains were cosy and compact, with a capacity to seat six to eight people, and they were accessed from a common corridor traversing one side of the entire length of each carriage. Everyone soon became acquainted in such an enclosed setting, and that made the journey pass that much quicker. If you were ever uncertain about when your station was reached, there was always plenty of free advice from your fellow passengers to ensure that you did not miss your destination.

Who has ever heard of Thorneywood located not far from Nottingham in the county of Nottinghamshire in the East Midlands region of England? I would suggest far more would recognise Nottingham and the famous Sherwood Forest by comparison. However, Thorney Wood as it was originally known is just as significant, particularly from the following commentary published in 1813:

> It appears that the [Sherwood] forest was anciently divided, or rather known, by the names of Thorney Wood, and High Forest; the first of which, although by much the smallest, contained within its limits no less than nineteen towns or villages, amongst which Nottingham was included; and the High Forest is described as abounding with fine stately oaks, and being entirely free of underwood.
>
> The first time in which we find this forest particularly mentioned was in the reign of Henry the second, it being then, as we have before noticed, a place of royal resort, and also famous as the principal haunt of Robin Hood and his trusty bowmen.[3]

Thorneywood was also eventually to become the location for a railway station on the Nottingham Suburban Railway, a relatively short line of only 3.65 miles (5.9 kilometres) in length, comprising three stations (Sherwood, St Ann's Well and Thorneywood) with four intervening railway tunnels. It would link other rail lines located at its northern end at Daybrook station and at its southern end at Trent Lane station in Sneinton.

In the 1880s, the city of Nottingham had expanded into its surrounding villages and hamlets, which, in turn, had expanded into suburbs, requiring connection to a suitable railway network to fulfill its requirements for industrial traffic and transporting of passengers.

Thorneywood station opened in 1889 and only operated until 1916, when it was closed to passenger traffic as a supposed wartime economy measure to close intermediate (secondary) rail stations and reduce services during World War I.[4] However, although steam trains continued to operate along this short line providing goods and passenger services after the war, the advent of more direct railway lines into the Nottingham city centre from 1900, and the progressive introduction of new electric tramcar services around the Northern Suburban Railway line between 1901 and 1915 offering quicker improved passenger transport ultimately resulted in its progressive demise.[5]

The last time a regular passenger train used the line was in 1931, whilst the goods service carrying domestic coal traffic finally ceased in 1951, as did the last-ever passenger train that was chartered by a group of rail enthusiasts.[6]

Due to the hilly terrain along the rail line, Thorneywood station was constructed in a deep cutting immediately south of the 408 yard (353 metre) Thorneywood tunnel, which was almost one quarter of a mile in length. The station also had an extensive siding accommodation, a goods shed and a short branch line to a nearby local brickworks.[7] It is further understood that the goods yard was the busiest on the entire line and handled a full range of traffic including livestock. Today, this station and its railway tracks are long since gone, demolished and removed, and the tunnel backfilled and obscured for various residential and industrial redevelopments of the area.

However, in the 1960s and 1970s when the system was clearly no longer in use, and especially after 1951 when the line was initially abandoned, largely unsubstantiated local lore cites strange and inexplicable sightings, sounds and smells emanating from the deep cutting that housed the station, as well as the rail tunnel:[8]

> The smell of train smoke evident, the clanking of carriage couplings and steam train engine noise distinguishable, and flickering lights observed near the old platform. Occasionally, a phantom train pur-

portedly emerged at night from the mouth of the tunnel despite the entrance being enclosed with bricks. Local school boys who used the tunnel as a shortcut before its enclosure are said to have felt cold and experienced an eerie feeling whenever inside the tunnel, as if there were something sinister about the site. On one such visit, the sound of footsteps were apparent following them deep inside the tunnel yet no-one was ever detected.[9]

Of course, there could be various explanations for much of this reporting, particularly the feelings of intense cold and dread/anxiety experienced when one is deep inside a long and disused railway tunnel. This can be a most natural reaction to such a lonely and dark place located deep below the ground. Even sounds inside such an empty tunnel can become exaggerated and one's imagination may take over.

Flickering lights at night may indicate someone simply exploring the old rail line perhaps with a torch. The sounds and smells of steam trains on the disused line may be from other neighbouring rail networks which under certain weather conditions prevailing at night might be evident across a considerable distance. The phantom train appearance, however, requires some research.

So what significant and traumatic events possibly occurred in the past at Thorneywood station that may have given rise to a spectral steam train? It has been said that during World War I, wounded soldiers arrived at the station by special trains from there were transported to local hospitals, and the bodies of the fallen were transported for burial.[10] On the night of 8 May 1941, during Nottingham's worst air raid blitz of World War II, considerable damage was done in the Sneinton area immediately south of Thorneywood, with a bomb landing on the southern section of the line and blowing away an embankment.[11] The Sneinton tunnel on the Nottingham Suburban Railway was located just south of the Thorneywood station. However, although casualties around Sneinton were heavy, with 159 people recorded as killed in this raid,[12] there appeared no such issues of damage and personal injuries associated with the railway line around Thorneywood.

If the phantom train and other strange occurrences are in some way related to the earlier transportation of injured and deceased soldiers from World War I at Thorneywood station and its nearby tunnel, it remains to be seen. Given the relatively short-lived operational services at the Thorneywood station (only 26½ years), no passenger services through the adjacent tunnel after 41 years, and no recorded calamitous train accidents around this station or tunnel as a possible cause to suggest a ghostly train, the tales will probably always remain simply local lore.

Few people today would even be aware that the Northern Suburban Railway, its few stations and tunnels even existed, with scant evidence of the line remaining or still accessible and easy to recognise. The rail line's course between Thorneywood station and the Sneinton tunnel is now a footpath, the rail tracks are gone, the station demolished and the sites largely redeveloped.[13] The Thorneywood tunnel has been packed with rubble spoil from the embankment to the north of the tunnel, and its portal covered with earth.[14] All of which I would surmise renders any further appearances by a spectral steam train somewhat unlikely.

Remarkably, another somewhat longer tunnel of 662 yards (605 metres)[15] known as the Sherwood Rise Tunnel and located not far from the Nottingham Suburban Railway line, also appears to have allegedly had an inexplicable phantom presence. This new north-south rail link known as the London Extension, was opened over ten years later in 1900 by the Great Central Railway to provide an even more direct route through the centre of Nottingham, although passenger and goods traffic were actually operating on the line by early 1899.[16]

The Sherwood Rise Tunnel was perched between the stations of New Basford at its north end and Carrington at its southern end, with much of the overall railway route laid underground due to built-up areas, such as this tunnel that had to traverse Sherwood Rise.[17]

A phantom man swinging a lamp was supposedly seen in the 1950s emerging from the northern portal of the Sherwood Rise Tunnel near the New Basford station and walking a short distance along the track before vanishing. He was thought to be an engine driver killed during the 1890s.[18] However, scrutiny of train accident records for that distant historical period did not indicate any calamitous events occurred directly along this section of the line, including during the construction period of the tunnel. Indeed, any reported train-related deaths on the rail systems throughout the Nottinghamshire region rarely appear in such formal records up to the eventual closure of the line, and none identified around the Sherwood Rise area.

If the fleeting apparition was actually that of an engine driver, it was certainly unlikely to recur as use of the tunnel ceased in the late 1960s, and eventually the original cutting was infilled to the present modern day height, partially burying the northern portal that had been encased in brickwork. The tunnel mouth remains effectively sealed off and inaccessible.[19]

EERIE FOG

When one thinks about fog, several adjectives come to mind regarding this climatic phenomenon, including gloomy, murky, misty, chilly, surreal, and sometimes even creepy. The meteorological scientific explanation is quite clinical and explicit about how fog forms and what it comprises. What this explanation does not provide however is why the appearance of fog, whether over land or at sea, can generate considerable apprehension in some people. I suppose that it has much to do with the subtle manner in which some fogs can slowly develop on a clear calm early morning or on a still night, and completely envelop you. It may have something to do with the nature of fog.

Thick, dense fog banks can totally isolate you from your surroundings without providing any way for you to know when it might disperse, all whilst sending a chill through your body. A light misty fog can subtly saturate you with moisture, leaving your hair and clothing drenched in water droplets. The apprehension you feel may also have to do with the extreme quietness that you encounter once in the fog, only shattered by the diffuse sounds somewhere in the far distance, perhaps from passing traffic or other people.

I suspect that the association with mysterious 'otherworldly' or supernatural forces might have some influence on your nervousness. Countless fictional works and mythical folklore concerning spectral apparitions and ghostly phantoms describe weird mists or fogs surrounding them, or ghost ships, horse-driven coaches and horsemen looming out of such fogs. Certainly there has been a fair share of horror movies generated utilising the important suggestive powers of something evil lurking in the fog, and about to strike. So let me delve deeper into the fog and attempt to find what appears to make it so unusual.

I start with fogs out to sea that have plagued mariners for thousands of years, including the intrepid Vikings who ventured far and wide in open longboats rowed by hand. These raiders encountered dense fog banks for days on end, and records of this date as far back as the 7th century, particularly between Iceland and Newfoundland in Canada. The Vikings certainly did not have the benefit of a fog-gun fired at regular intervals from the neighbouring shoreline to warn passing mariners of the proximity of land during impenetrable fogs. For this example of sea fog, the following few incisive selected verses from the prolonged poem entitled *The Fog-Gun* in the 1839 publication *Poems written in Newfoundland* by Henrietta Prescott are provided:

> ... They drift along before the gale
> Whither, they cannot know,
> For the fog is hanging like a veil
> Around them as they go.
>
> Darker and darker grows the day,
> Louder and more loud the storm,
> The fog so dense each sailor may
> Scarce see his neighbour's form –
> The brave turn pale to think that night
> May yield them to the wild Sea's might ...
>
> ... Again! again the welcome sound,
> Nearer and nearer still!
> It cometh from their native ground,–
> The steep and well-known hill ...
>
> ... They pass at length the guarded fort;
> They pass the rocky height;
> And now, within the sheltered port,
> They're safe from Ocean's might.
> One cheer, one loud, long grateful cheer
> Bursts forth from ev'ry lip,
> As, in their welcome rest they hear

The sound that led their ship, …[1]

Unsurprisingly, the Grand Banks off the Canadian island of Newfoundland remain one of the foggiest places in the world, and of course, were amongst the most treacherous for shipping in the bygone days of sailing ships. The fogs in this area are generated by the climatic influence of a constantly shifting atmosphere above and the torrid mixing below of cold northern waters of the Labrador or Greenland Arctic current with the substantially warmer southern waters of the Gulf Stream across these relatively shallow but extensive shoals. The other scary feature about this locale is that fog banks can form rapidly in the right weather conditions, mainly during summer, and dissipate just as quickly or simply enshroud the region for days. The fog rarely penetrates inland.[2]

For some historical context, I summarise the diary comments of the Bishop of Newfoundland who opted to sail around this island in 1849 visiting his clergy and experienced the dreaded fog banks first hand. His brief sea voyage along the south-western coastline between two harbour settlements should have taken 4 hours, but by mid-morning on the first day, a thick fog descended on their square-topsail schooner, effectively shrouding the coastline entirely. Although it lifted briefly that afternoon to indicate the 70 ton (64 metric tonnes) vessel was nowhere near land, the voyage resumed but the fog returned late in day and was so impenetrable, the captain opted to stand off from the shore for the night.

The morning of the second day was calm, permitting the noise of breakers crashing on the shore to be heard through the persistent fog. Eventually, the fog lifted later that morning, only to reveal that the vessel appeared to have travelled well westwards past its intended destination, and consequently they turned around. However, they then encountered another vessel which had also gone astray in the fog. The Bishop's schooner was so far off course, and actually much further westwards along the coast than initially assumed, that they subsequently settled for another harbour which was nearest to schooner's present location. Even such a short journey turned out to be a major exercise due to the fog of the Grand Banks. The aforementioned commentary was prepared from a journal with a title almost as lengthy as my book: *Journal of a Voyage of Visitation in the "HAWK" Church Ship on the coast of Labrador and round the whole island of Newfoundland in the year 1849.*[3]

Given how lost that schooner became in the tricky fog, the following old maritime quotation seems rather sensible to me. 'If you are looking at a chart you are not looking at what you should be doing. You don't need a chart unless you don't know where you are. If you don't know where you are, you have no business being out there.'[4] Of course in modern times, detailed information on coastlines and prevailing weather conditions is tracked by sophisticated electronic monitoring tools on board, and fog banks no longer pose such a mysterious threat. On land, however, fog can be an entirely different situation, and depending upon its location, can be the perfect basis for an enthralling horror or adventure story.

If one was to take the United Kingdom as a reasonable example, it is surrounded by the relatively cold waters and inclement weather patterns of the North Atlantic Ocean, the Irish Sea and the North Sea, resulting in transient fogs around the coastal fringes at various times. These sea mists can permeate well inland before dissipating, shrouding much of the hinterland in dense fog. Many a tale has been told over time of smugglers and pirates using these passing fogs along the coast to conceal their clandestine activities of landing contraband and eluding the dreaded government 'customs/revenue officers'. One only has to look at the names of some of the local hostelries, such as Smuggler's Inn, Longboat Inn and the Bell Inn, to savour those times.

However, my next tale about sea fog was first published in 1911 by Charles K. Ober and was entitled *Out of the Fog – A Story of the Sea*. It does not concern swashbuckling pirates nor canny smugglers off the English coast, but rather two young fishermen from a fishing schooner out on the Grand Banks of Newfoundland. The trawler had a crew of fifteen and six rowboats for checking for fish on any of the six trawl lines which extended from the stern of ship 'like the spokes on a wheel'. A buoy stationed about 1 mile (2 kilometres) from the schooner marked the outer anchor of each trawl line. On this particular day and for two weeks previously, there had been no fog. Then not long after the two men started rowing away from the schooner, a massive dense fog bank descended on the area, totally cloaking everything in their proximity.

It was not a concern as the men had clearly sighted the outer buoy in the distance before the fog appeared and continued to head in that direction rather than turn back. Two kilometres seems a long way to row in a fog so thick and dense that one could not see the other rowboats in the vicinity. After rowing for their estimated time to reach the buoy, it came as quite a surprise to realise the buoy was nowhere to be seen. It certainly had not been passed, so the rowboat must have drifted off course. Still no problem really, so they decided to head back to the schooner instead, and here comes the interesting twist. In fog, it is as important to have a known point of departure as it is to know the destination point. Shouting loudly from the rowboat summoned no reply whatsoever. Rowing back towards the general direction of the schooner made no difference. Usually, a crew member on board the mother vessel was assigned to continuously ring an alarm bell in these circumstances, but the men heard no bell.

The men concluded that the fog bank was so impenetrable that any sound from the schooner was probably being blocked. This was only the start of their problems, as an exceptionally strong sea current now pulled their boat along swiftly. Realising that such fog banks can last for days, the men started to panic but needed to remain calm. The other bad news was that the rowboat they selected had no food provisions, fresh water, anchor, compass or fishing line. Could it get worse? It really depends upon your perspective. Early on the first day, they sighted a sail through the foggy mist and rowed vigorously towards it, but the vessel appeared to be sailing away from them and disappeared. This was somewhat strange, as the prevailing breeze was not strong enough for the vessel to speed away.

Shortly afterwards, the same vessel reappeared only to glide back into the fog. Despite the men hailing the sailing ship on each occasion without a response, the vessel always remained out of their reach. By early evening, the mysterious phantom ship had gone without further trace, leaving the men despondent and feeling distinctly chilly as night temperatures plummeted. The next problem to encounter was that their rowboat was leaking, requiring frequent bailing of the seawater, and making sleeping somewhat difficult.

On the fourth night adrift, they were passed by another sailing vessel which was blowing its fog horn, but as the winds were very strong, no amount of shouting would have been heard and the fog bank continued to shroud their presence. This was followed on the fifth day by an ocean steamship which also bypassed them. Occasional passing showers provided essential rainwater for drinking but only rarely, and the men remained without edible food, despite sea fowl landing on the sea around the rowboat from time to time. Strangely, these birds always remained just out of their reach, even if using a boat's oar as a club.

Once shark fins started to appear behind the drifting rowboat and pursue them, it was definitely becoming desperation time. No food also means hunger awakens the wolf in us all eventually. Between midnight and dawn of the ninth day, the fog finally lifted to be replaced by a gentle rain. Then right on dawn, as if summoned to appear, an anchored sailing vessel came into their view in the far distance. It was a French fishing brig from the English Channel and it meant rescue.[5]

I have attempted to embrace this harrowing tale as succinctly and respectfully as possible, and to the best of my ability have kept to the key elements. However, I think the following brief excerpt taken from the western classics book *The Sea Fogs*, compiled by Robert Louis Stevenson in 1907, is particularly poignant, given the previous tale: 'Even in its gentlest moods the sea salt travails [painfully difficult effort], moaning among the weeds or lisping on the sand; but that vast fog ocean lay in a trance of silence, nor did the sweet air of the morning tremble with a sound.'[6]

Of course fogs and mists can also occur over land as well. The innumerable moss bogs of the moorland regions (the 'moors'), and low-lying marshlands of other areas are subjected to frequent ethereal mists which may only rise to shallow heights above ground, but nonetheless, still create a very eerie atmosphere at times. Universal Pictures' Sherlock Holmes detective mystery movie of 1944 entitled *The Scarlett Claw* was about such a marshland terrain in French Canada. Filmed in black and white for optimum dramatic effect, the movie had the perfect setting for mysterious or unexplained happenings, including a small village ominously named La Morte Rouge (The Red Death) full of terrified inhabitants, and a legendary luminescent monster residing somewhere in the gloomy mists of the nearby marshes.

This creature had supposedly reappeared at night as a glowing apparition and resumed savaging local livestock and villagers alike, with chilling and gruesome results. Member of the local gentry Lady Penrose contacted the famous British detective and super-sleuth Sherlock Holmes by letter, desperately seeking his help, but she was viciously killed by the claws of the phantom marsh monster before Holmes arrived in the village. Although the case was finally solved by the dynamic duo of Holmes and his bumbling offsider Dr. Watson, the enjoyment of the movie lies in the great atmospheric effects of the misty marshes and the mystical phantom that roamed relentlessly therein. The following Sherlock quotation said it all: 'Consider the tragic irony: we've accepted a commission from a victim to find her murderer. For the first time we've been retained by a corpse.'

A thick impenetrable fog can become not just eerie but downright creepy when it occurs late at night in large cities, blanketing the streets, parks and even the buildings. Cast your mind back to those distant times, in the 19th century for example, when streets were illuminated using gas burners which had to be lit individually by hand, when road travel still relied upon horses and carriages rather than automobiles. The illumination from such street lights was very restricted, with long stretches of intervening darkness between lamp posts. Now add a dense shroud of chilly fog to complete the picture of a gloomy atmospheric night. Try walking along one such foggy deserted street on your own late on a calm evening in winter, leaving the comforting illumination offered by each street lamp for those dark and foreboding long stretches of road between lamps. In such a fog, each lamp resembled more a beacon than a street light, signalling the next lamp post with a hazy diffuse glow. There was no passing traffic or other pedestrians, and everything was dead quiet.

Now imagine someone approaching you in the opposite direction. In the fog, it was only a vague outline of a shadowy figure looming out of the darkness, and you could not tell if it was a man or woman at such a distance. However, the figure seemed to be strangely very low to the ground, as if hunched over or possibly crouching. As you got closer to the figure and your heart started racing, you hoped that you would pass each other directly under the next lamp post and not in the dark. By good fortune only, you did pass each other under a street light, only to realise that the oncoming person was a short woman pushing a large pram, which in the fog resembled something entirely different. There goes that wild imagination again. Just your wishful thinking at work you supposed. Time to take a very deep breath and continue on into the darkness. Must be close to your destination by now surely. Oh fear and dread, somebody else approaching and this time you would pass each other in the darkest stretch of the street.

For another old black and white cinematic thriller about the decidedly creepy effects of fog and ground mists, the 1939 movie entitled *The Hound of the Baskervilles* made by 20th Century Fox and set in the desolate moors of Devonshire in west England was electric. This Sherlock Holmes film was one of his best and superbly combines the effects of a terrifying and blood-thirsty mythical 'hound from hell' on the rampage, with the foreboding and mysterious atmosphere of the bleak moorland at night. The fog-shrouded, shadowy landscape with its many hidden swampy bogs and stark skeletal trees provided the perfect eerie, almost supernatural setting to the main story of the legendary and gigantic demonic dog in the relentless pursuit of victims. Walking alone on these moors at night in dense fog was definitely not for the faint-hearted.

Who among us have not been in some rural area of the country late in the afternoon towards say the end of autumn or in winter, perhaps for a casual stroll through the nearby forest or woodlands to soak up the ambience of the wilderness? When you first started your walk, the weather was fine and calm with no hint of a breeze, the air was crisp yet cool, and the hazy sun was low in the sky. You only intended to stroll briefly for about 15 minutes, but the intoxicating lure of the fresh air of the forest this late in the afternoon tempted you to walk on just that little further. The birdlife in the surrounding bush was frenetic as the sun started to drop below the horizon, and you felt totally relaxed meandering slowly onwards following a rough pathway perhaps trodden by countless other bushwalkers.

With dusk approaching and the forest canopy closing around you, time to turn around and head back to where you started. It was only then that you noticed a subtle wisp of mist floating through the trees ahead, with a hint of fog likely. After a few more minutes of walking and with daylight fading, the mist quickly developed into a cold fog that pervaded the forest. Now your stroll had increased to more like a brisk walk and the pathway was no longer discernible. Have I wandered off the path or was it simply that the bush seems to have closed in around me? The fog continued to increase as you progressed and air became noticeably damp and chilly. No more bird sounds were apparent in the woods as they had sensibly retired for the evening.

In the half-light gloom of dusk, the forest appeared distinctly strange in the fog, taking on an entirely different look. Individual trees seemed to loom out of the fog with stark branches that almost reached out towards you. The silence was now entirely pervasive except for the sound of your own footsteps on the ground. Surely you must be close to where you started this walk. Then, almost upon command, the forest gave way to an open paddock and you saw the twinkling lights of your dwelling subtly beckoning you in the distance. As you quickly reached the front door of your accommodation, you turned briefly to observe the thick fog bank that appeared to stop on the very edge of forest, almost alike some spectral guardian of the woodlands. You were certainly was glad that you reached home before nightfall and got out of that creepy fog.

Best to play safe when confronted by a fog, as the contemporary American writer and poet Robert Brault suggests in the following quote: 'There are moonlit nights when the dead send their ghosts to haunt us – and dark, misty nights when they come themselves.'[7]

Figure 14: The Eerie Fog (*Courtesy of Shutterstock*)

THE POSSESSED

Ghosts have been known to haunt a specific dwelling, landscape and even particular people for various reasons, including a past association with that place or relationship with that person in their previous existence, Consequently, it should not seem at all weird that said ghosts may also choose to haunt an object such as a doll. After all, a doll can be an image of a living being, and if the ghost was emotionally attached to this human figure in life, it seems a somewhat natural progression for haunting.[1] Of course, dolls can take many shapes and sizes, are manufactured from a vast array of materials and are sometimes portrayed as fanciful images of perhaps folktale or imaginary characters. The principle, however, always remains the same: to create a lifelike and lovable toy to delight and fascinate children and sometimes adults throughout the world.

I am sure that when most people thought about a doll, it usually conjured a mental picture of an adorable (usually female) and attractive figure, with a youthful baby face, large realistic eyes which opened and closed, soft hair, and probably with the ability to utter human sounds. However, there are other types of dolls which warrant a review of this description, particularly where they are more than simply toys. These are working dolls. Of this group, I include ventriloquist dolls, marionettes or puppets, and my favourite doll: the life-size mannequins. Their prime purpose is to resemble living beings for the intention of entertainment or display. If one reverts to ancient times, an archaic word to describe a doll was a *poppet* which is related to *puppet*, which could easily be expanded to encompass the preceding diverse group.[2] Now combine these dolls with the use of magic, as was so widely practised over many centuries by witches for casting spells and incantations, and we are dealing with very special figures indeed.

When an inanimate, motionless doll is provided with physical movement, for example as a puppet or when operated by a ventriloquist, it effectively appears to have 'a life of its own'. To anyone watching the performance, it would appear as if the doll was talking and moving by itself, without external assistance. Of course, unless the doll is powered by batteries or some other internal power source, such puppets do not move on their own without human intervention. In the movies, however, this can be changed to provide a very scary outcome.

One such famous horror movie titled *Dead of Night* produced by Ealing Studios in England in 1945 depicted a ventriloquist who was dominated by his theatrical doll or 'dummy' known as Hugo. In various crucial segments of the story, the dummy appeared to speak independently of the ventriloquist, sometimes even from inside its enclosed storage cabinet. The two argued and bickered about matters of little importance, ultimately culminating in some chilling and suspenseful outcomes for the viewing audience. Was this dummy actually alive and possibly possessed in some way? The unexpected haunting finale evokes a suppressed demon probably present in each and every one of us.

Now that I have your attention, it is time to share a story about repairing a damaged doll, and fortunately not a ventriloquist's dummy. It involved an unhappy child whose doll's interior mechanism had been damaged, preventing it from crying when its stomach was pressed. To address the problem and cheer-up the child, a friend offered to repair the defect, but '… instead of fastening the spring to the crying machinery, he secured it to the tongue, so that when the doll was squeezed, it ran its tongue out of its mouth instead of crying'.[3] Now what does a child do with a doll that is constantly poking out its tongue? She naturally becomes particularly annoyed and rather unforgiving.

What are the tell-tale signs that your favourite doll may be possessed? Usually if a doll has realistic glass eyes that remain permanently open, or perhaps has eyelids that open and close, then you may be in trouble. From various accounts of troublesome dolls over history, there is usually a common connection to the eyes. Some say that their doll's eyes were open when the owner left them alone, only to discover later that one or both eyelids were closed. Others reported the eyes were no longer looking forward but inexplicably had moved to look to the left or right side of the doll. Perhaps the scariest accounts mention that when one entered the same room as the doll, its eyes appeared to follow you to wherever you were in that room.

In my case, I was given a new yellow stuffed teddy bear by my mother as a child in the mid-1950s which I still proudly keep on display at home some sixty years later. I called the bear 'Ted' and because he appeared so much like a real bear, we became inseparable in my early childhood. Ted only stood about 50 centimetres (20 inches) tall on his paws, had arms and legs that moved independently of his torso, and the deepest brown glass eyes that you could imagine. The strangest thing about Ted was that no matter how or where you positioned him in a room, the bear always seemed to have moved ever so slightly when you returned to that room.

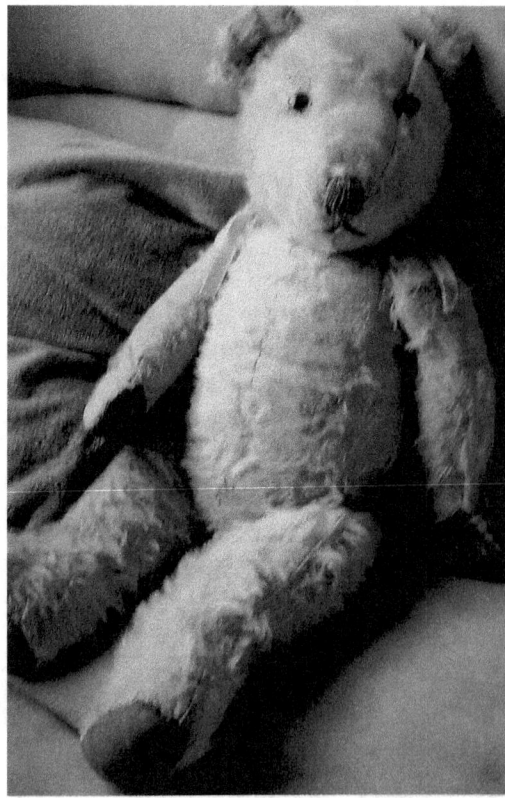

Figure 15: I Am Waiting for You

His head would to be tilted towards you when you entered the room and those piercing brown glass eyes followed your movement no matter where you stood. The bear's body parts had been lovingly repaired by hand over the years as he deteriorated with excessive handling, but somehow he survives intact to this day. I managed to retrieve Ted from the family home when my mother eventually passed away many years ago, and he remains close to my heart as always. Now Ted has a room for himself but I rarely visit him because I know that he will have moved ever so slightly yet again, and those glass eyes will be watching my every move. In bygone days, certain teddy bears were fitted with a mechanism known as a Growler, which when pressed, emitted a low but friendly growl. The purpose of the acoustic implant was probably to provide those bears with a simple means to communicate with their owners, albeit somewhat briefly.[4] These bears never growled without due pressure being applied, or so it appeared to most people.

My personal experiences differ somewhat. I found that a growl might be emitted when such a bear inadvertently toppled over. It would sound almost like a disgruntled growl, much like when someone fell over and became angry about such clumsiness. At other times, applying manual pressure to the bear with my fingers did not result in any growl occurring, despite numerous attempts. It seemed at times that the bear just did not want to communicate at all. Then again, I could have been simply imagining these matters, given my young age at the time.

Another tell-tale sign of spiritual possession of a doll can be its previous history of ownership. If the doll was inherited or procured second-hand, perhaps from a garage sale, exchange market, antique shop, it was probably unlikely that much will be reliably known about the doll. Why is this history so important? For most dolls, it does not matter at all, but for those unusual ones that come along once in your lifetime, it is critical. Take for example a doll that was previously owned by someone who was totally devoted to it but who subsequently perished or perhaps had some direct association with hauntings.

There have been stories throughout the world of nondescript dolls that have continued to exhibit inexplicable behaviour regardless of who owns them. Such stories often link the doll with a young child who owned it, sometimes dating back to over one hundred years or more. The doll may have displayed rather unusual behaviour, including becoming interactive or moving unassisted when no-one was around. The spiritual connection with the doll may be associated with the place where the hauntings originally occurred, or the paranormal activity may be directly emanating from the toy itself.

Two of the world's most famous haunted dolls include Robert, a well-worn, reputably cursed 1906 doll, and Mandy, the broken-faced baby doll from the 1920s era, both of whom have been the inspiration for successful horror movies. Rather than meticulously detail the litany of strange behaviours that plagued their respective owners, I am far more interested in the type of behaviour reportedly exhibited by a few extraordinary dolls.

Passive doll behaviour ranged from opening or shutting windows and moving furniture sight unseen, preventing cameras from working or photographs being developed of them, and other nuisance activity, through to making human sounds (including conversations), changing facial expressions or moving about without ever being observed. These activities closely resemble that of poltergeists who are intent on disturbing the living.

Active behaviour, on the other hand, could be quite confronting, with the dolls supposedly attacking their owners. Perhaps to keep this antagonism in perspective, it appears that such behaviour from a supposedly inanimate but possessed doll has more to do with one's personal beliefs and less with curses or spells. If the doll is disturbed from what it may want to do at the time, perhaps it reacts poorly.

Who has not heard of 'creepy clown dolls'? If ever there is a doll that you do not want left under your bed at night, or possibly seated in a chair and staring directly at you across the bedroom in the evening, it is a creepy clown doll.

Figure 16: Be My Friend

It would make no difference whatsoever if the clown was friendly in physical appearance or had a cheerful expression, at night everything changes and even shadows can appear sinister and almost ominous. After all, they are only lifeless dolls, are they not? The 1988 American low budget horror movie *Killer Klowns from Outer Space* by Chiodo Brothers' Productions was based upon a bizarre alien species who weirdly resemble circus clowns in physical appearance. With their permanent smiles and odd and lethal behaviour, the Killer Klowns certainly captured the essence of this phenomenon.

Another life-size doll worthy of further scrutiny is the mannequin traditionally used for displaying clothing. These dummies are manufactured to represent the human body as realistically as possible, including intricate facial features and hair, thus providing a practical way to model new clothing. They are inanimate dolls that do not speak nor move unassisted, with moulded faces that generally are expressionless. You can observe them on display throughout the world in most shop windows of fashion departments that sell clothing.

You probably walked past such mannequins virtually without even noticing them. They became part of the natural background. If one was to stop and take a closer look at a mannequin with its signature 'blank stare', it was to inspect the fashionable clothing being displayed rather than the model itself. However, every so often, you might inadvertently notice one mannequin that is unusual compared to those around it. There may be something slightly different about its facial expression, perhaps with the hint of a smile or the tilt of its head, or maybe its clothing did not appear as tidy as that of the other mannequins.

Then as you looked closer, you realised that this mannequin has probably been displayed in the wrong clothing section, or had been damaged in some way, as its clothes were dishevelled and not fitted correctly. It must be a shop assistant playing a practical joke on the customers. As you turned to walk away, you caught a faint glimpse of the mannequin from the corner of your eye, and it appeared to have moved and was now directly facing you. No, that cannot be right. You must have imagined that it was facing the opposite way surely.

Remarkably, the mannequin was now definitely smiling or did you imagine that as well? You had better get your eyesight checked out sooner rather than later, because we all know mannequins cannot move or smile, can they? Maybe it just needs some adjustment, as indicated in the following verses from the poem *My Little Doll*, about a very important doll. It was written by the Reverend Charles Kingsley in 1862 and taken from his children's novel *The Water Babies: A Fairy Tale for a Land Baby*:

> I once had a sweet little doll,
> The prettiest doll in the world;
> Her cheeks were so red and so white, dears,
> And her hair was so charmingly curled.
> But I lost my poor little doll, dears;
> As I played in the heath one day;
> And I cried for more than a week, dears,
> But I never could find where she lay.
>
> I found my poor little doll, dears,

As I played in the heath one day;
Folks say she is terribly changed, dears,
For her paint is all washed away,
And her arm trodden off by the cows, dears,
And her hair not the least bit curled:
Yet for old sakes' sake she is still, dears,
The prettiest doll in the world.[5]

For the creepiest doll in the world of the living, the voodoo doll certainly takes my award if there was ever such an accolade in the doll kingdom. The history of this type of doll is far too extensive and complex for this book, and encompasses a myriad of ancient and even modern cultures throughout the world. To be as succinct as possible, let me simply call the doll an instrument for sending a message to the spirits.

Usually the practice of voodoo involves benevolent intentions, such as overcoming illness, improving well-being or perhaps providing other blessings to protect one from harm, and is only occasionally for malevolent purposes. Why would someone wish to transmit such a message remotely? It is something to do with magic and all that such paranormal behaviour suggests. There are some fundamental rules associated with these dolls. If you encounter one, do not assume because it is made of rags, straw, wood or something as basic as moulded clay, that it is simply a doll. Use the rule of thumb that the basic model is still as powerful as a sophisticated version.

A voodoo doll is definitely not a plaything, but rather 'a symbolic living image or representation' to the spirits. Importantly, the doll is also indirectly delivering a message or sentiment. Exercise caution in handling and if in doubt, return to sender. I have no experience on these matters but the next rule seems obvious.

If it is hand-made rather than manufactured in a factory as are so many dolls today, it definitely involves a very personal message. Some of these models have unusual facial features or something else peculiar that you immediately notice. Human beings are complex but voodoo dolls are not. If the doll is possessed, you will soon know. If the doll is simply a charm or other beneficial messenger, you should relax.

The next rule is straight to the point. A human is composed of flesh and bone, and a doll is usually manufactured of inert materials, such as porcelain, plastic, clay, wood, cellulose, cloth and even rubber. So if an inanimate object like a voodoo doll is capable of inflicting some unexpected alterations to one's life, there is something else going on in the universe. As the famous English poet and playwright William Shakespeare once wrote 'There are more things in heaven and earth, Horatio, than are dreamt of in your philosophy [or learning]'.[6] Time to turn up the volume on your life. If you do come into possession of such a doll, it would be relatively abnormal.

The remaining rule is somewhat critical because it really determines if you take any of the preceding commentary seriously. If the voodoo doll was actually possessed by some spiritual force, would you believe it? Some people are always be non-believers or at the very least, sceptical of such matters. Even if there was an inkling of something weird going on, then perhaps all that misfortune or, alternatively, good fortune means something.

I recall a rather prophetic episode of the popular English BBC television science fiction series Doctor Who produced in the 1970s, in which the Doctor encountered an inert clay effigy of a small doll. Most of the time, this doll remained inactive and harmless. However, this deadly doll could certainly eliminate people efficiently. I recall when such putty-like modelling clay known as Plasticine™ was fun to use as a child, rather than being used as a potentially destructive alien force. Times have certainly changed.

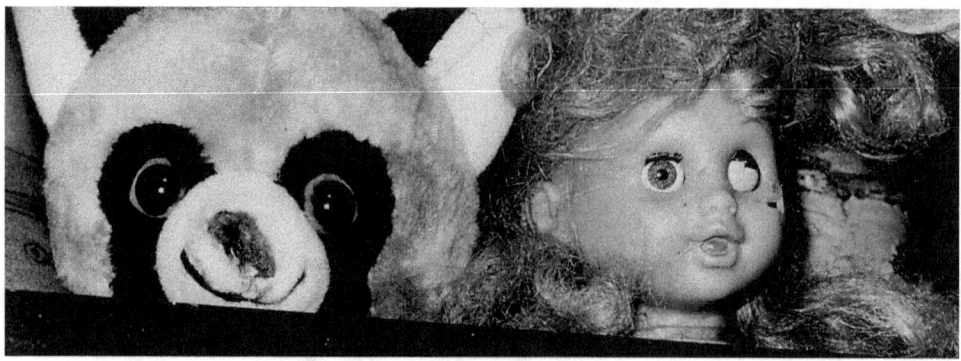

Figure 17: Strange Happenings

Perhaps one daunting thought about possessed dolls and the topic of ventriloquism may be found in the fragments of ancient Greco-Roman history by the following explanation. Unlike the usual modern signification that a ventriloquist is an entertainer who throws his voice into a sinister dummy, the original meaning from those archaic times is that of a person whose stomach is inhabited by a ghost or demon that speaks through his mouth.[7] This seems to capture my sentiments exactly. There is also another concept that such an entity may prevail between the living and the dead; an in-between wisp of existence that possesses ethereal qualities of a living spirit but lacks any physical shape or form unless within the body of an inanimate doll, mannequin or dummy. All the more reason to avoid such dolls wherever possible.

MASQUE

Most of us have at some time worn a special celebratory mask to a costume party, a masquerade ball, a Halloween celebration or perhaps even a bacchanalian local carnival. Why do we disguise ourselves for the night and indulge our senses in this unusual behaviour? One source believes it is so we can become another person or being, and that putting on the mask permits us to enter another realm or portal. Masks are shamanic tools that enable spiritual possession.[1] They are perceived as a possible means to permit us to communicate between the human and spirit worlds, as well as to appease the spirits. This is probably partially accurate, because maybe we all like pretending that we are someone else, albeit for one night. The mask provides us with that moment to become someone else.

Masks are the most ancient means within human culture for effectively changing identity, of displaying a second face/skin to the world, and probably most importantly, of disguising and transforming into something else, such as an animal, monster or freak for a range of reasons or purposes. It provides us with a new persona to behave as if we were another lifeform.[2]

Of the incredible diversity of masks throughout the world, I remain particularly interested in those symbolic creations that characterise spiritual entities, and there are an infinite variety throughout the history of human beings. People really enjoy wearing animal masks, particularly if said animal faces appear ferocious, malevolent or just plain scary. It is possibly more associated with the spirits of the animals rather than the physical depiction of wild beasts. Nonetheless, various carnivals in Europe and on the American continent do appear to focus on the masks of wild beings and monster-type portrayal of various animals.

When we think about Halloween for example, the celebratory masks usually conjure thoughts of something sinister or perhaps clandestine. They may represent ghouls, ghosts, skeletons, witches, demons or other fright-a-night characters, yet it is not about who is behind the mask, but rather what it truly represents. Halloween is all about celebrating new harvest and its change of season, as well as the supernatural spirits that assisted in such agricultural success. The ancient superstitious origins on that particular night involve the aforementioned spirits roaming the night playing pranks on the living.

To prevent this persecution by the dead, most people would supposedly disguise themselves in scary costumes and masks that were critical to this illusion. A night of transition between the past, when the souls of the deceased gather on this final night, and the beginning of a new year shared with the living ever so briefly.

The unpredictable weather in the northern hemisphere in October could also contribute greatly to the atmospheric effects on such a night. The Halloween mask certainly provided the necessary symbolic deception to fool evil spirits, particularly if it was as frightening as possible. The only limitation would be one's imagination in creating it.

For this tale about just such a mask, I relate to a particularly blustery evening on Halloween night and the usual progression of young costumed people seeking confectionary sweets in the local neighbourhood. The first small group of children arrived just before sunset and politely knocked on the front door. They were dressed as little witches and ghosts wearing bedsheets and left reasonably content with their treats. At dusk, two teenagers announced their arrival with ghoulish shrieks and howls, followed by flickering flashlights. Their masks were certainly fearsome, with skeletal hollow eyes and gruesome features. By now, a storm was brewing, with the occasional clap of thunder heralding the impending tempest. The two teenagers departed the premises well satisfied with their bounty of sweets.

I foolishly thought that the approaching storm would deter any further nocturnal visitors, and for a brief time, it was correct. Then as the rain started and the wind increased, three more teenagers knocked on the front door. One was dressed as a demon, the next as the Shadow and their companion as a beastie. Unfortunately, they were all soaking wet from the rain and keen to depart. Now the tale became creepy.

After about an hour without any more visitors, it was probably time to retire for the night. The thunderstorm had passed, the heavy rain had stopped and a full moon had appeared in the night sky. Even the gusty winds had eased. Then came a single loud knock on the front door, almost like someone thumping with a clenched fist. Before I could open the door, a second loud knock followed. To my complete surprise, when the front door opened, there was a solitary figure standing in the shadows shrouded entirely in black and almost indistinguishable in the gloom.

The visitor wore a distinctive mask that was both weird and grotesque, almost primeval. A primitive ghastly mask that had been crudely manufactured by hand with exaggerated and distorted facial features. I immediately noticed the bulging eyes that appeared to be staring straight through me, and a pronounced evil grinning expression. The visitor stood quietly, saying nothing. An awkward silence followed and I pondered, what next?

Then the visitor shuffled forward, very slowly raising one arm towards me with a beckoning open hand, as a gesture possibly for some sweets. This was not your usual nocturnal visitor on Halloween night. Could it possibly be someone or something from beyond? At first, I provided a few sweets as a courtesy, but then requested the lonely figure demonstrate a suitable prank in return for further rewards. This was a major blunder on my behalf. After pausing for a few more seconds, the visitor slowly and cautiously removed the mask to reveal who was underneath.

The unmasked face was far scarier than the malevolent façade being worn, with bizarre decorative markings, strident facial features and intense black colouration around the strange piercing eyes. With such an eerie, almost haunted face before me, it seemed that this being may not be of our world. Please, please put the mask back on. The visitor was amply rewarded with the rest of my remaining sweets and quietly glided back into the darkness. I did not answer the door again for the rest of that night.

The late American poet, novelist and playwright of the late 19th century,

Paul Laurence Dunbar, captured the moment in the first two opening verses of his poem *We wear the mask*:

> We wear the mask that grins and lies,
> It hides our cheeks and shades our eyes,—
> This debt we pay to human guile;
> With torn and bleeding hearts we smile,
> And mouth with myriad subtleties.
>
> Why should the world be over-wise,
> In counting all our tears and sighs?
> Nay, let them only see us, while
> We wear the mask.[3]

Figure 18: Look Behind The Mask

The contemporary Turkish playwright, novelist and thinker Mehmet Murat Ildan was also certainly on target when he quoted the following sentiment: 'Masks cannot change the real faces!'

Carnival masks are amongst the world's most prolific type of mask and are evident across many cultures since recorded history. The gaiety and flamboyance of these masks to depict various animals, such as bears, bulls, wolves and herd animals, or symbolic cultural characters, can also have a darker side. This may range from ritualistic parades involving the role of certain animals in legendary folklore, to the festivals of the dead, where the celebrations appease the deceased. To understand why such masks are important, one needs to appreciate their history.

Since the beginnings of human societies have tended to believe in the existence of a spirit world.[4] Ancient drawings dating back thousands of years have confirmed the process of mask-wearing across various cultures for a diversity of purposes associated with the spirit world, such as for ritualistic sacrifices, rites of transitional passage into the afterlife or for crop harvest and life cycle fertility purposes, to nominate a select few. In other instances, mask wearing may represent the appearance of strangely dressed outsiders who were considered to be visiting spirits. Tribal rock art has been known to depict such beings wearing modern helmets in some countries, akin to a technological mask to primitive peoples. Helmets came to be known as masks of the industrial culture that flourished in the early 20th century, and included protective full face, metal and fabric respirators for fire fighters or toxic gas/biological germ warfare face masks for example. The designs were stylish and highly decorative, extolling the spirit of a mechanised modern technology.[5]

In the World War 1 of 1914-1918, trench warfare was common throughout the conflict in the Europe, with soldiers on both sides often confined to a network of deep narrow trenches between physical attacks from ground troops or incessant shelling from artillery. The trenches could become rather inhospitable places, particularly after rain when extremely muddy conditions prevailed. On some occasions, it was possible for the enemy to release noxious gas known as 'sulphur mustard gas' that required Allied soldiers to wear fitted gas masks for suitable protection from exposure to such harm. This gas was used to incapacitate victims by causing debilitating burns. The safety mask usually comprised a cloth fabric to totally enclose the entire head, with two small clear circular eye-pieces for vision and a hose-attached canister of absorbent material for purifying the contaminated air. When combined with a helmet, the soldier's face was virtually obscured from anyone in proximity.

Late one particular day, three Allied soldiers were crouching in their trench when the enemy mounted a surprise attack using mustard gas. The companions were all wearing their protective canister 'masks' and survived the initial assault. Others in their trench did not fare as well and were all evacuated, leaving the three men alone in this section of trench. The men had become very close friends since arriving in Europe and looked after each other throughout the war. Shortly afterwards, on dusk, the enemy mounted a ground assault on their trench and despite ferocious fighting, one of the companions was killed and a second fellow seriously wounded. The remaining unharmed Allied soldier realised that it was time to evacuate his wounded friend before it was too late, and managed to drag him out of the muddy trench and crawl away from the intense fighting.

Despite attracting intensive enemy gunfire as they struggled through the thick soggy mud towards the next Allied trench in darkness, the brave soldier kept crawling on his stomach, relentlessly dragging his wounded comrade behind him. Eventually, by a superhuman feat of endurance, both men managed to safely reach the next trench and literally fell into it. Throughout the crisis, neither man spoke a word to the other.

Medics immediately attended to the seriously wounded soldier's injuries whilst his companion, with his face still obscured by his gas mask, sat propped against the trench wall, not speaking. Eventually, the medics turned their attention to this courageous survivor and attempted to remove his gas mask and helmet. To their astonishment, there was no-one sitting opposite them but an empty uniform, complete with a gas mask and helmet. It was as if the soldier had evaporated into the darkness, leaving only his uniform behind.

The following morning an inspection of the original Allied trench revealed the bodies of the wounded soldier's two companions, who had obviously both perished in the initial attack. Who will ever know the face behind the mask that saved one man's life under such traumatic circumstances? In the darkness of night during such a crisis, strange inexplicable things can occur that defy reason and logic, and who am I to question them?

Masks worn by the living symbolically depicting the dead or perhaps even malevolent spirits can be somewhat disconcerting in some cultures. They sometimes resemble the inner spirit too realistically for many of us.

> There is a world in which we dwell;
> And yet a world invisible!
> And do not think that naught can be,
> Save only what with eyes ye[you] see;
> I tell ye, that, this very hour,
> Had but your sight a spirit's power,
> Ye would be looking, eye to eye,
> At a terrific company! [6]

It must be appreciated that the one who resided behind the mask in many instances should remain disguised, lest in unfortunate circumstances, a truly ghastly spirit is unleashed.

One of the strangest yet most popular science fiction and fantasy cult classic movies was released in 1974 by 20th Century Fox and was entitled *Zardoz*. It featured terrifying 'exterminator' masks worn by some survivors of a future post-apocalyptic Earth, set at the close of the 23rd century. These survivors known as 'Exterminators' were literally armed savages who resided in a harsh wasteland (the Outlands), and were selected to maintain a sense of order amongst the remaining survivors known as the 'Brutals'. The remainder of the population were an elite group of 'Eternals' who were apparently immortal and lived a luxurious existence segregated from these barbaric survivors.

The striking exterminator masks resembled artefacts produced in the ancient Greco-Roman era, displaying considerable malevolent intent in their fearsome and grotesque facial expressions. Such masks were similar to the colossal masks affixed to keystones of the facades of ancient Roman temples and other buildings to honour their gods.[7] Those architectural decorations were almost straight from the Hellenic era of Greek culture around

300 BC, but reinvented for 23rd century use. The ritualistic masks were worn as an inspiration for the Exterminators, representing the symbolic image of a god-like benefactor named *Zardoz* who routinely supplied them with their weapons (in exchange for the food grown by the Brutals) to wreak their carnage. In this particular case, the mask was definitely far more terrifying than the face behind it.

Celebratory masks that effectively disguised ('guising') the wearer's identity during festivals have been popular perhaps as early as the Roman Empire around 400 AD, and possibly even as far back as pre-historic times in the case of wearing animal-head masks.[8] In Venice, where the *Carnevale di Venezia* originated in the late 13th century, this tradition of public celebration continued until almost the end of the 18th century when Napoleon's occupying government banned mask-wearing.[9] Wearing of a carnivalesque mask, perhaps with a tricorn hat, hood and cape, provided the ideal disguise for those preferring anonymity during such festivals. The addition of appropriate headwear, such as a magnificent plumage of feathers or perhaps a medieval hat, and the shrouding provided by a dark cape, always concealed the wearer's identity. To wear this costume in festival would be to terrify people who immediately associated it with imminent death.

The creepiest historical masks appear to have been the *volto* (ghost/mask) which originally covered the entire face and had no mouth, and the 'plague doctor's' mask. The *volto* could be worn with an enveloping veil known as a *bauta* usually attached to the mask, and comprising a large, black full-cut mantle extending from one's head over the shoulders to half-way down the body. Sometimes white, the *volto* made the wearer appear almost ghost-like, assisted by the addition of lots of shimmering gilding for extra effect.[10] The 'plague doctor's' mask was equally fearsome, somewhat resembling an oversized bird mask with an extended curved beak protruding well forward on the wearer's face. In reality, the hollow beak was originally intended to protect the wearer from being infected from airborne diseases such as the plague and any associated putrid evil smells. The beak would be lined with aromatic herbs to minimise potential infection and the round eye-holes covered with clear glass.

When one hide behind a mask in its various forms to disguise their identity, it was not too dissimilar to becoming invisible to others around them. In classical mythology for example, the helmet given to *Hades* or *Pluto* possessed the power to render the wearer invisible. It conferred special powers to become unseen and thus enable one to behave without any constrictions. Combine the mask with a dark hood and cape to shroud one's physical shape, and then one appeared as somebody entirely different altogether. In effect, a new *persona* has been created, and so it should not be surprising to note that in ancient Rome, the word persona actually meant 'a mask'. Of the myriad of meanings and origins across various countries and cultures, I prefer the Medieval Latin term of *masca* that translates into 'mask, spectre, nightmare'.[11]

It was the ancient Romans who used moulded wax portrait-masks of the deceased nobility or *imagines* for the tradition of tracing their ancestors. However, it was the use of masks in maintaining an element of mystery and almost spiritual power that contributed vastly to the next tale. This story concerned a most unfortunate fellow who went looking for a suitable gothic horror-mask to wear at a local county festival and found far more than his purchase price.

Hoping to discover something rather original that would impress his friends, the fellow tried the usual second-hand clothing thrift shops for his original item without any success, and was about to quit when he eventually uncovered a mask buried at the base of a shabby cardboard carton in one such shop. It looked relatively old yet unused, and had a rather creepy look about the facial features. The shop's proprietor knew nothing of the mask's history and sold it to him for a pittance.

The fellow was elated at such a treasure, for it certainly was exactly what he wanted, except that the facial features seemed almost too realistic. The forehead was frowning as if in a grimace, the mouth gaped with protruding sharp teeth and the hollow eye sockets were set well back in the face. It appeared to have a contorted expression of glaring pain and anxiety, but it would suffice. All of his friends commended him on his choice but curiously avoided him during the festival. In fact wherever he walked, people seemed to quickly move away as if not wanting any contact. After the festival, the fellow wisely decided to discard the mask as he had no further use for it and dumped it in a rubbish bin at the local shopping centre.

A few days later, as he was clearing out some old clothing from a cupboard in his bedroom, he discovered to his astonishment *that mask* hidden underneath the clothes. How could this be the same mask recently discarded? Perhaps he had not thrown it after all, but certainly would this time. The fellow immediately grabbed the mask and took it to a remote part of the local town where he threw it off a cliff. The mask floated briefly on its descent before landing in thick shrub at the base of a steep escarpment. That was surely the end of the tale.

When he arrived home, the fellow discovered the mask on his bed. Would this nightmare ever end? He next tried tearing the mask to pieces but it was made of a very durable rubber compound and resisted such attempts. The fellow even returned to the original thrift shop and offered it to the proprietor who politely refused. With nowhere left to turn, he asked his friends for advice.

The mask now proudly adorns the top of his bedroom cabinet where it shall sit *ad infinitum* until someone else ever wants to own it, which is highly unlikely given its grotesque appearance. This time around, the mask was definitely scarier than its wearer.

Throughout recorded history the true symbolic intent of wearing a mask has been to transform the wearer almost magically into something or somebody represented by the mask. The wearer shared their identity with that of the mask, connecting directly with the spirit or persona being portrayed. It revealed rather than concealed much about the wearer, who became free to act as if one with this persona/spirit. Contemporary masks, however, are used more for entertainment purposes, to disguise and conceal rather than be treated as living things. As a consequence, masks may have lost much of the sacred and symbolic meanings so important in portraying their powerful messages.[12]

HOBBINS AND BOBBINS

Everyone has experienced something that is totally inexplicable at least once in their lifetime, and for a few people, such encounters have probably been considerably more frequent. Phenomena that are beyond the scope of normal scientific understanding may be relegated to the realms of remarkable coincidence, predetermined destiny or perhaps simply a case of déjà vu, where one has a strange feeling of having been in the same situation or place before. When it comes to matters of coincidence, meeting old friends or previous acquaintances you haven't seen for many years in most unusual circumstances have to be amongst the weirdest encounters.

I had not been in any contact with a former friend for almost 15 years since leaving a small Australian country town and moving interstate, and was totally unaware of his whereabouts, until one day whilst working in a capital city. In this exceptionally rare circumstance, I had just moved into a new commercial office and was sitting at my desk while some air conditioning servicemen worked in the ceiling compartment above me. Despite not seeing either of these people, I immediately recognised the voice of one of them as my former friend who then promptly stuck his head through the open ceiling panel above to greet me, and was equally astonished. We kept in mutual contact for many years after that fateful encounter.

The next encounter borders on the bizarre, and involves an acquaintance whom I rarely saw, although we lived in the same capital city. On this occasion, I was visiting a suburban government office for only the second time, and not long after it had opened for the day. As I walked into the entrance foyer, another person followed me into the building and stood directly behind me in the short queue awaiting service. I did not turn around nor speak at any stage whilst in the queue, and was eventually served by counter staff. The person who had been standing behind me then approached and to my amazement, I realised it was the same acquaintance. Had it been an hour earlier or later, on a different day or even at a different office in another nearby suburb, there would have been no encounter at all. A strange coincidence of sorts no matter how one considered it.

As I was to discover later, this was more than simply a coincidence, as the acquaintance later fell gravely ill a few weeks later and was unlikely to ever recover. This rare meeting as it resulted was indeed very fateful.

My remaining example is about an unlikely encounter that appears to be almost pre-determined to occur. It could be with a complete stranger who astonishingly advises you with the precise information you were seeking about a matter. For example, you are on foot and have become lost in the crowded streets of a foreign city seeking an obscure address and are unable to communicate in the local language. Out of the masses a stranger appears who actually speaks your language and directs you precisely to your destination, removing any likelihood of becoming lost again. It almost seems as if that person was somehow sent to assist you out of your frustrating dilemma. Before you can thank the stranger for the help, the person has melted back into the crowd and gone.

If one is seeking answers to such peculiar matters, I think a very useful starting point would be the popular supernatural myths and traditional rustic folklore embraced by various generations. Sometimes fictional matters may originate from a basis of fact rather than simply from a vivid imagination. For the ultimate tricksters and mischievous spirits capable of dealing humans some unusual twists, what about hobgoblins and bogies (also known as bogles, bug-a-boos or boggarts)? Goblins on one hand are traditionally thought of as evil and malicious spirits, with a grotesque appearance, but hobgoblins (household or countryside goblins) are more akin to a tribe of friendly spirits who present as kindly, beneficent and only occasionally mischievous spirits. On the whole, they are good-humoured and ready to be helpful, but are fond of practical joking and rather nasty to annoy.[1]

Figure 19: Up Close and Personal (*Courtesy of Shutterstock*)

Bogies, bogles, bug-a-boos and boggarts are names given to a whole class of mischievous, frightening and even dangerous individual and solitary spirits whose delight it is to torment mankind. Some bogies can be malicious and fiendish, whilst bogles are mischievous but relatively virtuous creatures choosing not to be malevolent, and the bug-a-boos or boggarts are the most harmless of all.[2] The boggart is almost exactly like a poltergeist in his habits, whereas the bug-a-boo is regarded more as a nursery bogie to scare children into good behaviour.[3]

According to various folklore, hobgoblins are often found within human dwellings and associated with human activities, which could go some way to explaining their mischievous habits. If these fanciful pranksters really existed, such impish sprites would certainly have gained considerable enjoyment out of organising unexpected reunions (such as my experiences between people where anything could eventuate), and from watching the people involved puzzling over the reason for such a bizarre meeting at all. Contemporary American writer and poet of thoughts and observations Robert Brault certainly raised a doubt in the following quote: 'I don't know that there are real ghosts and goblins, but there are always more trick-or-treaters than neighbourhood kids.'[4] Could a few of these tricksters actually be something other than children?

So what special tools does the goblin of the hob or 'the household goblin' possess? As a prankster, it was quite capable of making ordinary inanimate objects, such as furniture, windows, doors, crockery and pictures, move without any explanation; it could set dogs howling and cats screeching, or change shapes to appear disguised as a person or animal. As a terrifying bogie, it could wreak havoc and fear in many with very little effort. Fortunately, this was all folklore and supposition. The best way to describe their behaviour is by the following simple tale.

Have you ever misplaced an item and searched relentlessly for it without any success, only to have it appear in the most obvious place? Sometimes you knew that you checked that particular place and the item was definitely not there at the time, or perhaps it really was after all. This tale involves a bag of glass marbles and a small boy who was on a picnic in the countryside with his mother.

After eating, the boy wanted to go exploring and left his precious bag of marbles beside the picnic hamper with his mother in case he might lose them. When he returned, the marbles were no longer there, and despite an extensive search of the area, remained missing. His mother had not been out of sight of the picnic hamper at any stage whilst the boy was exploring. On their way to the bus stop, the boy suddenly decided to return to the picnic site, exclaiming 'They *are* there, I must go and get them.' He ran back the half-mile (800 metres) and retrieved them, shouting 'Here they are, Mummy, and *two* new ones!' The mother subsequently explained that '... I have heard it is a tricksy place, where everybody loses something'.[5]

If one needed to look further than the mischievous 'Hobbin and Bobbin' fictional spirits of folklore and superstition for a suitable explanation, then it may be found in the supernatural and spiritual messengers from outside of our physical material world. Such messengers were believed in some ancient cultures to harness the necessary supernatural forces to communicate with us, and perhaps the examples provided earlier were such subtle messages from beyond. So who or what are these messengers that choose to orchestrate these 'coincidental meetings' between people?

They simply have too many names across various cultures and countries and throughout history for just one book. Spirit guardians, guides, or even deceased relatives may be responsible if one truly believes sufficiently enough. However, who is really to ever know if such odd encounters are merely coincidental or pre-determined destiny? Without venturing any further along this path, I would prefer instead to reflect on an ancient mythical entity/elemental spirit in folklore known as the will-o'-the-wisp (Willy Wisp): the luminous phenomena known as spirit lights.

What makes this ethereal spirit so interesting is its physical appearance is only indicated by a strange ghostly flickering light at night that is difficult if not impossible to approach. Try as you may, each time you reached out to grasp this flickering light, it always moved further away from you and usually disappeared. The simplest explanation of this entity is that of a natural eerie atmospheric glow-light seen at night over certain bogs, swamps and marshes.

The various causes attributable by modern science to this phenomenon can be quite complex, and include the effects of accumulated marsh gases, bioluminescence of microorganisms, spontaneous combustion of gases or geological origins to name a few.[6] Spontaneously combustible gas arising from the decaying matter usually plentiful in marshes and boglands, as well as some cemeteries, seems to have been the most popular reason attributable to the naming of these 'flickering corpse candles'.

However, I much prefer the folklore aspect to this strange glow. A will-o'-the-wisp is believed in some cultures to use this strange flickering light almost like a lantern to lure unfortunate travellers into the night, then leave them to their demise in pitch darkness in the marshes by extinguishing the light.

> How Will a' wisp misleads night-faring clowns,
> O'er hills, and sinking bogs, and pathless downs.[7]

So if such a spirit exists, was it considered malicious or perhaps simply creating harmless mischief for people? The probable answer lies in the story. Spooky lights and eerie unnatural glows in the night are certainly a great indicator of something weird. Add an ample dose of superstition and imagination then sprinkle it with the gloomy misty atmosphere often found hovering over swamps and marshes, and you have the right answer.

However, if you ever do find yourself lost in the woods at night and a strange flickering glow-light beckons in the distance, head in the opposite direction, just to be sure. After all, those will-o'-the-wisps can be somewhat unpredictable to say the least. Sometimes this lantern-bearing sprite simply gambols [frolics] and dances by itself in swampy meadows and bogs, or:

> Hovering and blazing with delusive light,
> Misleads th' amaz'd night-wanderer from his way
> To bogs and mires, and oft through pond or pool,
> There swallow'd up and lost, from succour [assistance] far.[8]

An interesting opinion amongst others about these mysterious beings commonly identified in folklore was that they could be restless spirit masqueraders, that in the past, we called fairies, elves or nature spirits. These entities or 'in-between beings' have interacted with humans for centuries by appearing in many guises to deceive humankind about the truth that they are phantoms. From time to time, these entities may even pose as humans, visiting us possibly from other parallel dimensions; intruding into our world from a universe that may almost be a mirror image of our own.[9] This is probably a difficult viewpoint to substantiate, but certainly raises many intriguing possibilities.

THE SCARECROWS ARE WATCHING

They mostly resemble people, they stand patiently forever in open fields or enclosed paddocks to protect precious arable crops from avian predators, and they always remain silent. That is what makes scarecrows so scary. No matter how carefully you constructed them, the face always seemed to have different expressions than you originally intended. Sometimes the expressions even appeared to change ever so slightly with the seasons.

A scarecrow spends endless days standing perched against a pole in the sweltering heat, chilled by the cold, drenched by the rain, pelted by hailstones, buffeted by strong winds and wild storms, covered by frosts and snow, and of course, hounded by those pesky birds. A scarecrow is supposed to be a deterrent, a decoy, a trickster for the ravenous birds, but nobody informed the birds. Why do birds insist on perching on a scarecrow's head, shoulders, arms or meticulously extracting the straw from the scarecrow one piece at a time? The war between the decoy and the predator is relentless.

The opening verses to the 1925 poem *The Hollow Men* by the English poet TS Eliot provides a great indication of these straw men:

> We are the hollow men
> We are the stuffed men
> Leaning together
> Headpiece filled with straw. Alas!
> Our dried voices, when
> We whisper together
> Are quiet and meaningless
> As wind in dry grass

Or rats' feet over broken glass
In our dry cellar

Shape without form, shade without colour,
Paralysed force, gesture without motion; ...[1]

A scarecrow is that which frightens without doing any physical harm. The more terrifying the straw man (hay-man), supposedly the more likely it will be to discourage ravenous birds from farm crops. To become such a fearsome spirit, scarecrows probably need faces with stark and gaunt features, or perhaps more subtle features like large wide eyes, a long nose, a stitched mouth and a grimacing expression or menacing frown.

It is likely that that most birds are probably not frightened in the least by such faces, and that they were constructed more to satisfy the farmer's wishes. The body shape and extremities of the scarecrow and its stance can best produce a far more threatening attitude to those pesky scavengers. If one assumed at least some birds may be deterred by the presence of a motionless and silent figure standing in the field, then scarecrows with arms horizontally extended only really provide the ideal perch for those birds for landing and observing the crop about to be devoured at close quarters.

If you have an inherent fear of scarecrows, it may be preferable to avoid the tiny Japanese village of Nagoro located in the rugged mountain landscape of the southern island of Shikoku, with a shrinking human population of fewer than 35 but a scarecrow presence of 350. Not only are they found throughout the village and its surrounds, but also occupy an abandoned school where they sit at their desks and stare at their lifeless scarecrow teacher.[2] It has become an eerie village on the edge of replacing its entire aging population as they die or relocate with life-sized, scarecrow-like mannequins. They seem to be everywhere, huddled in the bus stop, in the streets, outside of shops, on fences and roadsides, in houses and the trees, and even greeting you entering the village.

For those who enjoy being surrounded by scarecrows, an even better place to visit would have been the world's largest recorded gathering of scarecrows—3812 of them. The event was held at the National Forest Adventure

Farm (UK) in Burton-upon-Trent, Staffordshire on 7 August 2014.[3]

Of course, although scarecrows have been most successful for bird scaring since ancient times, a raft of modern alternatives have progressively replaced this benign straw man. These include a vast array of visual and auditory technological devices, selective use of live animals and chemicals, and even computer-activated, pop-up scarecrows complete with a propane gas gun. Not to worry, the original is still the best for sheer creepiness and the maximum eerie effect. Even though they are usually made of disused clothing carefully filled with straw, grass or wool, a crossbar for arms, and a head made from hessian sacking or a pillowcase, with an old hat flopped on top, the scarecrow always appears to assume a persona of its own. Supported on a wooden post or pole in the middle of a field, or simply propped against a fence, the scarecrow rises out of the surrounding ground almost like a phantom spectre.

For the more daring, a scarecrow's hands protruding from its clothes can be made particularly stark and bony by using thorny bare sticks for fingers, the face can be gaunt and strained by clever use of tucks and folds, and the expression made piercing and ominous by inserting dark, lustrous or reflective shiny eyes. The protector of crops is known by many unusual names throughout the United Kingdom, such as a *Hay-Man* (England), a *Tattie Bogle* (Scotland), a *Gally-bagger* (Isle of Wight), and just to be different, a *Bwbach* (Wales).[4] The definition of the Bwbach from Celtic mythology is that of a Welsh supernatural creature, a solitary fairy or ghost who may be helpful, mischievous or awesome, a primitive spirit of nature.[5] Strangely, the term also describes a bogy as well as the scarecrow, suggesting the ability to frighten and that is what most scarecrows do well.

is the term that describes a scarecrow on the Isle of Wight[6], the largest island in England and located some six kilometres off the southern coast. However, unlike the *Gally-bagger* whose role is to frighten away birds from the crops, in British folklore there is also a *Galley-beggar* that translates to a frightening/scary ghostly apparition;[7] a hazy, glowing and headless figure in the darkness. The *Galley-beggar* has been described as a ferocious, headless skeleton apparition which originates from the Somerset and Suffolk regions.

It has a scream capable of freezing a man where he stands, and seems to exist for the sole purpose of terrifying anyone who sees it.[8] If that does not get you shivering, then perhaps the following tale might suffice. It was reported that a *Galley-beggar* with a sense of humour and a most unusual pastime would toboggan on a simple sled down a hill between two villages in Somerset in South West England. He is described as follows: '...his head tucked firmly under his skeletal arm and shrieking with laughter. It was only on dark nights that he rode, but a strange light surrounded him, and he would slide, yelling with laughter ...'[9] He sounds very much to me like an entity to be avoided.

When one shifts to other languages defining a scarecrow, the translation seems to lose its scary appeal somewhat. Other names for scarecrow are *vogelscheuche* (German), *épouvantail* (French) *espantapájaros* (Spanish) or *fågelskrämma* (Swedish). Regardless of languages, the scarecrow certainly embodies the raw spirit of its creation; to protect crops by any means.

The one consistency about these straw men is that they are unable to walk and simply stand in the fields with outstretched arms to scare the scavenging birds. When I was about eight or nine years of age, I recall my mother taking me to a farming property slightly more than a mile (two kilometres) from where we lived to collect some fresh produce. As we did not have an automobile in those days, it was a very long walk. On this property, the farmer had erected a solitary scarecrow in the middle of his largest paddock surrounded by rows and rows of vegetables.

From all accounts, this scarecrow worked well, as there was virtually no evidence of any crop damage from the local birds. However, when it came to crop destruction the local rabbits were apparently a different story. Nonetheless, a scarecrow can only do so much. With not much to keep me interested on the farm, I decided to trudge out in the paddock on my own to inspect this scarecrow at close quarters and found it particularly daunting and somewhat fearsome. To describe it as sinister in appearance would be complimentary at best.

It had obviously been attacked by birds at various times and bore the damage inflicted by their persistent sharp beaks and talons, somewhat like battle scars. These included numerous small ragged tears in the clothing and in its hat, loose strands of straw dangling from its various body parts, and one arm strangely contorted, almost as if scarecrow had tried to swat the birds like a person does with annoying flies. However, it was the weird expression on the scarecrow's face that caught my attention immediately. It was more like a grimace than anything else. It made me think that this scarecrow had been through some serious bird attacks. I returned to the farmhouse and asked the farmer why there was only one scarecrow in such a substantial paddock to protect so many crops? He slowly turned towards me and responded very quietly that he had only ever needed one scarecrow because this one was special. I enquired about what made this one so special? Surprised by my insistence for answers, he replied that he would tell me, but requested that it be kept secret, otherwise people would think that he was crazy.

His explanation was that no matter where the scarecrow was initially positioned in the paddock, a few days later it would be found elsewhere around the field. Sometimes it was towards the extreme ends, other times along the fence line or perhaps only a mere few metres away from its original location. The farmer added that, eventually, he did not bother to ever return the scarecrow to the middle of the paddock as it appeared to be protecting his crops so well across the entire field, and had left it to continue to do so. I took this comment to mean the scarecrow knew best. It was a very long time ago and of course, I was a young and impressionable boy with quite an imagination, but that explanation certainly seemed plausible to me. Given the healthy crops in that paddock, who was I to ever doubt the paranormal abilities of the grimacing scarecrow?

Very few important occupations would be as lonely as that of the scarecrow that traditionally stands alone in the fields, continually exposed to the harsh unforgiving extremes of the weather until eventually succumbing to the elements and finally disintegrating. A fitting tribute simply entitled *Scarecrow* is provided to illustrate one's feelings about such forlorn spirits:

Scarecrow, oh scarecrow
lonely you must be,
forced to scare away
your only company.

Out in the open
surrounded by fields of ears,
but no-one to see you smile
or hear you cry your tears.

Now your clothes are only tatters,
your bounty almost grown,
but the only thing that matters,
is you spend your time alone.[10]

So much doom and gloom about the forlorn, lonely straw man makes you wonder whether there were some less frightening versions who simply enjoyed their job. The diversity of scarecrow construction—often from simple and reusable materials—around the world is almost worthy of a separate book. Many wear disused apparel to represent the appearance of a person in various guises, whilst other versions may simply be more basic models of a scary figure. For those with a spirited sense of humour and creative skills, the scarecrow may take on a mischievous even comical look, not that the birds would ever notice or care.

Figure 20: The Lonely Scarecrow (*Courtesy of Shutterstock*)

Has anyone ever wondered what a scarecrow does at night after all those pesky birds have departed for the day? With no birdlife to frighten, a scarecrow must have considerable free time on its outstretched hands. Perhaps the scarecrow uses the night to repair any damage to its body inflicted by the random bird attacks, or simply adjusts its clothing to retain some appropriate dignity, or just prepares for the following day's onslaught. Perhaps if there are any other scarecrows nearby in the same field, it may communicate with them about the day's events. It may even scan the crops in the field to select a better location to scare the birds. How would we know what a scarecrow does at night, as most likely almost all of us would be asleep anyway.

This tale, as related to me by an acquaintance, involved a night spent researching the nocturnal activities of a scarecrow in a field of crops long since left by the local landowner who had relinquished his property. The crops had been left to perish due to a severe economic downturn in the region, and consequently, the local birdlife relentlessly feasted on the remaining live plants. Surprisingly, the resident scarecrow remained unscathed as the birds focused entirely on decimating the crop each day.

The acquaintance spent the earlier part of the evening with virtually nothing to do as the scarecrow remained completely inactive, as one would expect. Not a sound nor movement could be detected in the field, other than the crackling noise caused by the acquaintance trampling over the layers of dry dead crops underfoot. Perhaps this was all a waste of time after all.

Sometime after midnight on that cloudless night, a slight gentle breeze commenced and the sound of the rustling of leaves of the dead crops became only just distinguishable. Patience was going to be required now as the night hours passed. With dawn approaching in a couple of hours, the acquaintance noticed that something strange was underway. The slight breeze wafting through the field had now ceased entirely, yet the rustling sounds persisted. Could it be the sounds of rodents or insects feeding on the fallen crops accumulated around the scarecrow? A visual inspection in the darkness identified no movement or any sign of rodents or insects scurrying around on the ground. Who or what was causing these incessant sounds?

By listening intently to the rustling sounds in the darkness, the acquaintance subsequently recognised it to be murmuring; an almost indistinct whispering of discontent. There were no discernible words but rather a subdued grumbling, much like someone who quietly expressed dissatisfaction under their breath. Could it all be in one's imagination given the lateness of the hour and a lack of sleep?

Over the remaining hour before dawn, the rustling sounds progressively decreased and then suddenly stopped as soon as the daylight returned. With the departure of the darkness of the night, and the resultant glare of broad daylight, the silence was only broken by the clatter of birds descending on the field, and of course, the sounds of insects foraging through the stricken crops. Back to work for Mr Scarecrow.

The acquaintance provided an interesting twist to his nocturnal story about the grumbling scarecrow just to add some more flavour to his tale. Although he could not confirm it due to the thick layers of crop debris underfoot, the acquaintance was convinced that the scarecrow had possibly moved ever so slightly from its original location in the field, perhaps contributing to some of the discernible rustling noise. I agreed that this story was best left to one's imagination, as I was certainly not ever going to share a night with that old Mr Scarecrow.

You probably did not need to be superstitious about scarecrows to enjoy them, but it certainly would not go astray. Sometimes it provided you with a distinct advantage should you encounter the next unfortunate situation. It is a tale about a lone farmer who started constructing a few scarecrows to preserve his crops from the voracious birds, and continued to make more and more, just as a pastime. Eventually, each field had several of the straw figures, all slightly different in appearance with perhaps a cap, hat or no hat, and dressed in various old discarded clothing.

The farmer then added more of them around his isolated property, including beside the farm buildings and his cottage, standing under various trees and even one to greet any visitors at the front entry gate to the farm. To any outsider, it would seem that the farmer was obsessed with these scary sentinels, but living a solitary and lonely life, he craved company and I can only suppose that these artificial figures provided such comfort.

Given the remoteness of the place, it was quite rare for anyone to visit, but on this occasion, a traveller who was seeking directions to a nearby town arrived at the front gate on dusk in winter. As this visitor entered the property and drove his car along the long winding track towards the farmhouse, he could not avoid noticing in the evening gloom how many scarecrows were located along the route. These shadowy figures were probably every twenty to thirty metres apart and positioned along both sides. Each was facing the track and glaring intently in his direction. Upon reaching the farm cottage, the traveller was greeted by the farmer and, given the lateness of the day, was invited to stay overnight. This invitation was willingly accepted as the visitor was extremely exhausted from his travels and very unsure of safely driving any further at night in the wintery conditions. It was a night of passing rain showers and blustery wind. Not a night for travelling on remote, unlit country roads.

After parking his car in the nearby barn, the visitor noticed two more scarecrows at the entrance to the building, almost acting like a pair of vigilant silent guards. They were simply everywhere on the property. A hearty country meal was enjoyed by the farmer and his visitor, who then settled in the cottage lounge room around a warming log fire in an open brick hearth. It was around this time that the visitor noticed that there was a scarecrow positioned outside each window of the lounge. Strangely, they all appeared to be peering through each window. When questioned about this unusual arrangement, the farmer simply dismissed the inquiry stating that 'all these scarecrows were his friends.' As the evening progressed, the shadows generated by the flickering flames of the open fire created a remarkably eerie atmosphere around the lounge room. All the visitor noticed at this time were those staring faces with dark sinister eyes at each window. It would be a very long night.

As it was getting rather late, both men retired to their respective bedrooms for the night and the wintery conditions deteriorated, with a howling wind and frequent heavy downpours of rain. The windows and doors rattled incessantly and the cottage timbers creaked intermittently from the force of the wind. These were not the only noises evident through the night, but in any stormy weather dwellings tend to make strange, inexplicable sounds. The visitor tried to sleep but something kept him awake most of the night. It was his enduring thoughts about those uncanny menacing looks on the faces of each of the scarecrows. By morning the inclement weather had passed and the day dawned with clear sunny skies. The farmer was nowhere to be found and the visitor assumed that the man had probably gone out early to tend his crops in the fields.

After retrieving his car from the nearby barn, the visitor noticed the scarecrows were no longer at the building's entrance, perhaps blown away by the strong and gusty winds. However, as he drove along the winding track to leave the property, there seemed to be far more scarecrows dispersed along the route than when he first arrived. He was probably mistaken about the original number as it had been on dusk and he was very tired, so maybe his imagination had simply played tricks on him. After he passed through the farm's front gate, the visitor glanced in the car's rear view mirror and to his astonishment noticed a scarecrow now standing on either side of the gate entrance. There were two scarecrows instead of the one solitary scarecrow that had initially greeted him upon arrival. There was no mistake about that observation. He drove on at an increasing speed and did not look back again.

MOMENTARY RESPITE OF SILENCE

Imagine you were on a passenger jet being buffeted by a turbulent storm late at night, lashed by rain and shocked by spontaneous bolts of lightning. Your fellow passengers were nervous and exceptionally quiet, whilst you were downright terrified. The plane bucked and thrusted through the incessant turbulence, flexing, straining and twisting seemingly every rivet and panel. The chief pilot assured the passengers everything was fine and the bumpy ride would be over soon, overlooking the fact that he had already stated the same wishful thought 30 minutes earlier. You were gripping the seat's armrests as if riding in a roller-coaster in a fun park and fellow passengers were doing the same. How much longer would this last?

Suddenly the jet took a rapid descent ever so briefly and then the pilots eventually regained control. By now, you were not the only one turning a whiter shade of pale and perspiring profusely. Why did you take the late flight when you could have been sleeping soundly in a comfortable bed on the ground? As the plane ploughed on through the night and the tempest, it occurred to you somewhat vividly that we all have a limited time for our lives and that this journey was certainly not helping this experience. In this period of thoughtful reflection, you suddenly realised others onboard were also very pensive, perhaps realising that time was ultimately running out for all of us.

Why did the plane not climb to higher altitude above the inclement weather or perhaps even return to the airport? Almost instinctively, the chief pilot announced that 'we could not turn around now as our fuel would not suffice and we were not far from landing at our scheduled destination'. You immediately wondered if his definition of the term 'landing' meant the same as your definition. Worry continued unabated as did that period of total silence amongst the other worried passengers.

The plane started its descent as an announcement was broadcast in a booming voice that passengers needed to prepare for landing by returning to their seats and fastening their seatbelts, as if we have all been frolicking like new-born lambs in the aisles during the flight. Everyone tightened their respective seatbelts as if they were in a spacecraft preparing to crash-land on a strange alien planet. The lights of the airport below became visible through the clouds, although the plane continued to twist violently from side to side through the turbulence. This was going to be a rough landing, and you crossed fingers just as an extra precaution.

The silence amongst fellow passengers was overwhelming, with not even the mildest whimper discernible as the airport tarmac loomed. Finally you touched Mother Earth, albeit in a series of bumps and bangs as the plane grasped the tarmac and the lightning cracked one more final time as if ceremoniously announcing our safe arrival. As we taxied toward the arrivals terminal, a brief announcement was made over the plane's sound system affirming that we had arrived safely and the silence was forever broken by a communal sigh of relief. What were you so worried about? Next time, however, you would drive even though it would the entire day. After all, life can be far too short.

For a similar tale with a markedly different outcome, the episode entitled *Nightmare at 20,000 Feet* from the incredibly popular 1963 science fiction television series The Twilight Zone would take some beating.[1] It also involved a plane journey through a storm at night, only in this instance, one of the passengers had just spent the past six months recovering from a complete nervous breakdown. The man's breakdown occurred during his last flight under near-identical conditions, so this journey already presented him with considerable anxiety. Once the flight was underway and the storm increasing, the passenger noticed something very peculiar out on one of the plane's wings that appeared to be tearing pieces off the aircraft.

Despite alerting the crew and other passengers to this weird creature that appeared to have landed on the wing, he was unable to convince anyone else of its presence. Their silence and scepticism about his outrageous claims became overwhelming for him. It appeared as if only he could see this winged gremlin-creature that moved freely outside of the aircraft even at this altitude. Each time others tried to detect the creature, it simply disappeared from their view. Convinced that he was now suffering the onset of another breakdown and behaving somewhat hysterically, the frustrated passenger desperately attempted to prevent the 'imaginary' creature from further damaging one of the aircraft's engines. He smashed a cabin window to reach the gremlin and prevent certain disaster, only to have it directly confront him face-to-face, whereupon he was able to shoot it.

The plane was forced into an extreme emergency landing because of the intense cabin de-pressurisation caused by this passenger's bizarre behaviour. In a final twist to the tale after landing safely, the distraught passenger was taken to a medical facility in an ambulance amid concerns for his mental state. However, this was followed by the last haunting scene of the episode showing the wing of the grounded plane concerned with considerable metal peeled off or torn away from around the engine. Better late than never, as the saying goes, for this flight's final destination.

Total and prolonged silence in certain circumstances can be particularly daunting for some individuals, including myself. Take the very early hours of the morning after midnight, for example, when the passing traffic noise in the local neighbourhood becomes virtually nonexistent, likewise the shrill clatter of the local birdlife non-existent, and most people are deep in slumber. If the weather is calm with no breeze to disturb the nearby trees or rattle your windows, it can be a time when even the slightest noise inside your dwelling is magnified. Perhaps this slight noise is a house clock chiming occasionally, a dog barking somewhere in the far distance, or even the building in which you are sleeping creaking as the timber expands/contracts in hot or cold temperature climates. So what could awaken someone from such a peaceful sleep when the silence is almost blissful?

Sometimes the total uninterrupted silence was so prolonged, I might awaken late into the night and wonder if the entire world was asleep. Then, the daily newspaper delivery van shattered my solitude as it arrived around 4 a.m. in the morning to cast a rolled newspaper into my driveway with what seemed a thunderous jolt. Not being the only one awake at such an early hour may be reassuring for some. In those few quiet hours between midnight and dawn, when most of the people living in my region were asleep, my mind was also at rest and untroubled by life's routines. It could be a thoughtful time to reflect upon many things without unnecessary distractions. Then without any warning, there were two loud distinctive knocks as if someone has just knocked twice on my front door in rapid succession. But my front door is downstairs and I could not possibly have heard knocking from my bedroom on the second storey. Who could possibly be at my front door at that early hour?

Then I realised that the knocking sounds actually appeared to originate from inside the bedroom and in reasonably close proximity to me. I lay still, patiently anticipating more knocking to follow. It did not eventuate and I slowly drifted off to sleep. In the harsh light of the morning, I decided that it had all simply been in the imagination and there had been no loud noises.

However, a few weeks later on a calm night and at a similar time between midnight and dawn, two more loud knocks were heard in my bedroom. Someone or something was trying to communicate and I was now listening with both eyes wide open. Several weeks later around 2 a.m. and again on a calm still night, I lay awake and clearly heard around six loud knocks in quick succession, as if something was trying very urgently to attract my attention. This was far more persistent than experienced on previous occasions but did not ever recur. Quite a conundrum to solve.

The following story originated from the county of Hertfordshire immediately north of London in southern England in late 1967. It is about a lone male road traveller who usually undertook a uneventful short car journey between the homes of his immediate relatives. The weather was mild and it was late in the evening as his car approached a T-Junction and yet started to slow down despite his best efforts. No matter how much he tried to control the vehicle's steering wheel and accelerator, the car continued to slow as if seemingly controlled by an overpowering force, and almost came to a halt. Already exasperated, confused and feeling helpless by what had just happened, the driver could only watch in disbelief as an oncoming car approached from the left side of the T-Junction, which was hilly and steep. This car sped downhill across his direction of travel, and surely would have collided with him had it not been for his car slowing. Immediately afterwards, his car's controls returned to normal.

Upon regaining his composure, the driver then resumed the journey, but upon approaching a distant crossroad a few minutes later, the vehicle started to slow yet again regardless of what he did. The car would not respond to anything that the driver tried, as if he had lost all control to some mysterious intervening force. To his amazement, just before his car reached the crossroad, a large truck sped through the intersection without warning and definitely would have collided with him had he kept his original speed.[2]

Now he experienced that eerie silence of intense thoughtfulness that one incurs when cheating death twice in such a very short time. Something had slowed his car sufficiently to avoid two separate collisions on the same night and had thus prevented him from perishing. The driver was unable to explain such a weird and shocking experience, and perhaps most importantly, was unable to comprehend what unknown force had been temporarily controlling his vehicle on that night.

Perhaps the following variation of the rhyme from William Shakepeare's *Midsummer's Night Dream* may provide some comfort:

> Over hill, over dale,
> Through bush, through brier,
> Over park, over pale,
> Through flood, through fire,
> I do wander everywhere. [3]

ENCOUNTERS OF THE ANIMAL KIND

There have usually been many memorable and unusual encounters with animals for most people, because animals are relatively unpredictable. The encounters that interest me significantly are when you enter the animal realm to share their view of the world, and thus become part of that reality. Given the extreme diversity of animals on this planet, it would not be unreasonable to assume that even animals might experience paranormal circumstances, given the right conditions.

Sensory perceptions of certain species are far superior to those of mere humans and consequently, these species could be highly sensitive to outside influences that we simply do not notice. Domesticated dogs and cats that share our everyday lives can exhibit almost psychic abilities when exposed to the right situations. They instinctively recoil from some strangers and become overtly friendly towards others. Cats in particular have been known to do the strangest things without reason or explanation, yet to them, it appears most appropriate. There is probably much we still have learn from animals as to why they react to situations which we may find simply unimportant.

My most memorable encounter with 'an animal' is without doubt something that would fill most of us with a shivering dread. It involved one of the world's most primordial creatures, the Australian saltwater crocodile (*Crocodylus porosus*), the largest of all living reptiles and one of the most frightening riparian/marine predators. These prehistoric survivors usually have a lifespan of around 70 years with few natural enemies to disrupt their lives. This is predominantly due to their scaly protective armour, and in Australia they have been proclaimed as a protected species since the early 1970s to prevent their eventual decimation by crocodile hunters. As a consequence, such predators have been known to grow to enormous lengths, upwards of five metres.

Although their preferred habitat is in the tropical regions of Australia, these predators can travel extensively throughout such areas via the ocean currents and nearby waterways, and have even been found well inland in freshwater billabongs/ponds of creeks and rivers. They are adept hunters whose stealth in stalking their prey is a combination of extreme patience and subtle camouflage, sometimes submerging their entire body for lengthy periods without surfacing. Although appearing rather cumbersome, saltwater crocodiles can actually move very rapidly over short distances and will tenaciously grip their prey with powerful jaws. A formidable foe for any unwary swimmer in the tropics or perhaps a camper beside an isolated billabong.

Many years ago I lived in the remote, isolated and relatively unpopulated Kimberley coastal region of Western Australia that was frequented by a considerable number of marine crocodiles. To travel anywhere along this coast required a boat as roads were rare in such an inhospitable terrain. The area was also subject to one of the highest tidal ranges in the world, with mean spring tide rises/falls of up to 10-11 metres possible in consecutive six hour periods at various times of the year. Boating on these tidal variations typically meant that when anchoring your boat at a beach, eventually the tide would retreat totally leaving your boat 'high and dry' on the sand below. Consequently, you had to dispense excessive anchor rope to safely compensate for the incoming rising tide when the boat did eventually refloat.

On a particular night whilst camping on one such a remote beach, it was brought to my attention that some important provisions had been inadvertently left on board my six metre half-cabin cruiser that was now afloat, but about a distant 50 metres from the beach. With the large incoming tide still rising, this sea distance between our camp and the boat would eventually have extended to about one hundred metres of water and become too far to sensibly reach by swimming. So as you do in these situations, I opted to swim out the short distance to the vessel to retrieve the important items.

It was a cloudless night with no moonlight or breeze, and a dead calm sea with not even a ripple evident as the tide slowly advanced. It was also deathly quiet with the only sound evident to me, as I cautiously entered the water, being the tide gently caressing the shoreline.

I carefully breast-stroked the short distance out to the boat, without splashing and with minimal disturbance of the water. After all, if there was a crocodile lurking on the incoming tide, it was better to be cautious then adventurous. As I approached the boat, I looked back towards the shore and our bright campfire burning in the darkness, and thought how distant the scene appeared. In the dark, it felt as if the campfire/beacon of light was more like a kilometre away rather than a mere 50 metres. Having gathered the provisions from the boat, I quietly slipped back into the sea to return to the beach. That is when the nightmare began.

Before I even took a stroke, I sensed an audible sonic signal transmitting through the water. It was barely perceivable but certainly distinctive. It sounded much like the humming noise from an inquisitive bee but more consistent in tonal character. Fearing that I might definitely have a marine visitor prowling somewhere out there in the dark, I immediately turned onto on my back and simply floated motionless on the incoming tide. I would let the tide eventually return me safely to the beach. Over the ensuing minutes, the sonic signal fluctuated as if probing the seawater for me. It would stop briefly then resume, as if seeking out my form much like an underwater sonar device.

Figure 21: The Night Swimmer

Slowly, ever so painfully slowly, I drifted closer towards the beach and the relative safety of the shore. Laying on one's back in the darkness and being 'at one' with the incoming tide, provided an unusual sense of serenity in the midst of such a nightmare. Then when I was almost to the beach, the sonic signal dramatically ceased. I immediately imagined that the crocodile was in such close proximity to me that it was about to attack, so in sheer panic, I stood upright in the shallows and sprinted the remaining few metres to dry land. The mind can play tricks on one in such circumstances, but I went with my intuition at the time to be certain.

I estimated that it took me about twenty minutes to float back to the shore but it seemed like an eternity to this day. In the early morning before leaving that beach camp, I scoured the sea around the beach for any sign of a crocodile without success, although those predators are experts are remaining invisible. Perhaps there had been no crocodile out there that night after all. However, when one was in the same habitat as the predator, in the dark and alone, it was always wise to acknowledge why they have survived far longer than us and forget such nocturnal swims when in the tropics.

I have written at length about the extraordinary qualities of cats not only as witches' familiars but because of their unique abilities. For my next encounter, I shall describe a very special male cat indeed. But then again, are not they all special?

This black and white cat seemed relatively innocuous when I first acquired him many years ago. Until he arrived home that was. As a kitten, he was always demanding the maximum attention but with a distinctive attitude to life in general, and later as an older cat, he pronounced himself as the Lord of the Manor. In keeping with his self-proclaimed status, the cat expected to go anywhere at any time without question or control. The tough no-nonsense attitude towards anybody questioning his rights would be displayed abruptly. Such was the magnetic power of the black and white moggie.

On a particularly hot day, he could be found in the most obscure indoor locations, such as in an alcove beside a brick chimney, in a closet or perhaps a shopping basket. It was also possible for him to occupy an outdoor poolside deck chair if so inclined. On colder days, the cat would become ensconced anywhere inside where heat was generated, such as directly in front of a fireplace, on a mantelpiece above the aforementioned fireplace, burrowed deep into your favourite comfortable lounge chair, or in front of a portable heater.

Whenever the weather was indifferent, the cat intentionally sat on your lap or in some other way distract you to garner your attention. His powerful claws could also make short work of attractive wall coverings and selective soft furnishings. These sharp claws were sometimes used to full advantage if you passed too close by him. An inherited attitude to intimidate others around him immediately made this cat the chieftain of the local neighbourhood. As the cat aged and his ability to conduct his daily routine of ruthless control over the household declined, much more time was spent in sleeping rather than in irritating those around him.

Sadly his eventual demise was unexpectedly sudden and in most unfortunate circumstances. However, the cat's remains were ceremoniously buried on my property and he shall always remain quite a character for his special way of getting his own way most of the time. Beware the dreaded claw of the cat if passing by.

I am reminded of an ancient superstitious omen that is as follows: 'That it is a very unfortunate thing for a man to meete [meet] early in the morning *an ill-favoured man or woman, a rough-footed hen, a shag-haird [hair]dog, or a black cat.*'[1] Once again, the poor black cat receives the unjust criticism merely for being a black cat. However, the ominous warning about a rough-footed hen is certainly worth heeding.

Of course not all animals are subject to paranormal influences or exhibit bizarre, almost inexplicable behavioural patterns. Some select examples which immediately come to mind include aardvarks, hamsters, platypus, hedgehogs, wildebeests, buffalo and even goats, but then again, even the humble goat has its moments. As a young boy raised on a semi-rural property in the 1950s, I still have very vivid memories of our female domesticated 'Nanny-goat' (*Capra aegagrus hircus*) who we kept for maintaining the outdoor yard in a clean and tidy state, as well as for producing her delicious goat's milk. That goat ate/chewed virtually anything, including even disused tin cans as I recollect. As a result, any edible litter or domestic waste never quite made it off the property, and most importantly, no grass/weeds grew outside our house more than a few centimetres (inches) in height before the eating machine nibbled her preferred diet of greens to ground level.

However, this particular goat did have her ways about her and was duly treated with considerable r-e-s-p-e-c-t. From time to time, she took an extreme dislike to strangers visiting the property and would blindly charge at them. Many a visitor performed amazing feats of athleticism to escape the oncoming goat. Now I always thought that the male 'Billy-goats' did all the stampeding and head-butting tasks, but our Nanny-goat assumed this role perfectly. As it eventuated, her mood swings were not always predictable, and at times she played hide-and-seek with our family, as if not wanting to be tethered or constrained in some other way. On other occasions, the goat was as placid as a lamb (albeit awaiting her next cunning move). The goat's natural curiosity and a relatively placid nature most of the time made her an ideal and mostly loyal companion animal on the property, until of course, there came a twinkle in her eye as another visitor approached the house. As the old western saying of the Lone Ranger goes: 'Hi-yo, Silver, away!'

It has always puzzled me whether one's pets eventually become like their owners over time, or the owners simply become more and more aligned to their pets. It has been said by some that owners of certain pets may start to resemble their animals, but that could be taken as being rather insensitive. Although birds are not animals, I do know of many cases of pet birds, such as parrots, cockatoos, budgerigars/parakeets and others able to communicate readily, who display rather peculiar abilities, perhaps acquired by consistently being in the company of people. Sometimes their cognitive understanding of human language and ancillary sounds can be quite embarrassing and colourful, whilst at other times, it can be downright hilarious when such birds mimic people's speech.

Putting expletives and other saucy nautical phrases sometimes used in the old maritime pirate days of sailing aside, some of the birds can utter the most obscure phrases, usually without prompting or for any other explicable reason. In rare cases, these birds can also differentiate meanings between selective words and phrases. Then there can be the tricksters who actively encourage you to put your fingers through the bars of their cage only to try snapping them in their beaks. As the saying goes: 'Who is a clever bird then?'

So is all simply mimicry amongst the birdlife or is it something more clandestine and paranormal? Is it true that only some species are capable of speech, or are we simply not listening intently enough? A complex topic involving human intervention to provide incentives for birds to learn words and phrases, and the careful selection of particular bird species may be part of the answer. On the lighter side of talking birds, let me simply add that any bird that can be taught to generate 'an evil-sounding laugh' like a villain, or even provide you with some wistful, colourful but discourteous advice regarding your personal appearance, has got to be on the smarter side of the world's avian flocks.

On the subject of birds, not much has ever been written about paranormal encounters with the humble domestic fowl/chicken or 'chook' as they are known in Australia. Many tales have been compiled throughout the world about visitations from phantom dogs, spectral horses and spooky black cats, but I cannot recall a single story about the haunted hen or rampant rooster. Perhaps they have flown under the literature radar so to speak? As a young boy growing up in semi-rural Australia in the 1950s, it seemed every house kept at least a few chooks and always a rooster for that early morning crowing (in lieu of an alarm clock of course).

The hens produced a prolific number of eggs, usually hidden somewhere throughout your property, as these chickens were free to 'roam the range' and predators like foxes were rare in those days. It would one of my daily chores to relentlessly search for these eggs/hidden treasures and recover them. It was also my responsibility to hand-feed the chooks with grain and provide clean potable water. Periodically, chicks hatched from a few selective eggs and the ritual would resume all over again. Every so often, one of the plumpest chooks was selected as the main course for the traditional Sunday roast dinner, and this was where my encounter commenced.

Even in a large brood of domestic chickens, it seemed to me that every one of them had a personality of sorts and a distinctive behaviour. You became accustomed to them and they relied upon you for their daily supplementary feed when not foraging for worms, insects, seeds and other nutrients. I had my favourites and also admired the chooks who were not necessarily as likeable. To despatch a chook for the Sunday dinner in the most humane manner was a most delicate task, and was almost always assigned to my father as head of the family.

My role was to first catch the unfortunate fowl and to provide any further assistance should a fowl manage to escape. On one such rare occasion, the chook selected did escape my father's clutches and avoided many attempts at recapture. Another chicken took its place instead. Eventually, weeks later, the elusive escapee's turn arrived again and this time, there was no magical reprieve.

I had trouble sleeping for days afterwards, thinking about losing this unusual character from the brood. To placate me, my father allowed me to select one of the brood who would remain the family pet and never meet such an end. As my favourite, this chook prospered and grew quite plump whilst others in the brood eventually met their end. At least I had my favourite. Unfortunately, my pet chook eventually grew so large that it attracted the attention of a predatory fox new to our district. All we eventually found were some feathers spread over a wide area. I suppose, ultimately, the chook had a good life until its number came up. Rest In Peace, Chook.

As a comforting end to the tale, my father gave me a really cute hatchling chick shortly afterwards and it remained the new family pet forever as I recollect. It followed me everywhere and I was not even its mother.

THE STRANGE ONES

There has always been that 'strange one' throughout my life. Sometimes it was a strange elusive friend who was always in the background and occasionally appeared without warning at your party or social gathering. Nobody knew exactly what that person did for a living nor cared for that matter. Sometimes it was a total stranger who sat next to you on the train or bus, and for some unknown reason, appeared to enjoy chatting incessantly with you and no-one else sitting nearby. It could be someone in a crowd who approached you to enquire about something innocuous, such as the time of day. They were possibly all that same person that I shall name as 'the strange one'.

Have you ever wondered why they select you for this temporary alliance? Why do these unusual people insist on being so close to you yet strangely distant at the same time? Perhaps they are messengers from elsewhere with something to say, or as some would philosophically surmise, it is just a co-incidence. Delve deeper and it may surprise you. We are all different in so many ways yet similar. Some of us are definitely different yet we may not actually recognise it until we meet the strange one.

If you were the offspring of somebody with real mystical powers or with a direct historical connection to the supernatural, then this story probably does not relate to you? It concerns those people who attract interest for no apparent reason whatsoever. They are the quiet and pensive ones who you passed in the street without a second glance or thought. They blended into the crowd so convincingly that it is miraculous anyone noticed them at all. Yet the strange ones noticed them and sought them out. Thereby starts my story about such beings.

It has been said that we all only have one life, but nobody tells you which life and for that matter, how long we have in this life? Suppose for a moment that a relative, friend, work colleague or simply a casual acquaintance passed away. In some cultures, notably Japan, it was believed that when someone's spirit left this physical world for an eternal world or afterlife beyond, the spirit may linger for some time before attaining this destination. Whilst detained in this state, a spirit can become restless or unhappy, intent upon haunting or otherwise disrupting those with whom it feels a strong connection. This may continue until someone or something released them to resume their journey.[1]

Now assume that this entity was originally known to you in the physical world such as a relative or friend, but now has an entirely different and unrecognisable appearance. The stranger who singled you out for special attention, a new acquaintance or perhaps a new friend who shared so much in common with you may actually be this entity. This strange one who seemed to have something different about them compared to most people, yet was disquietingly familiar to you at the same time. Is there really such a thing as a coincidence that you should encounter such a person, or have they sought you all along?

Take the curious story recounted in Ireland in late 1913, when a lady went into her local town for some business and noticed a small group of four people standing on the pavement engaged in conversation. She only noticed them because her brother and sister were standing in the group. As the woman was in a hurry to get her business done, she did not join the group but recalled later that her sister was wearing the clothes she had worn before, and was heard to distinctly laugh, although not to speak. The rest of the group appeared to be listening intently to the woman's sister. It would only be later back at the family home that the tale took a bizarre deviation.

The woman casually remarked to her brother about seeing him and his three companions in the street, only to be corrected by the man that there were only two companions with him. The sister had not been with them as she was not in town that day. Despite the woman describing all the group accurately, including their clothing and position in the group, her brother assured her that the sister had not been present, and that no-on present had been laughing. To add to the mystery, the woman checked with her sister the following day, and the sister confirmed that she had indeed not been in the town on that day and so was equally mystified.[2] Could the woman have been mistaken in her rush to get her business done, or was this fourth companion an inexplicable vision of her sister, known as "a double"? She was an entity that was present but not obvious to the rest of the group. In Germany, such a manifestation is called a *Doppelgänger* or double-goer.

To attempt to provide some natural explanation of what may have occurred, consider an entity known as a *Wraith*, of which there are various kinds. Most people would know a wraith as a ghostlike, exact image of a living person, a shadowy apparition or perhaps a waft/waff, a passing shadow or phantasm. To see one's own wraith was considered an omen of death, whilst to see the wraith of a friend would indicate that person had just died or about to die.[3] The two kinds of most interest to me are the ominous wraith that is a "double" or shadow of oneself that appears as a portent of the imminent death of a dying person, and the strange *visitant* that is a non-ominous wraith seen elsewhere than the body of the person concerned. The visitant does what the person wants to do, but is unable to do so in their own body.[4] This type of wraith is an exact likeness of the person, even as to details of dress. In the story of the inexplicable vision of fourth companion, the sister's visitant appeared on her behalf without the woman even being aware of it, without any deadly consequences.

A similar story of a sea captain and a mysterious sailor provide further insight into such visitants. As the story went, a sea captain was on a lengthy ocean voyage when one of his sailors informed him that there was a strange man inside the captain's cabin seated at a table, writing with his back to the door, and so not clearly distinguishable. The captain ordered the sailor to return to the cabin to discover who this stranger might be, but the crewman duly found that upon his return, the person had disappeared. However, the stranger had left a mysterious message written in ink which was still wet and read "Steer due south".

As the captain was not pressed for time on this voyage, he opted to change the ship's course southwards and before long came upon '... a ship long disabled and whose crew were in the last extremity.' The captain of this ship told his rescuers that one of his crew '...was a very strange character...' who had actually been found on a deserted ship and taken aboard. However, this crew member had eventually fallen into a cataleptic trance, and when he recovered, recounted that during the trance, he had been in another ship, begging its captain to come to their assistance.

When pointed out to the sailor who had first sighted the stranger in the cabin writing the mysterious message, the sailor recognised him immediately as their own visitor.[5] Whilst this strange character had been on board the disabled ship, his out-of-body visitant seemed to have been temporarily on another ship leaving a written plea for rescue. On the other hand, ominous wraiths are not quite as appealing, and have been known to manifest themselves to the friends of a dying person near the time of death, even at considerable distances. A wraith is usually an apparition of the ailing person, but sometimes may even be of some other startling appearance.

An acquaintance once recounted to me a first-hand experience of an ominous wraith that appeared before him in a hospital on the evening just before his father passed away. He described the wraith as completely shrouded in dark/black clothing, with a dark shadow for a face, and quietly seated on a bench just outside his father's hospital room. Despite standing with a small group of other people in this corridor, the acquaintance was the only person to see the entity for a few brief seconds, but clearly recalled the detail in his description. He rarely mentioned the sighting to others afterwards, to avoid possible ridicule.

Figure 22: Patiently Waiting (*Source Unknown**)

For a most fitting verse concerning the dreaded wraith, I again turn to the late American poet, novelist and playwright Paul Laurence Dunbar for the following extracts from his profound poem entitled *The Wraith*:

> Ah me, it is cold and chill
> And the fire sobs low in the grate,
> While the wind rides by on the hill,
> And the logs crack sharp with hate…
>
> …Oh, the logs they crack and whine,
> And the water drops from the eaves;
> But it is not rain but brine
> Where my dead darling grieves.
>
> And a wraith sits by my side,
> A spectre grim and dark;
> Are you gazing here open-eyed
> Out to the lifeless dark?
>
> But ever the wind rides on,
> And we sit close within;
> Out of the face of the dawn,

I and my darling, – sin.⁶

In far earlier and less learned times, around the early 1800s, these two distinct species of apparition were recognised in some local county English folklore by somewhat simpler terms. One type of spectre would not attempt to disguise what it really was and either stood still, appearing and vanishing in the same spot, or glided along without moving its feet. The other type imitated living people even in their walk, to the extent of limping or otherwise walking awkwardly.

Of course, there were people in those times who never claimed to have seen these apparitions, and did not believe there was anything to see anyway. Strangely, many would rather not venture near certain places after nightfall, for fear that there should be something to be seen there.⁷ This says so much about the human species. So how does one vanquish an apparition if it were to be encountered?

An enjoyable and jaunty story of such an encounter, which occurred in bygone days in an English town, involved a very curious character named Tommy who was sought by a householder to deal with a troublesome apparition that plagued a particular room in his very large, old house. Although Tommy appeared to be relatively simple, he was very clever when it came to hauntings. His only request was to be left alone in the same room with an empty bottle, a bottle of brandy with a small glass, and a pitcher of water. With a fine fire in the room for such a cold winter night, Tommy locked the door behind him and settled in to pass the time drinking the warm brandy and water.

On midnight, he was roused by the appearance of the apparition standing before him and was surprised when it greeted him by his actual name. Tommy enquired about how it had gained entry to the room, given the door was locked, and was informed by the apparition that it had entered through the keyhole. In disbelief, Tommy reiterated that this was not possible and demanded the apparition prove what it was stating. He pointed to the empty bottle, which he pretended to have emptied, and requested that if the apparition could come through a keyhole, then it could certainly enter the empty bottle. The onus of proof was now on the spirit.

By now, the apparition appeared very angry at being so doubted about its powers, and entered the empty bottle to prove the point. Tommy immediately corked the bottle tightly to ensure this entity would not escape and subsequently threw the bottle off a nearby bridge where the river was wide and deep.[8] If only it was that easy to vanquish the spectre! Nevertheless, it remains a popular story perhaps recounted more for its ingenuity than for any sensible practicality.

To those people who are rationally convinced that wraiths have never existed, except in the minds of those who professed to have seen them, it is far easier to accept that the sightings were figments of imagination. Your imagination can trick you into believing just about anything, given the right circumstances, or so it would appear. Superstitions concerning wraiths and similar apparitions can persuade some people to imagine the worst, particularly where lonely rural dwellings, cemeteries or perhaps some other desolate location involving the departed may be involved. Combine the superstition with the cloak of night, and the atmosphere definitely became downright creepy. I recall from my impressionable early childhood days, when the only household lighting was provided from paraffin or kerosene lamps rather than electricity, it would not be wise to venture out at night beyond the circle of the lamp-light. It was a childhood superstition that assumed no spirit of the departed would dare enter within this circle, and it certainly kept you inside the house.

This sad story pertains to the mid-1700s in the county of Northumberland in the north-east of England, and concerns a lone farmhouse that was visited regularly by a pedlar (seller of petty wares) of some wealth as he travelled throughout the local county. The pedlar met an untimely demise at the hands of the farmer's wife who disposed of his corpse in a deep well nearby, after relieving him of his money. The body was later retrieved by the farmer and him and his wife buried it on the property. Satisfied that no-one would ever suspect them, the pair commenced spending the money.

However, neither were to experience any happiness from their bounty. The farmer fell from his horse a few years later and perished from a broken neck, whilst his wife was seized by fits of terror which continued unabated until her untimely death. What gave rise to these seizures? As the story goes, the farmer's wife confessed just before her death to frequently seeing the wraith of the pedlar in the kitchen where he had met his demise. Despite moving houses, the wraith continued to appear to her: '... he used to sometimes seat himself opposite to her, with his hair wet and hanging down over his face, as he appeared when she and her husband drew him from the well '.[9] The torment eventually got the better of the farmer's wife, who had hid the corpse in a well but could not hide from herself.

The wraith or *wauf* as it is frequently called in Northumberland, is the apparition of a person which appears as a portent *before* their death. There has also supposedly been a person who saw and spoke to his own wraith (without receiving an answer), and who died the next day.[10] In the story of the farmer's wife, however, it seems to me that this wraith with the ghastly visage was more akin to a solitary messenger from beyond, patiently awaiting the impending demise of his former assailant.

For any of you who have not wandered in company with a wraith, through the ghost-realms of the mystic past, I offer a suitable extract of *The Wraith's Warning* by 19th century American poet Isaac Newton Phipps, as published in 1895:

> O hark you, fair maiden, and heed it,
> The Wraith she will sing you a song,
> Which if you will heed, maid, indeed it
> May save you a sorrow life-long.
>
> From a land that is far hence that I sprung,
> I lived in the time of earth's prime;
> To the maids of all ages I've sung,
> And the fair ones of every clime.
>
> My song is a warning, and weighted
> With caution each maiden should know;
> With sorrow it is freighted,
> But sorrow that mitigates [reduces] woe.

...So, maiden, if thou wouldst be pleasured,
Think well of the step thou wouldst take,
For each step in life's way is measured,
And sorrow treads close in its wake.[11]

Probably a rather prophetic echo far too late for the farmer's wife to heed.

PARANORMAL MAGICIANS

The definition of the term 'magic' and its associated elements as derived from the ancient Greeks can vary considerably, so I select the following succinct interpretation as most suitable: 'A superior power that arises from harnessing inner power and supernatural forces and beings to effect change in the physical world.' It should not be confused with sorcery, as 'magic is the knowledge that teaches the practical application of the lowest laws of nature to the highest laws of spirit.'

It is as old as humanity and began in attempts by humankind to control environment, survival and destiny either by using natural forces or appealing to higher powers to help.[1] Magic was the foundation of the whole mystical and scientific universe of primitive man.[2] Conversely, sorcery, by definition, is the art, practices or spells of a person who is supposed to exercise supernatural powers through the aid of evil spirits; black magic; witchery.[3]

Magicians are the skilled practitioners of magic, who were either born into their powers or trained themselves to acquire power. For others, they became magicians through their physical peculiarities/infirmities, extraordinary gifts (such as juggling, ventriloquism and tumbling), or were brought to public notice by their neurotic delusions about possessing special powers. Such individuals were believed to possess magical powers not directly attributable to these causes, but more a consequence of society's attitude towards them.[4]

The magic practised by these people should not be considered as inherently good or evil, but rather as neutral and more reflective of the intent of the magician. The credibility of magicians was dependent on their success in performing their duties, and if their conjuration of spirits, divination, incantations, spell-casting or magical medical remedies failed, their future was not so bright.

I adore the following abbreviated discourse concerning a sorcerer/magician from the 1600s which succinctly identified the true spirit of a paranormal magician intent on entrapping a ghost as follows:

> …What sort of creature is a conjurer?
> Why, he's made much as other men are,
> if it was not for his long grey beard.
> – His beard is at least half a yard long;
> he's dressed in a strange dark cloke, as black as a coal.
> He has a long white wand in his hand…
> … But what will he [the conjurer] do with him [a trapped ghost]…?
> Why then he'll overpower him [the ghost] with his learning.[5]

I am reminded of the magic gifted to the young boy Icarus in Greek mythology who was provided with a fabricated set of wings like a bird, to escape imprisonment on an island. The wings comprised feathers secured only with thread and wax but were suitable for flight, on the condition that Icarus did not fly too high in order to avoid the scorching sun's heat melting the wax, or too low for the seawater to wet the feathers. Poor Icarus soared upward as if to reach heaven, the wax softened, his feathers came off, and despite fluttering his arms, the boy plummeted to his demise in the sea. The following excerpt paints the picture most aptly:

> … with melting wax and loosened strings
> Sunk hapless Icarus on unfaithful wings;
> Headlong he rushed through the affrighted [arousing fear] air,
> With limbs distorted and dishevelled hair;
> His scattered plumage danced upon the wave,
> And sorrowing Nereids[sea nymphs] decked his watery grave;…[6]

A subject yet to be fully appreciated about magicians is the conjuration of spirits: the practice of raising or evoking spirits, ghosts, demons and even storms by means of carefully formulated rituals. In particular, this included the practice of ghost-laying or diverting ghosts away from haunted places and to prevent these entities from harming people. This was not exorcism of individuals, but rather a purification of the spiritual environment.[7] Of course, this feat could also be often accomplished by magical adepts like sorcerers and witches, or other ghost-layers such as psychics, mediums and priests, but let us not mince words.

Why do ghosts and demons frequent places such as cemeteries, marshes, woods, and crossroads? Rubbish heaps too, can you believe, as they were considered impure. They also haunted any other places where the spectre was trapped or earthbound. The banishment of the restless ghost or ghosts did not always involve ritualistic magic, and certainly did not always succeed, but certainly formed an integral part of a magician's expertise.

In ancient Greek religion and mythology, the potent but protective three-faced goddess of crossroads; goddess of the Earth, Moon and the Underworld [mythical abode of the dead], was known in Latin as *Hecate* (from the Greek 'Εκατη or *Hekatē*, possibly derived from *Hekas* meaning 'operates from afar').[8] She was a mysterious divinity representing amongst many things, the darkness and terrors of the night, associated with ghosts, infernal spirits, the dead and necromancy (evocation).

Evocation is the supposed practice of magic involving communication with the deceased, either by summoning their spirit as an apparition or raising them bodily for the purpose of divination; seeking knowledge of the future or unknown by supernatural means. This may have included imparting the means to foretell future events or discover hidden knowledge, bringing someone back from the dead, or even using the deceased as a weapon, such as in witchcraft.[9] *Hecate's* great powers of magic and witchcraft as well as association with ghosts and spirits made her known to haunt tombs and crime scenes.[10]

Shrines to *Hecate* were placed at entrances to homes and cities in the belief that it would protect their inhabitants from the restless dead and other spirits. As a goddess she was expected to avert harmful or destructive spirits from homes and cities, as well as protect the individual inhabitants. *Hecate* might also refuse to avert the demons or even direct them against unfortunate individuals.[11] By any account, this goddess had quite some responsibility, particularly concerning matters of ghostly spirits and witchcraft.

So what defines these magical entities or spirits conjured by such a deity or sorcerer? A complex topic across many cultures and far too involved for this book, so I shall restrict it primarily to the ancient Greeks. The majority were embraced by the souls of the dead whose funeral rites were yet to be properly performed, had not been buried, perhaps died in a violent unnatural or untimely manner, perished during childbirth, or died as a hero/heroine or martyr.

Lesser known magical spirits are demons or genies that are not necessarily a synonym for devil, but rather specialised magical beings of all kinds, shapes and sizes, as well as both sexes. By the Middle Ages, medieval magic had embraced considerably more of these demon/genie spirits, including goblins, sprites, fairies and so many others.[12]

To an extent, in this discussion we cross-over into witchcraft, whose powers were believed to supposedly include shape-shifting, aerial flight, visions, controlling weather and the ability through creating elixirs and potions to change physical appearance and emotional outcomes. However, unlike the ancient Greeks, Romans and Egyptians who admired and respected those so blessed by their gods for such powers, witchcraft subsequently became reviled in many cultures.

The summoning of spirits of the dead to appease or 'lay a troublesome ghost', known as evocation, or necromancy in ancient Greece, required completing unfinished business that may have included reburial of the corpse or perhaps a purification ritual to cease the haunting process. In order for evocators or 'soul-drawers' to conduct the ghost-laying by a cleansing/purification process and then placating any restless spirits, it was crucial to recognise the type of spirit involved. Sometimes there were many shadows of dead spirits at a location, and in some cases, dark demon spirits unwilling to be placated or laid-out. This was where the 'magic' was truly required by such practitioners.

For our suitable tale, I revert to ancient Greece in the late second century AD and a house long since rendered uninhabitable and rather dilapidated due to the presence of its terrors: a restless and terrifying spirit that successfully scared away whosoever attempted to enter the building. One brave soul who was a philosopher of superhuman wisdom and was possibly interested in the supernatural and magic, took on the challenging task to spend a night in this dreary darkened abode despite the fearful spirit. He armed himself with a considerable collection of Egyptian books to assist in dealing with issues of the occult. [13]

Of course not long after entering the premises with a lamp in hand, this wise man was confronted by the ghost, best described as '…squalid, he had long hair, and was blacker than the dark'. The ghost had materialised in attack and proceeded to beat the man on all sides, as well as to scare him by taking on different shapes. To purify the house and thus appease the spirit, the man let out a blood-curdling incantation (the most fearsome formula in Egyptian gleaned from his books), '…driving the ghost into a corner of the dark room, and laid him with the charm'.

The man noted where the ghost had gone down in the room, and in the morning, along with others who returned keen to view the results of his visit, they dug in the same spot with picks and shovels. Buried some six feet below, they uncovered a mouldering corpse of which only the bones lay together in order. By exhuming the remains and providing a proper burial, from that time onwards, there would be no further trouble from phantoms in that house.[14]

The magician from that ancient period has been variously described as 'one who creates delusions in the minds of other men' (and presumably women), then 'sorcerer', and 'one who deludes the masses', and in the first half of the third century AD is mentioned alongside performers/utterers of incantations, astrologers, diviners, interpreters of dreams and makers of amulets[charms worn to ward off bad fortune].[15] Quite a mixed bag of occupations by any stretch of the imagination, and in some cases, different ways of referring to the same person. Another succinct interpretation is that of a magic-maker with '… a number of stock formulae that he uses in these spells, both in season and out of season'.[16] Oh, the paranormal world of the sorcerer and his divination.

By the middle of the third century AD, there was commentary on some practising magic who '... used incantations to make the higher powers obey them and do their bidding and more specifically, that the incantations in question were songs, cries, breathings-upon, hisses, and other noises ... that were said to have a magical effect'.[17] Such strange sounds, including whistling and popping noises, were deemed to be a most important part of magic rituals. Of course, not all practising magic were of fixed abode, but rather obscure wanderers who told fortunes on street corners and in marketplaces, and as a consequence could be branded as scoundrels or rascals.

For the application of ancient magic in foretelling the future, it would difficult to beat Prognostication [prediction] by Thunder, as depicted in text based on that found in the manuscript *MS Cotton Vespasian D xiv, fol. 75v* in London's British Library. Such predictive texts were popular in England and continental Europe from the eighth century onwards, and have been transcribed below in part for some of the calendar year:

> ...If there is thunder in February, it means that many people will die; and the rich most of all.
>
> In March, it means strong winds will come, and crops will grow well; but there will be no agreement amongst people.
>
> If it thunders in April, the year will be happy, and the wicked will die.
>
> Thunder in May means a year of hunger.
>
> In the month of June, thunder warns of strong winds, and madness amongst lions and wolves...[18]

For those of you choosing to be outdoors during thunderstorms, particularly in June, please remain vigilant of any mad lions or wolves roaming your neighbourhood.

In the Middle Ages throughout Europe, practitioners of magic attempting to influence the future by using either spiritual or natural forces had a profound link with the sciences. Some were also proficient astrologers who provided a connection in the physical world between the cosmos and humankind. Other magicians were alchemists as well and developed potions and elixirs to cure illness, or perhaps they were doctors of sorts who used natural magic, such as the positive power of one's imagination, to effect healing.

Perhaps one of the most powerful and complex magicians and healers of ancient times was considered to be Odin, the pagan deity of Germanic and Nordic mythology; he was also known as the true magician's deity. He possessed an insatiable thirst for knowledge and was renowned for his shamanistic abilities and astral travel, and as well as being a shape-shifter, was most accomplished in the extent of his magical knowledge and as the father of incantations.

Such were Odin's qualities; 'It was thought that Odin may have been a real person whose myth grew over the passage of time.'[19] The following description in part of such a person, as portrayed in literary works, would be somewhat difficult to exceed: 'I am the unknown Will [willpower], The Anger that threatens glory and ruin: Lord of Storms am I, in heaven high and caverns deep… Wayfarer, wanderer, beggar, king…'[20] However, as the saying goes, 'there is no magic when one no longer believes.'

In Celtic Britain (600 BC to 50 AD), various magical processes were employed in seeking knowledge of the future or of the unknown by supernatural means, using spirits of any kind rather than those specifically of the dead which seemed a rare occurrence. To achieve this magic, they relied upon 'the spirit call', which was a spiritual echo or response as from a distance. The magic involved taking the unfortunate participant (frequently selected by drawing lots) to an appropriate remote location, or one reputed to be haunted, or otherwise likely to possess such spirits, such as at a waterfall, and leaving them alone overnight and perhaps wrapped in animal hide in order to receive these mystical communications.[21]

In one extreme case reported from the Isle of Lewis (the largest island of the Western Isles/Outer Hebrides' archipelago in Scotland), the participant certainly received something quite unexpected '… during which time he felt and heard such terrible things that he could not express them…' Furthermore '…that for a thousand worlds he would never again be concerned in a like performance'…[22] If one expects to dabble in the realms of the supernatural, then be prepared to reap the whirlwind.

As an interesting conclusion to my book, I add a personal note concerning the name *Sibyl* (from Latin *Sibylla*) eventually adopted by my mother as alternative to her original birth-name. As she was a most gifted fortune-teller who in the 1950s and 1960s freely volunteered her unique and harmless skills at local community fairs for charitable purposes, such a name befitted her special gift. As the ancient Greeks and Romans aptly realised, such a woman was a soothsayer/oracle, possessing powers of prophecy and divination, and who am I to disagree?

Figure 23: Still Watching You (*Courtesy of Shutterstock*)

EPILOGUE

Wraiths, spectral spirits, eerie shadows or spooky visitations may all potentially conjure fear and dread in the minds of the beholder, regardless of the location and the era. One does not necessarily have to believe in their presence to be truly frightened. Now combine the medium for communicating by such apparitions, such as a possessed doll, a moving scarecrow, perhaps a phantom ship or train, or even a familiar animal such as a cat or dog, and we have the right ingredients for a suitable haunting.

The questions to be asked, however, are whether these ethereal spirits are simply visiting us for a brief intermittent period or are actually amongst us most of the time? What is their intent and why do we have so many recurring incidents throughout the recorded history of humanity? Why do a few people clearly perceive the ghostly whispers and other almost inexplicable signs of their presence, whilst the majority of us do not? Perhaps part of these answers can be sourced from ancient folklore and superstitions concerning these 'otherworldly' spiritual messengers?

It could probably be acknowledged that olde world terms such as *galley-beggers, barguests, bogies* or *boggarts* were handed down over generations through oral folktales and did have some substance to them originally. However, as with many historical stories, exaggeration and distortion of the facts can sometimes get in the way when reciting these tales. Nonetheless, the tales are consistent about the sighting of various paranormal 'characters' or whatever you wish to name them. Scrape away the layers of superstitious elements to most of these folktales and you will possibly still find something else altogether.

Witches' familiars have been dealt quite an unenviable hand in the world of superstition and legend, particularly given most are simply animals or birds with peculiar or unusual traits. The cat, bear, wolf, fox, horse, monkey, hare, lamb, toad, raven, crow, owl, and so very many other fellow beasts/avians certainly appear to have been singled out for a rather unfavourable focus.

It may also be difficult to accept that in various ways, human perceptions actually play a major part in paranormal appearances. When one is faced with imminent death or has a near-death experience, the human psyche traditionally 'kicks-in' and we survive, but not always of course. Perhaps some of us are merely convenient receptors for the 'otherworldly' beings and their communicative transmissions/whispers/shadows.

The final thought about this bizarre and contentious field of visitations is aptly described by the following sentiment:

> The hall is booked,
> The band is playing,
> Time to dance, said the ghost to the other ghost,
> and what a dance it surely shall be.

REFERENCES

CHAPTER 1: Reflections of the Other Side
1. Illes, *The Weiser Field Guide to Witches*, 2010, pp.103-4.
2. Reader's Digest, *Into the Unknown*, 1982, p.175.
3. Back Seat Ghost, https://www.newsfromthespiritworld.com/ghostly-pics-the-back-seat-ghost, 23 January 2013.
4. Longfellow, H.W., *Haunted Houses*, 1858
5. Hudson, 'Alone', *Halloween: Stories and Poems*, 1992, p.3.
6. Ross, *Supernatural and Mysterious Japan: Spirits, Hauntings and Paranormal Phenomena*, 2015, pp.130-1.

CHAPTER 2: Spectres and Shadows
1. Cardin, *Ghosts, Spirits and Psychics*, 2015, pp.104-5.
2. Ibid, p.106.
3. Ibid, p.21.
4 Lipman, *Co-habiting with Ghosts*, 2016, pp.13-4.
5. Barrie, J.M., *The Little Minister*,1891.
6. Lipman, op.cit., p.13.
7. Thompson, R.C.,'Utuuki Limnûti, Tablet V,' *The Devils and Evil Spirits of Babylonia*, 1903, p. 53.
8. Ibid, 'The Seven Spirits', p.XLV.
9. Bainton, R., 'The Flying Dutchman', *The Mammoth Book of Unexplained Phenomena*, 2013, Part 6.
10. Wikipedia, *Flying Dutchman*, http://en.wikipedia.org, Retrieved 28 March 2017.
11. Beck, *Forklore and the Sea*, 1973, p.390.
12. Lipman, op.cit., pp.16-7.
13. Livingston,M.C., 'Wailed a ghost in a graveyard in Kew', *Halloween Poems*,1989.

14. Cardin, op.cit., p.104.
15. Stevenson, R.L., 'Shadow March', in Part XLI North-West Passage: No.2, *A Child's Garden of Verses*, 1910, pp.78-9.
16. Cardin, op.cit., p.114.
17. Ibid, p.107.
18. Story, W.W., *Ode on the Anniversary of the Fifth Half Century of the landing of Governor John Endecott*, Verse XXX, 1878, p.27.
19. Story, W.W., 'Shadows and Voices at Twilight', *Poems*, 1856, p.136.
20. Davis, *Haunted Asylums, Prisons and Sanatoriums*, 2013, pp. 23-5.
21. Guiley, *The Encyclopedia of Ghosts and Spirits*, 1992, pp.444-5.

CHAPTER 3: The Black Dog and Others
1. Lovecraft, H.P., 'From Beyond', *The Fantasy Fan Magazine*, Vol. 1, No.10, June 1934, pp.147-151, p.160.
2. Reader's Digest, op.cit.,pp.244-5.
3. Ibid, p.247.
4. Brown, T., 'The Black Dog in English Folklore', *Animals in Folklore*, 1978, p.45.
5. Brown, T., 'The Black Dog', *Folklore*, vol.69, 1958, pp.176-9.
6. Lear, E., 'The Owl and the Pussy-Cat', *Nonsense Songs, Stories, Botany, and Alphabets*, 1871.
7. Davidson, A., 'The Children of the Owl and the Pussy-Cat', *Edward Lear: Landscape Painter and Nonsense Poet*, 1938.
8. Josiffe, C., *Gef the Talking Mongoose*, Fortean Times, December 2010, Retrieved 2 Decmber, 2016.
9. Price and Lambert, *The Haunting of Cashen's Gap*, 1936, Chapter 2.
10. Gef, https://en.wiki2.org/wiki/Gef_the_Talking_Mongoose, Retrieved 2 December, 2016.
11. Price, H., *Confessions of a Ghost Hunter*, Putnam, 1936.
12. Gefmongoose.com.au/p/Gef_The_Eighth_Wonder_of_the_World, 2016.
13. Masefield,J., *Reynard the Fox*, Part II, 1921, p.116.
14. Seymour and Neligan, *True Irish Ghost Stories*, First Edition, 1914, pp.195-7.
15. For Want of a Nail, https://en.wikipedia.org/wiki/For_Want_of_a_Nail, Retrieved 15 February, 2017.

16. Anonymous, *Suffolk County Folk-Lore*, Printed Extracts No 2, ¶1893, p.169.
17. Ibid, p.202.
18. Seymour and Neligan, op.cit., pp.221-2.
19. Ibid, p.186.
20. Ibid, pp.187-8.
21. Morton, *Trick or Treat: A History of Halloween*, 2012, p.49, p.51.
22. Unexplained-Mysteries.com, *Phantom Coach*, https://www.ghoststories.org.uk.
23. Cheung, *The Element Encyclopedia of the Psychic World*, 2006, p.25.
24. The Ankou, https://www.mysteriousbritain.co.uk/folklore/the-ankou, Retrieved 5 September, 2016.
25. Cheung, op.cit., p.25.
26. Haining, 'Ankou', *A Dictionary of Ghost Lore*, 1982.
27. Wilde, *Ancient Legends, Mystic Charms and Superstitions of Ireland*, Vol I, 1887, pp.178-9.
28. Anonymous, *Suffolk County Folk-Lore*, Printed Extracts No 2, p.8.

CHAPTER 4: The Bear and the Wolf
1. Otten, *A Lycanthrophy Reader: Werewolves in Western Culture*, 1986, p.150.
2. Hallowell, 'Bear Ceremonialism in the Northern Hemisphere', *American Anthropologist*, 1926, p.149.
3, Ellis Davidson, H.R., 'Shape-changing in the Old Norse Sagas', *Animals in Folklore*, 1978, p.130.
4.Ibid, p.134.
5. Oten, op.cit., pp.148-9.
6. Ellis Davidson, H.R, op. cit., p.131.
7. Widdowson, J.D.A., 'Animals as Threatening Figures in Systems of Threatening Social Control', *Animals in Folklore*, 1978, pp.38-9.
8. Barguest, *Encyclopædia Brittanica*, Vol. 3, 11th Ed., 1911, p.399.
9. Brown, op. cit., 1978, p.47.
10. Henderson, *Notes on the Folk-Lore of the Northern Counties of England and the Borders*, 1879, pp.274-5.
11. Whitaker, *An History of Richmondshire in the North Riding of the County of York*, 1823, pp. 167-8.

12. Hazlitt, *Faiths & Folklore of the British Isles*, Volume II, 1965, p.663.
13. Ankarloo & Henningsen, *Early Modern European Witchcraft*, 1990, pp.270-1.
14. Illes, op.cit., p.234.
15. McKinstry, *Water Dark*, 2013, Excerpt from The Theory of Structure and Formlessness.

CHAPTER 5: Whispers

1. Field, E., 'The Night Wind', *Love-Songs of Childhood*, 1896, p.6.
2. Stokes, *Discoveries in Australia;With an account of the Coasts and Rivers explored and surveyed during the Voyage of the H.M.S. Beagle in the Years 1837-38-39-40-41-42-43*, Volume 1, p. 200.
3. Ingram, *The Haunted Homes and Famous Traditions of Great Britain*, 1897, pp.77-8.
4. Lister, 'Under the Stairs', *Halloween:Stories and Poems*,1992, p.63.
5. Rappoport, *Superstitions of Sailors*, 2012. p.55.
6. Bassett, *Sea Phantoms: Legends and Superstitions of the Sea and of Sailors in all lands and at all times*, 1892, pp.101-2.
7. Bottrell, *Traditions and Hearthside Stories of West Cornwall*, 1873, p.224.
8. Bassett, op.cit.,p.115.
9. Jeans, *Seafaring Lore & Legend*, 2004, p.313.
10. Shelley, P.B., *The Revolt of Islam, (previously Laon and Cythna)*, Canto VIII, 1817.
11. Brand, *Observations on the Possible Antiquities of Great Britain, Vol III*, p.239.

CHAPTER 6: The Last Moment

1. Coxe, *Halloween, A Romaunt with Lays, Verse LXIX*, 1845, p.47.
2. Brockie, *Legends and Superstitions of the County of Durham*, 1886, p.199.
3. Ibid, p.200.
4. Seymour & Neligan, *True Irish Ghost Stories*, 1914, pp. 166-8.
5. Brockie, op.cit., p.199.
6. Addy, *Household Tales, with other Traditional Remains*,1895, p.125.
7. Henderson, op.cit.,1879, pp.54-5.

8. Ibid, p.56.
9. Glyde, *The Norfolk Garland*,1872, p.29.
10. Cressy, 'The Old Mourner', *Birth, Marriage & Death, Ritual, Religon and the Life Cycle in Tudor and Stuart England*, p.119.
11. Ibid, p.445.
12. Hazlitt, op.cit.,1965, p.617.
13. R. Herrick,'The Wake', *Hesperides and His Noble Numbers*, 1648, Item 763.
14. Miller, 'The Broken Promise', *Scenes and Legends of the North of Scotland*, 1869, pp.359- 61.

CHAPTER 7: Ocean Wanderers
1. Masefield, J., 'Sea Fever', *Salt-Water Ballads*, 1902, pp. 59-60.
2. Beck, *Folklore and the Sea*,1973, p.18.
3. Bassett, op. cit., 1892, p.368.
4. Drake, *A Book of New England Legends and Folk Lore*, 1901, pp.418-20.
5. Hunt, *Popular Romances of the West of England*, 1881, p.359.
6. Truro News, 'Dreadful Shipwreck and Loss of Life', *West Briton Newspaper*, April Issue 1838.
7 Bassett, op. cit., 1892, p.290.
8. Bottrell, op.cit., p. 248.
9. F.H.McLean, 'Famous Phantoms of the Sea, *Washington Herald*, 2 June Issue, 1909.
10. Bassett, op. cit., 1892 pp. 353-4.
11. Ibid, p.344.
12. Beck, *Folklore and the Sea*,1973, pp.395-6.
13. Bradley, *The Romance of Wales*,1929, p.180.
14. Bennett, *Dollar Wreck: One of the Treasure Ships of Wales*, 2016.
15. A Compressed History of the Penarth Dock Area – Ice Age up to circa 1820, *https://www.penarthporthladd.org/documents/early-history*. Retrieved 19 December 2016, p.1.
16. Ibid, p.3.
17. Ings, D., 'North Beach and Kymin', *Penarth History Tour*, 2016, Section 23.
18. Beck, op. cit., p.287.

19. Beck, *The Folklore of Maine*, 1957, pp.206-7.
20. Ibid, p.207.
21. Leach, *Folk Ballads and Songs of the Labrador Coast*, 1965, pp.244-5.
22. Beck, *Folklore and the Sea*, 1973, p.99.
23. Purkiss, *The Witch in History*, 1996, p.125.
24. Ibid, p.127.
25. Herrick, 'The Hag', *Hesperides*, 1648, Item 645.
26. Blind, 'New Finds in Shetlandic and Welsh Folklore', *The Gentleman's Magazine*, volume cclii, March-April 1882, p.365.

CHAPTER 8: The Sea Marauders
1. Jeans, op.cit., 2004, p.231.
2. Beck, *Folklore and the Sea*, 1973, p.315.
3. Ibid, p.319.
4. Jeans, op.cit., p.228 and p.230
5. Masefield, 'The Ballad of John Silver', *Salt-Water Ballads*, 1902, p.71.
6. Hauck, *The International Directory of Haunted Places*, 2000, p.34.
7. Kirkstone Pass Inn, Ambleside, *The Ghost and Paranormal Stories of the World*, https:// www.facebook.com @ Ghostsandparanormal, 3 February, 2014.
8. Beck, *Folklore and the Sea*, p.327.
9. Jeans, op.cit., pp.118-120.
10. Wikipedia, *Peter Easton*, https://en.wikipedia/org, 4 February, 2016.
11. Eastwaters, *Newfoundland and Labrador's Maritime Heritage*, https://www.eastwaters.com/easton, Retrieved October 2016.
12. Jarvis, D., *Pirate ghosts haunting cabins and guarding treasure*, https://www.thetelegram.com/opinion/columnists/2010, 13 July 2009.
13. Ibid
14. Lemoine, *The Chronicles of St.Lawrence*, 1878, pp.36-7.
15. Patterson, *Wild Life on a Norfolk Estuary*, 1907, p.1.
16. Anonymous, *An Historical Guide to Great Yarmouth in Norfolk with the most remarkable events recorded of the town*, 1817, p.8-9.
17. Ghost Ships: Ghosts, Hauntings & the Paranormal, https://www.unexplained-mysteries/com/forum/topic/11562-ghost-ships, 31 January, 2004.

18. Anonymous, op.cit., p.43.
19. Beck, *Folklore and the Sea*, p.405.
20. Ibid, p.348.
21. Ibid, p.347.
22. Ibid, p.344.
23. Ibid, p.340.
24. Jeans, op.cit., pp.300-301.

CHAPTER 9: Mysterious Lighthouses
1. Reid, *From Dusk till Dawn : A history of Australian lighthouses*, 1988, pp. xii –xiii & cover leaf.
2. Ibbotson, *Lighthouses of Australia*, 2004, pp. 2-4.
3. Reid, op.cit., p.229.
4. Beck, *The Folklore of Maine*, 1957, pp.158-9.
5. US Department of the Interior, National Park Service, 'National Register of Historical Places Inventory – Nomination Form #PHO365416', *Owl's Head Light Station*, Rockland,1978, Item 8, p.1.
6. D'Entremont, 'New England Lighthouses: A Virtual Guide website', *History of Owl's Head Light*, Maine, https://www.newenglandlighthouses.net. Retrieved December 2016.
7. Ibid .
8. Lighthouse Friends, *Owl's Head Lighthouse*, Maine, https://www.lighthouse friends.com/light, Retrieved November 2016.
9. Steitz, *Haunted Lighthouses and How to Find Them*, 2008, pp.214-5.
10. Millburn, S. and Walling, M.,Top 10 Haunted Lighthouses, https://www. coastalliving.com/travel, Retrieved November 2016.
11. D'Entremont , op.cit.
12. Lighthouse Friends, op.cit., *Owl's Head Lighthouse*, Maine.
13. Wikipedia, *Brother Jonathon (steamer)*, https://en.wikipedia.org, 9 November 2016.
14. Wikipedia, *St.George Reef Light*, https://en.wikipedia.org, 25 August, 2016.
15. Lighthouse Friends, *St.George Reef Lighthouse*, California, http://www.lighthouse friends.com/light, Retrieved November 2016.
16. Ibid.
17. Dash, *The Vanishing Lighthousemen of Eilean Mór*, 1998, p.3.

18. Martin, *A Description of the Western Islands of Scotland*, 1706, pp.18-9.
19. The Flannan Isles, 'The Basement Geographer', https://www.basementgeographer.com/the-flannan-isles, 9 August 2013.
20. Dash, op.cit.,pp.1-38.
21. Hunt, op.cit., 1881, p.133.
22. Reid, op.cit., pp. 233-4.
23. Lighthouse Friends, *Sand Island Lighthouse, Alabama*, https://www.lighthouse friends.com/light, Retrieved December 2016.
24. R.Jones, *Haunted Lighthouses*, 2010, p.116.
25. Harrison, *The Hero of Horn Island Pascagoula*, Mississippi, http://www.Lighthousedigest.com/digest/archives/ Jul/Aug 2011.
26. Sable Island, https://en.wikipedia.org/wiki/Sable_Island, 4 December,2016.
27. Howe, J., 'Sable Island', *Poems and Essays*,1874, p.40.
28. Budge, 'Strangers in the Night', *Memoirs of a Lightkeeper's Son: Life on St.Paul Island*, 2003.

CHAPTER 10: Genesis of Witchcraft

1. Kors & Peters, *Witchcraft in Europe 400-1700*, 2001, p.12.
2. BBC, 'The Masque of Mandragora', *Doctor Who*, Season 14, Serial 1, Final episode aired 25 September, 1976.
3. Levack, *The Witchcraft Sourcebook*, 2004, p.90.
4. Ankarloo & Henningsen, Early Modern European Witchcraft, 1990, p.150 and p.169.
5. Levack, op.cit., p.69.
6. Guiley, *The Encyclopedia of Witches, Witchcraft and Wicca*, 2008, pp.325-6.
7. Levack, op.cit., p.3 pp.88-9.
8. Levack, *Demonology,Religion and Witchcraft*, p.21
9. Levack, *The Witchcraft Sourcebook*, p.231.
10. Ibid, p.129.

CHAPTER 11: Witches

1. J. Prelutsky 'The Witch', *Nightmares: Poems to Trouble Your Sleep*, 1978, p.22.

2. E.Jones, *On the Nightmare*, 1931, pp.205-9.
3. Kors & Peters, op.cit., p.145.
4. Goodare, *Scottish Witches and Witch-Hunters*, 2013, pp.160-2.
5. Ibid, pp.164-5.
6. Ibid, pp.167-8.
7. Levack, *The Witchcraft Sourcebook*, p.2.
8. Ibid, p.231.
9. Ibid, pp.88-90.
10. Ibid, pp.94-6.
11. Barry & Davies, *Palgrave advances in witchcraft historiography*, 2007, p.204.
12. Levack, *The Witchcraft Sourcebook*, pp.31-2.
13. Sharpe, J.A., 'Witchcraft and Women in Seventeenth-Century England: Some Northern Evidence, *Continuity and Change 6 (2)*, 1991 p.182.
14. Linton, 'The Witches of Scotland', *Witch Stories*, p.71.
15. Wreyford, 'Old Mother Moore', *Essex Villians: Rogues, Rascals and Reprobates*, 2012.
16. Bassett, *Sea Phantoms: Legends and Superstitions of the Sea and of Sailors in all lands and at all times*, 1892, p.111.
17. Williams, 'The Sea-witch (Leigh-on-Sea)', Chapter Four, *Essex Folk Tales*.
18. Ibid, The Sea-witch.
19. Anonymous, *The Life, Prophecies and Death of the famous Mother Shipton*, pp.10-11.
20. Ibid, pp.7-8.
21. Harrison, *Mother Shipton Investigated*, 1881, p.17.

CHAPTER 12: The Black Cat
1. Jeans, op. cit., p.315.
2. Bassett, op.cit., p. 110, pp.278-9.
3. Ibid, p.125 and p.429.
4. Ibid, p.430.
5. Bialoksy, J., *History of a Suicide*, 2012, p.104.
6. Linton, *Witch Stories*, 1883, pp. 265-6.
7. Ibid, pp.162-164.
8. Smith, K.C., 'The Role of Animals in Witchcraft and Popular Magic,

Animals in Folklore, 1978, p.97 and p.102.

9. Wilde, *Ancient Legends, Mystic Charms and Superstitions of Ireland*, Vol II, 1887, p. 22.

10. Ibid, p. 23.

11. Ibid, p.19.

CHAPTER 13: Crows and Ravens

1. Spence, *The Magic Arts in Celtic Britain*, 1995, p.82.

2. Saxby & Clouston, *Birds of Omen in Shetland with Notes on the Folk-Lore on the Raven and the Owl*, 1893, p.23.

3. Robinson, 'The Poets' Birds, Part IV Birds of Omen and Superstition', *The Gentleman's Magazine*, vol. CCLII, January 1882, pp.329-34.

4. Witchcraft & Wicca, www.witcheslore.com/magical-creatures-bookofshadows/familiars, 9 October 2010.

5. Longfellow, 'Part XIII Blessing the Cornfields', *The Song of Hiawatha*, 1855, ln.98-130.

6. MacDowall, *Asgard and the Gods*, 1880, pp.52-3.

7. Cowan, *Are You Superstitious?*, 1968, pp.100-1.

8. Bassett, op.cit., p.274.

9. Saxby & Clouston, op.cit., 1893, p.7.

10. Spence, op.cit., p.84.

11. Babson, *The History of the town of Gloucester, Cape Anne, including the town of Rockport*, 1860, p. 321.

12. Saxby & Clouston, op. cit., 1893, p.9.

13. Edmondston & Saxby, *The Home of a Naturalist*, 1888, p.221.

14. Lewis, M.G., 'Bill Jones, a Tale of Wonder', *The Life and Correspondence of M.G.Lewis*, Vol.2, 1839, ln 1-10.

15. Bannatyne, *Halloween: An American Holiday, An American History*, 1990, p.89.

16. 'Halloween', *Harper's Weekly, Vol.39, No.2033*, 1895, p.1069.

17. Bliss Carman, et al., eds, 'The Owl', *The World's Best Poetry*, Volume V, Nature, 1904, ln. 1-33.

18. A Wise Old Owl, https://en.wikipedia.org/wiki/A_Wise_Old_Owl, Retrieved March 2017.

19. Brand, op.cit., p.209.

CHAPTER 14: Enjoy the Ghost Train

1. Harper, *Ghost Chronicles: Ghostly Tales on Land and Sea*, 2010, pp.43-4.
2. Ackroyd, *The English Ghost: Spectres Through Time*, 2010, pp.108-9.
3. Hodgson and Laird, *The Beauties of England and Wales; or, Original Delineations, Topographical Historical and Descriptive, of each county*, 1813, p.55.
4. Swain,S. and Catford,N.,'Thorneywood', https://www.disused-station.org.uk/t/thorneywood, 31 August, 2014.
5. Swain, S., Northern Suburban Railway, https://www.forgottenrelics.co.uk/routes/nottsub, 2010.
6. Swain and Catford, op.cit.,31 August, 2014.
7. Marshall, *The Railway Magazine*, June, 1961, p.376.
8. Ghost Trains of Great Britain, https://strangedayz.co.uk/2007/10/ghost-trains-of-great britain, 23 October, 2007.
9. Smalley, J.R., 'The Thorneywood Legend', https://nottinghamhiddenhistoryteam. wordpress.com/2012/09/03/ghosts-of-nottinghamshire-railways, 3 September, 2012.
10. Ibid, 3 September, 2012
11. Swain and Catford, op.cit.,31 August, 2014.
12. Nottingham Blitz, https://en.wikipedia.org/wiki/Nottingham-Blitz, 10 November, 2016.
13. Swain and Catford, op.cit.,31 August, 2014.
14. Tunnels of Nottingham, https://en.wikipedia.org/wiki/Tunnels-of-Nottingham, 12 September, 2016.
15. Sherwood Rise Tunnel, L3454, https://www.railwayarchive.org.uk/the-last-main-line,17 May, 2004.
16. Great Central Railway, https://www.gcrailway.co.uk/brief-history, retrieved January 2017.
17. The Great Central Railway in Nottingham, http://www.leverton.org /tunnels/notts-gcr, 4 February, 2008.
18. Man with Lamp, https://www.paranormaldatabase.com /hotspots/nottingham, retrieved 11 January, 2017.
19. Buried Railway Heritage & Redevelopment in Nottingham, https://www.railwaymaniac.com>transport related articles, 10 January 2016.

CHAPTER 15: Eerie Fog
1. Prescott, H., 'The Fog-Gun', *Poems written in Newfoundland*, 1839, pp.144-7.
2. McGrath, *Newfoundland in 1911*, pp.181-2.
3. Feild, E., *Journal of a Voyage of Visitation in the "HAWK" Church Ship on the coast of Labrador and round the whole island of Newfoundland in the year 1849*, pp.18-21.
4. Beck, *Folklore and the Sea*, 1973, p.107.
5. Ober, *Out of the Fog*, 1911, pp.18-39.
6. Stevenson, *The Sea Fogs*,1907, p.7.
7. Brault, *Halloween Thoughts,Old and New*, A Robert Brault Reader-Rssing.com, 13 October 2012.

CHAPTER 16: The Possessed
1. Cardin, op,cit., p.104.
2. Illes, op.cit., pp.101-2.
3. Starr, 'Curious Customs and Tales of Dolls', *The Doll House*, 1908, pp.187-8.
4. Bull, *A Hug of Teddy Bears*,1984, p.5.
5. Starr, op.cit., p.214.
6. Shakespeare, W., *Hamlet (The Tragedy of Hamlet, The Prince of Denmark)*, 1603, Act 1, Scene 5, Lines 167-8.
7. Ogden, *Magic, Witchcraft, and Ghosts in the Greek and Roman Worlds*, 2002, p.30.

CHAPTER17: Masque
1. Illes, op.cit., pp.103.
2. Nunley and McCarty, *Masks: Faces of Culture*, 1999, p.13.
3. Dunbar, P.L., *Lyrics of Lowly Life*, 1896, p.167.
4. Nunley and McCarty, op.cit., p.30.
5. Ibid, p.287.
6. Coxe, op.cit., *Verse IX*, 1845, p.11.
7. Mack, 'Photo 90: Roman Empire Mask', *Masks:The Art of Expression*, 1994, p.322.
8. Brown, *Carnival Masks of Venice*, 2008, p.9.
9. Ibid, p.5-6.

10. Ibid, p.10.
11. 'Mask', *Online Etymology Dictionary*, 2017.
12. Guiley, *The Encyclopedia of Magic and Alchemy*, 2006, pp.189-190.

CHAPTER 18: Hobbins and Bobbins
1. Briggs, *A Dictionary of Fairies*, 1976, pp.222-3.
2. Ibid, pp.30-33.
3. Ibid, p.29 p.52.
4. Brault, 'Halloween', *rbrault.blogspot.com/there_is_child_in_every_one_of_us_who.html*, 2011.
5. Briggs, *The Fairies in Tradition and Literature*, 1967, p.137.
6. Wikipedia, *Will-o'-the-wisp*, http://en.wikipedia.org, Retrieved 10 December 2016.
7. Brand, op.cit., p.396.
8. Wright, 'Will-o'-the-wisp', *Rustic Speech and Folk-Lore*, 1918, p.201.
9. B.Steiger and S.Steiger, Ghosts, Restless Spirits and Haunted Houses, *Real Visitors, Voices from Beyond*, and Parallel Dimensions, 2016.

CHAPTER 19: The Scarecrows are Watching
1. Eliot. T.S., *Poems 1909 -1925*, 23 November 1925, p.123.
2. Jackson, C., 'Japanese Village Overrun By Nightmarish Scarecrows', *fangoria.com/new/camillas-beastly-bulletin-1-scarecrows-ax-murder-and-aliens-oh-my*, 20 March 2015.
3. *guinessworldrecords.com/world-records/largest-display-of-scarecrow*, 7 August, 2014.
4. Wikipedia, *Scarecrow*, http://en.wikipedia.org, Retrieved 12 December 2016.
5. MacKillop, *Dictionary of Celtic Mythology*, 1998, p.58.
6. Toms, *The Little Book of the Isle of Wight*, 2011, p.1.
7. Briggs, *A Dictionary of Fairies*, 1976, p.183.
8. Bane, *Encyclopedia of Fairies in World Folklore and Mythology*, 2013, p.155.
9. Tongue, *County Folklore*, p.122-3.
10. Scarecrow, *theteachersguide.com/readingcomp/poetry/scarecrow-001*, 2013.

CHAPTER 20: Momentary Respite of Silence
1. Nightmare at 20,000 Feet, *The Twilight Zone:The Original Series (1959-1964)*, Season 5, Episode 3, Aired 11 October 1963.
2. Scott, 'File No.13', *My true spooky files – Part 1 Phenomenal encounters of the mysterious, paranormal and supernatural kind*, 2007, p.30.
3. Bannatyne, op.cit., p.82.

CHAPTER 21: Encounters of the Animal Kind
1. Brand, op.cit., p. 204.

CHAPTER 22: The Strange Ones
1. Ross, op.cit., pp.128-9.
2. Seymour and Neligan, *True Irish Ghost Stories*, 2005, pp.136-7.
3. Leach and Fried, *Funk & Wagnalls Standard Dictionary of Folklore, Mythology and Legend*, 1972, p.1185.
4. Briggs, *A Dictionary of British Folk-Tales – Part B Folk Legends Vol.2*, 1971, p.487.
5. Hare, *In my solitary life*, 1953, p.36.
6. Dunbar, P.L., *The Complete Poems of Paul Laurence Dunbar*, 1913, p.186.
7. Jackson, *Shropshire Folk-Lore: A Sheaf of Gleanings*, 1883, p.104.
8. Ibid, pp.141-2.
9. Richardson, *The Local Historian's Table Book of Remarkable Occurrences, Historical Facts, Traditions, Legendary and Descriptive Ballads*, 1843, pp.34-5.
10. Ibid, p.36.
11. Phipps, I.N., *The Lay of the Wraith And Other Poems*, 1895.pp.2-3.

CHAPTER 23: Paranormal Magicians
1. Guiley, *The Encyclopedia of Magic and Alchemy*, 2006, p.175.
2. Mauss, *A General Theory of Magic*, 1972, p.13.
3. Sorcery, *https://www.dictionary.com/browse/sorcery*, Retrieved 19 February 2017.
4. Mauss, op.cit., pp. 27-8.
5. Brand, op.cit., p.59.
6. Bullfinch, *Myths of Greece and Rome*, 1980, p.188.

7. Guiley, *The Encyclopedia of Ghosts and Spirits*, 1972, p.196.
8. The Goddess of the Witches, *https://www.auntyflo.com/magic/hekate-hecate-goddess-witches*, Retrieved February 2017.
9. Hecate, *https://en.wikipedia.org/wiki/Hecate*, Retrieved February 2017.
10. The Goddess of the Witches, op.cit., 2017.
11. Hecate, op.cit., 2017.
12. Mauss, op.cit., pp. 82-4.
13. Dickie, *Magic and Magicians in the Greco-Roman World*, 2001, p.198.
14. Ogden, op.cit., p.154.
15. Dickie, op.cit., p.217.
16. Ibid, p.234.
17. Ibid, p.201.
18. Lawrence-Mathers and Escobar-Vargas, *Magic and Medieval Society*, 2014, p.98.
19. Adams, *The learned arts of witches & wizards: history and traditions of white magic*, 1998, p.98.
20. Balder, A., 'Invocations and Oracles', *Germanic Appendices*, Volume 5, The Teutoburg Saga, Retrieved 30 September, 2014.
21. Spence, op.cit., 1995, pp.96-7.
22. Martin, op.cit., 1706, pp.112-3.

BIBLIOGRAPHY

Ackroyd, P., *The English Ghost: Spectres Through Time*, Chatto and Windus, London, 2010.

Adams, A., and Adams, M., *The learned arts of witches & wizards:history and traditions of white magic*, Lansdowne Press, Sydney, 1998.

Addy, S.O., *Household Tales, with other Traditional Remains. Collected in the Counties of York, Lincoln, Derby and Nottingham*, David Nutt, London,1895.

Ankarloo, B. & Henningsen, G.(eds.), *Early Modern European Witchcraft: centres and peripheries*, Clarendon Press, Oxford, 1990.

Anonymous, *An Historical Guide to Great Yarmouth in Norfolk with the most remarkable events recorded of the town*, Barnes and Webster, Yarmouth, 1817.

Anonymous, *The Life, Prophecies and Death of the famous Mother Shipton*, J.Wainwright, London.

Anonymous, *Suffolk County Folk-Lore*, edited by Lady E.F. Gurden, Printed Extracts No 2, 1893; in Folk-Lore Society Publication Relics in Popular Antiquities, London, 1895.

Babson, J.J., *The History of the town of Gloucester, Cape Anne, including the town of Rockport*, Procter Brothers, Gloucester, 1860.

Bainton, R., *The Mammoth Book of Unexplained Phenomena: From bizarre biology to inexplicable astronomy*, Constable and Robinson, London, 2013.

Bane, T., *Encyclopedia of Fairies in World Folklore and Mythology*, McFarland & Co, London, 2013.

Bannatyne, L.P., *Halloween: An American Holiday, An American History*, Facts on File Inc., New York and Oxford, 1990.

Barry, J. & Davies, O., *Palgrave advances in witchcraft historiography*, Palgrave McMillan, Hampshire, 2007.

Bassett, F.S., *Sea Phantoms: Legends and Superstitions of the Sea and of Sailors in all lands and at all times*, Morrill, Higgins and Company, Chicago, 1892.

Bauer, C.F., (ed.) and Sis, P., *Halloween: Stories and Poems*, Harpercollins, 1992.

Bayless, R., *Animal Ghosts*, University Books, New York, 1970.

Beck, H.P., *The Folklore of Maine*, J.B.Lippincott Company, Philadelphia and New York, 1957.

Beck, H.P., *Folklore and the Sea*, Wesleyan University Press, Connecticut, 1973.

Bennett, T., *Dollar Wreck: One of the Treasure Ships of Wales*, Self-Published, 2016.

Black, G.F. & Northcote, W.T. (ed.), *Examples of Printed Folk-Lore Concerning the Orkney and Shetland Islands*, Folk-Lore Society: County Folk-Lore, vol. iii: Printed Extracts, no.5, Folk-Lore Society County Publications, London, 1903.

Blind, K., 'New Finds in Shetlandic and Welsh Folklore', *The Gentleman's Magazine*, volume CCLII, March-April, 1882.

Bottrell, W., *Traditions and Hearthside Stories of West Cornwall*, Beare and Son, Penzance, 1873.

Bourke, E. J., *Shipwrecks of the Irish Coast*, Volume 1,1105-1993, Self-Published, Dublin, 1994.

Bradley, A.G., *The Romance of Wales*, Metheun and Company, London, 1929.

Brand, J., *Observations on the Possible Antiquities of Great Britain*, Vol III, Henry G. Bohn, London, 1849.

Briggs, K. M., *The Fairies in Tradition and Literature*, Routledge and Kegan Paul, London, 1967.

Briggs, K.M., *A Dictionary of British Folk-Tales in the English Language - Part B Folk Legends Vol. 2*, Routledge and Kegan Paul, London, 1971.

Briggs, K.M., *A Dictionary of Fairies: Hobgoblins, Brownies, Bogies and Other Supernatural Creatures*, Allen Lane, London, 1976.

Brockie, W., *Legends and Superstitions of the County of Durham*, B.Williams, Sunderland, 1886.

Brown, T., *Folklore*, Vol.69, No.3, Folk-Lore Society, William Glaisher Ltd, London, 1958.

Brown, J.C., *Carnival Masks of Venice*, Artists' and Photographers' Press Ltd, Surrey, 2008.

Budge, W.G., *Memoirs of a Lightkeeper's Son: Life on St.Paul Island*, Pottersfield Press, Nova Scotia, 2003.

Bull, P., *A Hug of Teddy Bears*, The Herbert Press, London, 1984.

Bullfinch, T., *Myths of Greece and Rome*, Allen Lane, London, 1980.

Cardin, M., *Ghosts, Spirits and Psychics: The Paranormal from Alchemy to Zombies*, ABC-CLIO, Santa Barbara, 2015.

Cheung, T., *The Element Encyclopedia of the Psychic World*, Harper Element, 2006.

Clarke, R., *A Natural History of Ghosts: 500 Years of Hunting for Proof*, Penguin Books, London, 2012.

Cowan, L., *Are You Superstitious?*, Leslie Frewin Publishers, London, 1968.

Coxe, A.C., *Halloween, A Romaunt, with Lays*, Case, Tiffany and Burnham, Connecticut, 1845.

Cressy, D., *Birth, Marriage & Death, Ritual, Religon and the Life Cycle in Tudor and Stuart England*, Oxford University Press, Oxford, 1997.

Dash, M., 'The Vanishing Lighthousemen of Eilean Mór', Research Paper in Fortean Studies Volume 4, John Brown Publishing, London, 1998.

Davis, J.: *Haunted Asylums, Prisons and Sanatoriums*, Llewellyn Publications, Woodbury Minnesota, 2013.

D'Entremont, J., *The Lighthouses of Massachusetts*, Commonwealth Editions, 2009.

Dickie, M., *Magic and Magicians in the Greco-Roman World*, Routledge,London, 2001.

Drake, S. A., *A Book of New England Legends and Folk Lore*, Little, Brown and Company. Boston, 1901.

Edmondston, B. & Saxby, J.M.E., *A Home of a Naturalist*, James Nisbet & Company, London,1888.

Elder, A., *Tales and Legends of the Isle of Wight*, Simpkin, Marshall and Company, London, 1839.

Enright, D.J., *The Oxford Book of the Supernatural*, Oxford University Press, New York, 1994.

Field. E., *Love-Songs of Childhood*, Charles Scribner's Sons, New York, 1896.

Glyde, J., *The Norfolk Garland: A Collection of the Superstitions, Beliefs and Practices, Proverbs, Curious Customs, Ballads and Songs of the people of Norfolk*, Jarrold and Sons, London,1872.

Goodare, J. (ed.), *Scottish Witches and Witch-Hunters*, Palgrave McMillan, Basingstoke, 2013.

Gosse, P.H., *The Pirates' Who's Who: Giving Particulars of the Lives &*

Deaths of the Pirates & Buccaneers, Burt Franklin, New York, 1924.

Gosse, P.H., *The International Directory of Pirates, Buccaneers, and other Rogues*, Fireship Press, 2008.

Guiley, R.E., *The Encyclopedia of Ghosts and Spirits*, Facts on File Inc, New York, 1992.

Guiley, R.E., *The Encyclopedia of Magic and Alchemy*, Facts on File Inc, New York, 2006.

Guiley, R.E., *The Encyclopedia of Witches, Witchcraft and Wicca*, Facts on File Inc, New York, 2008.

Haining,P., *A Dictionary of Ghost Lore*, Prentice-Hall, 1982.

Hallowell, A.I., *American Anthropologist, Vol 28, No.1*, University of Pennsylvania, Philadelphia, 1926.

Harper, J. (ed.), *Ghost Chronicles:Stories of the paranormal*, David & Charles, Newton Abbot, Devon, 2010.

Harrison, W.H., *Mother Shipton Investigated*, British Museum, London, 1881.

Harr, A.J.C., *In my solitary life: being an abridgement of the last three volumes of The story of my life, as edited by M.Barnes*, Allen and Unwin, London, 1953.

Hauck, D.W., *The International Directory of Haunted Places*, Penguin Books, Ringwood, Victoria, 2000.

Hazlitt, W.C., *Faiths & Folklore of the British Isles*, Volume II, Benjamin Blom, New York, 1965.

Henderson, W., *Notes on the Folk-Lore of the Northern Counties of England and the Borders*, Folk-Lore Society, W.Satchell, Peyton & Company, London, 1879.

Hodgson. J. and Laird, F.C., *The Beauties of England and Wales; or, Original Delineations, Topographical Historical and Descriptive, of each county*, Vol. XII, Part 1, London, 1813.

Hunt, R., John Camden Hotten, London, 1881.

Ibbotson, J., *Lighthouses of Australia: Images from the end of an era*, Australian Lighthouse Traders, Surrey Hills, Victoria, 2004.

Illes, J., *The Weiser Field Guide to Witches*, Red Wheel/Weiser llc, California, 2010.

Ingram, J.H., *The Haunted Homes and Famous Traditions of Great Britain*, Gibbings and Company, London, 1897.

Ings, D., *Penarth History Tour*, Amberley Publishing, Stroud, Gloucestershire, 2016.

Jackson, G.F., Burne, C. S. (ed.), *Shropshire Folk-Lore: A Sheaf of Gleanings*, Trübner and Company, London, 1883.

Jeans, P.D., *Seafaring Lore and Legend*, McGraw-Hill, USA, 2004.

Jones, E., *On the Nightmare*, Hogarth Press, London, 1931.

Jones, R., *Haunted Lighthouses: Phantom Keepers, Ghostly Shipwrecks, and Sinister Calls from the Deep*, Globe Pequot Press, Connecticut, 2010.

Kors, A.C. & Peters, E. (eds.), *Witchcraft in Europe 400-1700: a documentary history*, University Of Pennsylvania Press, Philadelphia, 2001.

Lavatar, L., *Of Ghosts and Spirits, Walking by Night*, Thomas Creede, London, 1596.

Lawrence-Mathers, A., and Escobar-Vargas, C., *Magic and Medieval Society*, Routledge, Abingdon Oxon and New York, 2014.

Leach, M., *Folk Ballads and Songs of the lower Labrador Coast*, Ottawa, 1965.

Leach, M and Fried, T. (eds.), *Funk & Wagnalls Standard Dictionary of Folklore, Mythology and Legend*, One volume edition, New York, 1972.

Lemoine, J.M., *The Chronicles of St. Lawrence*, Dawson Brothers, Montreal-Quebec, 1878.

Levack, B.P.(ed.), *Demonology, Religion, and Witchcraft: New Perspectives on Witchcraft, Magic and Demonology*, Volume I, Routledge, New York /London, 2001.

Levack, B.P.(ed.), *The Witchcraft Sourcebook*, Routledge, New York/London, 2004.

Linton, E.L., *Witch Stories*, Chatto and Windus, London, 1883.

Lipman, C., *Co-habiting with Ghosts-Knowledge, Experience, Belief and the Domestic Uncanny*, Routledge, New York, 2016.

Luckhurst, R. (ed.), *Late Victorian Gothic Tales*, Oxford University Press, Oxford, 2005.

Lupton, H., *Norfolk Folk Tales*, The History Press, Gloucestershire, 2013.

MacDowall, M., *Asgard and the Gods*, Swan, Sonnenschein, Le Bas and Lowrey, London, 1886.

MacKillop, J., *Dictionary of Celtic Mythology*, Oxford University Press, Oxford, New York, 1998.

Mack, J. (ed.), *Masks: The Art of Expression*, British Museum Press, London, 1994.

Marshall, J.,'The Nottingham Suburban Railway', *The Railway Magazine*, Issue 107, June, 1961 Edition.

Martin, M., *A Description of the Western Islands of Scotland*, 2nd Edition, London, 1706.

Masefield, J., *Salt-Water Ballads*, Grant Richards, London,1902.

Mauss, M., *A General Theory of Magic*, Routledge and Kegan Paul, London, 1972.

McGrath,P.T., *Newfoundland in 1911*, Whitehead, Morris and Company London, 1911.

McKinstry, F.T., *Water Dark*, Wild Child Publishing, ebook, 2013.

Miller, Hugh, *Scenes and Legends of the North of Scotland*, Seventh Edition, William P Nimmo, Edinburgh, 1869.

Morton, L., *Trick or Treat: A History of Halloween*, Reaktion Books Ltd, London, 2012.

Nichols, J., *The History and Antiquities of the County of Leicester*, Vol IV, Part 1, John Nichols and Son, London, 1807.

Nickell, J., *The Science of Ghosts: Searching for Spirits of the Dead*, Prometheus Books, New York, 2012.

Noall, C., *Cornish Lights and Ship-Wrecks*, D. Bradford Barton, Truro, England, 1968.

Nunley, J. and McCarty, C., *Masks: Faces of Culture*, Harry N.Abrams, St. Louis, Missouri, 1999.

Ober, C.K., *Out of the Fog – A Story of the Sea*, Association Press, London and New York,1911.

O'Donnell, E., *Animal Ghosts: Animal Hauntings and the Hereafter*, The Floating Press, Auckland, 2012.

Ogden,D., *Magic, Witchcraft, and Ghosts in the Greek and Roman Worlds: A Sourcebook*, Oxford University Press, Oxford, 2002.

Otten, C.F.(ed.), *A Lycanthrophy Reader: Werewolves in Western Culture*, Syracuse University Press, Syracuse, 1986.

Parker, M., *Ghost Islands of Nova Scotia*, Pottersfield Press, Nova Scotia, 2012.

Patterson, A. H., *Wild Life on a Norfolk Estuary*, Metheun & Company, London, 1907.

Pickering, T., *A Discourse of the Damned Art of Witchcraft*, Cantrel Legge Press, Cambridge, 1610.

Porter, J.R., and Russell, W.M.S. (eds), *Animals in Folklore*, D.S.Brewer

Ltd, Cambridge, 1978.

Price,H., and Lambert, R.S., *The Haunting of Cashen's Gap: A Modern 'Miracle' Investigated*, Menthuen and Company Limited, Great Britain, 1936.

Purkiss, D., *The Witch in History: Early modern and twentieth-century representations*, Routledge, London and New York, 1996.

Rappoport, A.S., *Superstitions of Sailors*, Dover Publications, New York, 2012.

Reader's Digest Association, *Into the Unknown*, The Reader's Digest Association, Sydney, 1982.

Reid, G., *From Dusk till Dawn, A history of Australian lighthouses*, McMillan, South Melbourne,1988.

Richardson, M.A., *The Local Historian's Table Book of Remarkable Occurrences, Historical Facts, Traditions, Legendary and Descriptive Ballads, Volume 1*, J.R. Smith, London, 1843.

Ripley, G. and Dana, C.A.(eds.), *The American Cyclopædia: A popular dictionary of general knowledge*, Volume XIV, D.Appleton and Company, New York, Second Edition, 1879.

Robinson, P., 'The Poets' Birds', *The Gentleman's Magazine*, volume CCLII, January 1882.

Rogoziński, J., *Pirates!: brigands, buccaneers and privateers, in fact, fiction, and legend*, Facts on File, New York, 1995.

Ross, C., *Supernatural and Mysterious Japan: Spirits, Hauntings and Paranormal Phenomena*, Tuttle Publishing, New York, 2015.

Rushing, F., *Scarecrows: making harvest figures and other yard folks*, Storey Books, Vermont, 1998.

Saxby, J.M.E.& Clouston, W.A., *Birds of Omen in Shetland with Notes on the Folk-Lore on the Raven and the Owl*, AMS Press, Indiana,1893.

Scot, R., *The Discoverie of Witchcraft*, Elliot Stock, London, Reprint of First Edition of 1584, 1886.

Scott, B.J., *My true spooky files – Part 1 Phenomenal encounters of the mysterious, paranormal and supernatural kind*, Nollamara, Western Australia, Revised Edition, 2007.

Seymour, St. J.D. & Neligan, H.L., *True Irish Ghost Stories*, First Edition, Hodges, Figgis and Company, Dublin, 1914.

Seymour, St. J.D. & Neligan, H.L., *True Irish Ghost Stories: haunted houses, banshees, poltergeists and other supernatural phenomena*, Dover Publications, London, 2005.

Sikes, W., British Goblins: Welsh Folk-lore, *Fairy Mythology, Legends and Traditions*, Sampson Low, Marston, Searle and Rivington, London, 1880.

Simpson, J.C., *The Life and Prophecies of URSULA SONTHEIL better known as Mother Shipton*, Dropping Well, Knaresborough, Yorkshire, 1920.

Snow, E.R., *The Lighthouses of New England*, 1716-1973, Dodd, Mead, New York, 1973.

Spence, L., *The Magic Arts in Celtic Britain*, Constable and Company, London, 1995.

Starr, L.B., *The Doll Book*, The Outing Publishing Company, New York, 1908.

Steiger, B. and Steiger, S., *Real Visitors, Voices from Beyond*, and Parallel Dimensions, Visible Ink Press, Detroit, 2016.

Steitz, G.C., *Haunted Lighthouses and How to Find Them*, Pineapple Press, 2008.

Stevenson, R.L., *The Sea Fogs*, Paul Elder and Company, San Francisco and New York, 1907.

Taylor, D., 'Spaces of Transition: New Light on the Haunted House', *At the Edge Magazine*, No 10, Fairies and Ghosts Special Issue, June 1998.

The Encyclopædia Brittanica, Volume 3, 11th Edition, Cambridge University Press, Cambridge, England, 1911.

Thompson, R.C., *The Devils and Evil Spirits of Babylonia*, Luzac and Company, London, 1903.

Thomson, W.O., *Lighthouse Legends & Hauntings*, Scrapes Me, Kennebunk, Maine, 1998.

Toms, J., *The Little Book of the Isle of Wight*, The History Press, Stroud, Gloucestershire, 2011.

Tongue, R.L., *Somerset Folklore*, edited by K.M. Briggs, County Folklore Series;Volume VIII, Folk-Lore Society County Publications, London, 1965.

Towers, G., *St. George Reef Lighthouse*, Arcadia Publishing, Charleston, South Carolina, 2015.

Turi, J., *Turi's Book of Lapland*, translated from the Danish by E.G.Nash, Alden Press, Oxford, 1931.

Whitaker, T.D., *An History of Richmondshire in the North Riding of the County of York*, Vol I, Longman, Hurst, Rees, Orme and Brown, Paternoster-Row, London,1823.

Wilde, J.F., *Ancient Legends, Mystic Charms, and Superstitions of Ireland*, Vol I and Vol II, Ward and Downey, London, 1887.

Williams, J., *Essex Folk Tales*, The History Press Ltd, Stroud, 2011.

Wreyford, P., *Essex Villians: Rogues, Rascals and Reprobates*, The History Press Ltd, Stroud, 2012.

Wright, E.M., *Rustic Speech and Folk-Lore*, Oxford University Press, Oxford, 1918.

ABOUT THE AUTHOR

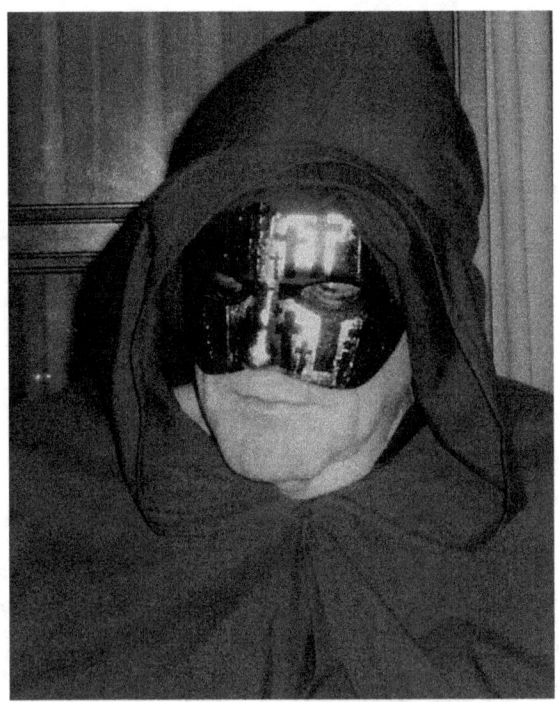

The Halloween Monk

Simon King is a geosciences career professional who has worked in various technical, managerial and consultative roles, particularly in mining. More recently he has been an industry consultant in occupational health and safety. He is now an emerging Australian author who has already published his debut book on the remote and pristine West Kimberley coastal region of Western Australia, where he spent a good part of his working life.

Simon's second book embraces the entirely different subject matter of paranormal/supernatural encounters and events as well as matters dealing with associated folklore, myths and legends that have arisen from his considerable interest in such phenomena. This has been augmented by his first-hand personal experiences and observations as well as a family history of such encounters to provide a realistic perspective to the topic.

Recent retirement from a long industrial career has provided him with the rare opportunity to extensively research selective interesting works previously compiled on this subject worldwide, and the maturity to view such extraordinary work objectively. Simon lives with his wife in Perth, Western Australia.

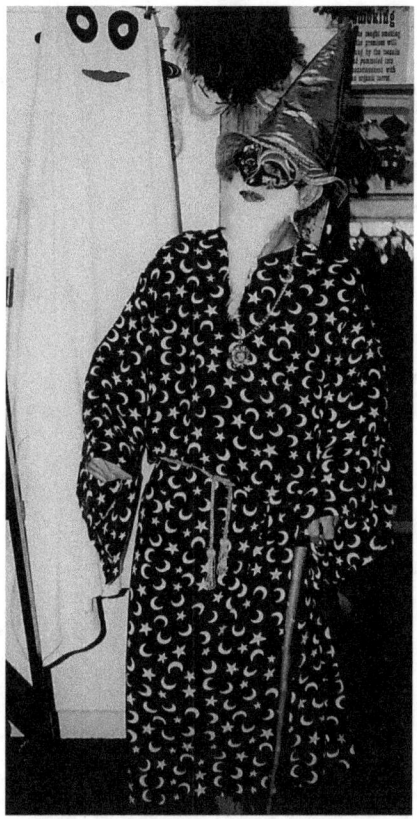

Merlin the Sorcerer

www.ingramcontent.com/pod-product-compliance
Lightning Source LLC
Chambersburg PA
CBHW071903290426
44110CB00013B/1267